'Progress' in Zimbabwe?

In this edited collection, scholars from Zimbabwe and abroad contribute essays that deepen our understanding of the causes, dynamics and consequences of Zimbabwe's current crisis. The volume includes considerations of the dynamics of accumulation and power in Zimbabwe, historiographical perspectives, civil society and state relations, workers' and peasants' responses to Zimbabwe's crisis, and debates on foreign investment, land reform and the relevance of the concept of the National Democratic Revolution to Zimbabwe and South Africa's relations with it. The theme of "progress" – a concept underpinning 'modern', 'liberal' and 'radical' perspectives of development – unifies these disparate issues. The book engages in debates about how the idea of "progress" informs present and past analyses of Zimbabwe.

This book was published as a special issue of the *Journal of Contemporary African Studies*.

David Moore is Professor of Development Studies at the University of Johannesburg.

Norma Kriger is a Researcher in the Federal Research Division of the Library of Congress in Washington D.C. and a Research Associate at the University of Johannesburg.

Brian Raftopoulos is Director of Research and Advocacy for the Solidarity Peace Trust, and Mellon Senior Research Mentor, Centre for Humanities Research at the University of the Western Cape.

'Progress' in Zimbabwe?
The Past and Present of a Concept and a Country

Edited by
**David Moore, Norma Kriger
and Brian Raftopoulos**

LONDON AND NEW YORK

First published 2013 by Routledge

2 Park Square, Milton Park, Abingdon, Oxfordshire OX14 4RN
711 Third Avenue, New York, NY 10017

Routledge is an imprint of the Taylor & Francis Group, an informa business

First issued in paperback 2018

Copyright © 2013 The Institute of Social and Economic Research

This book is a reproduction of the *Journal of Contemporary African Studies*, vol. 30, issue 1. The Publisher requests to those authors who may be citing this book to state, also, the bibliographical details of the special issue on which the book was based.

All rights reserved. No part of this book may be reprinted or reproduced or utilised in any form or by any electronic, mechanical, or other means, now known or hereafter invented, including photocopying and recording, or in any information storage or retrieval system, without permission in writing from the publishers.

Notice :
Product or corporate names may be trademarks or registered trademarks, and are used only for identification and explanation without intent to infringe.

British Library Cataloguing in Publication Data
A catalogue record for this book is available from the British Library

ISBN13: 978-0-415-59465-3 (hbk)
ISBN13: 978-1-138-38297-8 (pbk)

Typeset in Times New Roman
by Taylor & Francis Books

Publisher's Note
The publisher would like to make readers aware that the chapters in this book are referred to as articles as they had been in the special issue. The publisher accepts responsibility for any inconsistencies that may have arisen in the course of preparing this volume for print.

Contents

Citation Information	vii
1. Progress, power, and violent accumulation in Zimbabwe *David Moore*	1
2. ZANU PF politics under Zimbabwe's 'Power-Sharing' Government *Norma Kriger*	11
3. Narratives of progress: Zimbabwean historiography and the end of history *Ian Phimister*	27
4. Civil society and state-centred struggles *Kirk Helliker*	35
5. Anti-developmental patrimonialism in Zimbabwe *Martin Dawson and Tim Kelsall*	49
6. Foreign investment, black economic empowerment and militarised patronage politics in Zimbabwe *Booker Magure*	67
7. Teachers' and bank workers' responses to Zimbabwe's crisis: uneven effects, different strategies *Tapiwa Chagonda*	83
8. 'New realities' and tenure reforms: land-use in worker-peasant communities of south-western Zimbabwe (1940s–2006) *Vusilizwe Thebe*	99
9. Two perspectives on Zimbabwe's National Democratic Revolution: Thabo Mbeki and Wilfred Mhanda *David Moore*	119
10. Reflections on the concept of progress – and Zimbabwe *John Hoffman*	139
11. Shifting the debate on land reform, poverty and inequality in Zimbabwe, an engagement with *Zimbabwe's Land Reform: Myths and Realities* *Blair Rutherford*	147
Index	159

Citation Information

The chapters in this book were originally published in the *Journal of Contemporary African Studies*, volume 30, issue 1 (January 2012). When citing this material, please use the original page numbering for each article, as follows:

Chapter 1
Progress, power, and violent accumulation in Zimbabwe
David Moore
Journal of Contemporary African Studies, volume 30, issue 1 (January 2012)
pp. 1-10

Chapter 2
ZANU PF politics under Zimbabwe's 'Power-Sharing' Government
Norma Kriger
Journal of Contemporary African Studies, volume 30, issue 1 (January 2012)
pp. 11-26

Chapter 3
Narratives of progress: Zimbabwean historiography and the end of history
Ian Phimister
Journal of Contemporary African Studies, volume 30, issue 1 (January 2012)
pp. 27-34

Chapter 4
Civil society and state-centred struggles
Kirk Helliker
Journal of Contemporary African Studies, volume 30, issue 1 (January 2012)
pp. 35-48

Chapter 5
Anti-developmental patrimonialism in Zimbabwe
Martin Dawson and Tim Kelsall
Journal of Contemporary African Studies, volume 30, issue 1 (January 2012)
pp. 49-66

CITATION INFORMATION

Chapter 6
Foreign investment, black economic empowerment and militarised patronage politics in Zimbabwe
Booker Magure
Journal of Contemporary African Studies, volume 30, issue 1 (January 2012)
pp. 67-82

Chapter 7
Teachers' and bank workers' responses to Zimbabwe's crisis: uneven effects, different strategies
Tapiwa Chagonda
Journal of Contemporary African Studies, volume 30, issue 1 (January 2012)
pp. 83-98

Chapter 8
'New realities' and tenure reforms: land-use in worker-peasant communities of south-western Zimbabwe (1940s–2006)
Vusilizwe Thebe
Journal of Contemporary African Studies, volume 30, issue 1 (January 2012)
pp. 99-118

Chapter 9
Two perspectives on Zimbabwe's National Democratic Revolution: Thabo Mbeki and Wilfred Mhanda
David Moore
Journal of Contemporary African Studies, volume 30, issue 1 (January 2012)
pp. 119-138

Chapter 10
Reflections on the concept of progress – and Zimbabwe
John Hoffman
Journal of Contemporary African Studies, volume 30, issue 1 (January 2012)
pp. 139-146

Chapter 11
Shifting the debate on land reform, poverty and inequality in Zimbabwe, an engagement with Zimbabwe's Land Reform: Myths and Realities
Blair Rutherford
Journal of Contemporary African Studies, volume 30, issue 1 (January 2012)
pp. 147-157

Progress, power, and violent accumulation in Zimbabwe

David Moore

Department of Anthropology and Development Studies, University of Johannesburg, South Africa

> Zimbabwe's recent travails have challenged the concept of progress as it is popularly conceived, as they have forced social scientists to revisit many of the verities of nationalist history and the initial euphoria of Zimbabwean 'liberation'. Critics of 'fast-track' land reform and patriotism, however, have been as simplistic as the regime's academic praise singers, and often simply turn celebratory scholarship upside down. Historically rooted and specifically applied concepts of primitive accumulation can assist the understanding of the development of Zimbabwe's coercive networks of accumulation and their more recent manifestations, but they do not solve the problems of how to lessen violence and deepen democracy in the short term.

As Roger Southall raised the idea for this special edition of the *Journal of Contemporary African Studies* many years ago, the popular political theorist John Gray's gloomy reflections on the idea of 'progress' seemed to be very relevant to Zimbabwe. Gray's *Black Mass: Apocalyptic Religion and the Death of Utopia* (2007) spoke of theories of 'development' and 'modernisation' – surely 'scientific' syntheses of liberal philosophies of 'progress' in 'lesser developed' places such as Africa – as dreams. For Gray they are 'not scientific hypothesis but theodicies – narratives of providence and redemption – presented in the jargon of social science'. As such they are part of the economistic (sometimes 'neo-liberal') 'beliefs that dominated the last two decades... residues of the faith in providence that supported classical political economy' (2007, 75). Perhaps the political, economic and social collapse of Zimbabwe amidst the ability of its rulers to maintain – and perhaps even to gain – power, buttresses Gray's pessimism. Closer than Gray to Zimbabwe, Peter Godwin wrote that events in his homeland moved him to wonder if 'the whole idea of progress is a paradox, a rocking horse that goes forward and back, forward and back, but stays in the same place, giving only the comforting illusion of motion' (2006, 51–2).

It was in such a context that this issue's theme – and that of the approximately 150 person November 2010 Bulawayo conference that was its prelude[1] – came to be. A society in which the economy had plummeted to such an extent that the state no longer had a currency in its name, and even the thinnest form of democracy (elections) seemed still-born in the form of a 'transitional inclusive government', might have been a good place to test the optimism of believers in progress.

Aside from those who received middling or large plots of land in the 'fast-track' reform process,[2] a small elite within the accumulation networks within and beyond the ZANU-PF party, state and society complex benefitting from the tacky triumvirate of 'fast-tracked' land, finagled forex and bloodied diamonds (eg Mawowa and Matongo 2010), and perhaps a few in the top echelons of the diaspora, by late 2011 for whom in Zimbabwe had 'progress' unfolded? Very few indeed, it would seem. The vast majority had lost their jobs to 'work' in the informal sector if they were lucky, had migrated to South Africa and further abroad to work – often informally too – if they were somewhat luckier (although leaving Zimbabwe for South Africa put migrants at risk of xenophobia), while a significant minority who kept up their political opposition in Zimbabwe (or were even suspected of voting against the ruling party) and its counterpart in civil society (see Helliker in this edition for important theoretical considerations) suffered violent abuse or death (Sachikonye 2011; Staunton 2009; Orner and Holmes 2011). Many died from easily avoidable illnesses, such as those in the cholera epidemic of 2008–9, or ones that can be kept at bay in 'normal' circumstances. To be sure, the secular celebrants of the 'land to the poor' litany maintain their beliefs (Scoones et al. 2010; cf Rutherford in this edition[3]) but the statistical rebuffs to what appears to be their positivist rectitude are incubating. In general, even the most sanguine of those following the varied dicta of the 'national democratic revolution' – such as South Africa's former president Thabo Mbeki (2001; Moore in this issue) – could not apply the laws of deferred socialism to Zimbabwe easily, while John Hoffman in these pages (perhaps with post-NDR as well as post-liberal lines) can only offer us the hope that the momentum of progress, albeit stalled, *has* taken root in Zimbabwe and *will* appear more obviously again: but even in a post-Mugabe era there will be 'tremendous problems to overcome', needing a 'hard headed notion of progress, rooted in painful and complex realities'.

'Accumulation' is a 'hard-headed notion' indeed, as are those of power and the violence that accompanies it when widespread consent and legitimacy disappear, to emerge again only with a combination of coercion and patronage (see Kriger in this edition). Thus this issue – veering somewhat from the more varied topics at the Bulawayo conference – has moved towards bringing together the ideas of accumulation and power. As the time of publication approached, so too did the mirage of elections to take Zimbabwe out of its inclusive government impasse, and thus the reality of ZANU PF's increased intimidation: this time, the new twist seemed to be that marauding urban youth gangs headed by ZANU PF affiliates sought to control the once *laisser-faire* informal marketers captured so well in Chagonda's contribution to this issue (Moyo 2011), as well as deterring activists and electors from their preferred party choices.

As the transitional inclusive government or the 'government of national unity' mired deeper into its deadlock while a parallel form of governance emerged (Kriger, this issue), the links between violence and accumulation – and lack of the latter for some: those without access to alternative accumulation possibilities are easily recruited to brutal enterprises such as the *Chipangano*, as are they to the National Youth Service (contrary to Shumba 2006, 2010 more akin to a recruiting ground for torturers than a relatively benign site for 'identity construction') and the long-standing Green Bomber militias – were tightening as never before. Yet even this connection – a 'rational' and 'logical' association between the meting out of cruelty and the gathering of often excessive wealth amidst extreme scarcity – may still lock us into the development theodicy of which Gray speaks. We can attempt to *explain* Zimbabwe's violence in terms of the original sin of primary or primitive accumulation if we are Marxists, or the painful transition to modernity if we are liberals: as Ahluwalia, Bethlehem, and Ginio (2007, 2) take it from Mamdani, the 'notion of historical progress...ensures that our modern sensibility is not repulsed by the endemic violence that has marked the modern condition', but when that violence seems senseless – if it 'cannot be justified by progress' – it is much more disturbing; it becomes *explained away* as 'evil', a category too often applied to the Third World 'other' by denizens of wealthy capitalist countries whose historical memories have disappeared. Perhaps *explaining* is a lesser evil – or a better religion – than *explaining away*, so social scientists continue in that attempt. In any case, *explaining* means teasing out particularities rather than resting on general platitudes such as 'primitive accumulation is always violent' (the 'materialist' social scientists), 'Africans are always violent' (the racists), and 'liberation wars always lead to violent and predatory ruling parties and/or classes' (a version of the liberal view). Perhaps too, the movement of 'progress' can only be measured by examining standards of life rather than whether or not humanity's spiritual essence has improved: saints are quite often poor.

Those who live in Zimbabwe and who study it once invested much 'hope' for its progress on the possibility of its settler-colonial heritage of relatively advanced forces and relations of production negating the need for more violence than that expended in the first phase of primitive accumulation (the settler conquest) and the struggle to spread its gains to a new generation of differently coloured politicians and citizens (the 'liberation' war). In 1980, many feared the supposedly 'Marxist-Leninist Terrorist' Robert Mugabe (although not a few 'Marxist-Leninists' were fooled too). Yet his kind, if stilted (and, in retrospect, not so soothing), words on the dawn of independence – 'if yesterday you hated me, today you cannot avoid the love that binds you to me and me to you...the wrongs of the past must now stand forgiven and forgotten...we are all Zimbabweans now' seemed to dissipate those qualms as Mugabe was compared favourably with figures of Mother Theresa's stature (De Waal 1990; Kilgore 2009). When those dreams were dissipated during ZANU PF's 'third *chimurenga*', many were surprised. Robert Mugabe's bromides were remembered with a bitter nostalgia and he was turned quickly into a mendacious, if not mad, dictator. Some mourned the metamorphosis of 'nationalist' to 'patriotic' history,[4] (see Ian Phimister's account in these pages: for him there was no metamorphosis, but a nearly natural evolution in nationalist history – and histories of nationalism as some define them – far too silent on class and contradictions that we all should have seen coming) while others with some sense of that discipline saw the roots of all the current problems in the violence of the national/patriotic war. Yet many of those who wrote against the celebratory nationalist current were prone to seeing a mirror image.

Sithole and Makumbe, for example, wrote that the when the liberation war's 'philosophy of annihilation' was 'complimented [sic] with the monopoly of state power at independence' it was only a matter of time until violence – especially against opposition forces – resumed (1997, 133; see others cited in Moore 2009). This is a rather simplistic explanation: Uganda did not have a war of liberation, but had lots of violence well after independence; the Democratic Republic of the Congo's continuing devastation and death is not a result of battles against colonialism – and has elections, for what they are worth, alongside the simmering war; Mozambique experienced an anti-colonial war against the Portuguese *and* Frelimo and Renamo fought tenaciously thereafter – but Frelimo now bears faint resemblance, at least in the way it dispenses its state's monopoly on force, to ZANU PF. Nor has South Africa's freedom struggle led to a Zimbabwean-style denouement. To be sure, there were many characteristics of the Zimbabwean nationalist war that veered it far away from the trajectory of a 'just war', with propensities carrying through to the present (Kriger 1992, 2003). However, these traits and tendencies were uneven, and contested – and they did not proceed to the next era *inevitably*.

Other currents critical of the nationalist-patriotic hegemony over history emphasise so many bizarre ideologies within what might be called 'Mugabeism' that even those who attempt to chronicle it get confused: is Mugabeism a pernicious blend of nativism and Stalinism, or has it reinvented the old tropes of tribalism (Ndlovu-Gatsheni 2006, 2008, 2009a, 2009b, 2011)? Perhaps these confusing complexities, however, were also embedded in the nationalist strain of historiography, which seemed to take any espoused ideology on face value: on Mugabe's rise to the pinnacle of power Terence Ranger said he was a radical 'in the Castro fashion' (1980, 83), just as far to the left as the young Turks in the Zimbabwe People's Army (ZIPA) he had thrown out to Mozambique's prisons a few years before (Mhanda 2011): they needed teaching, Ranger said (1980, 89), although how that was to take place under incarceration was never revealed. Just a few years earlier an American emissary to Mugabe's own place of restriction in Quelimane (a pleasant house, however, not a prison) was impressed with his commitment to democracy and his antipathy to war, Mozambican militarism, and Soviet-style rule (Solarz in Moore, forthcoming). Politicians and diplomats were bamboozled just as easily as nationalist historians.

It is clear one cannot understand the Mugabe mode of accumulation by attempting to read his ideological mutterings and discerning whether or not his party follows them. However, if one examines the ways in which a historically particular Zimbabwean blend of violence and accumulation came together during the anti-settler struggle, a strand of continuity can be perceived that takes us right into the zones of accumulation outlined in different but complementary ways in this issue by Kriger, Dawson and Kelsall, and Magure.

There is a section in Lloyd Sachikonye's understated but very powerful *When a State Turns on its Citizens* entitled 'coercive accumulation' (2011, 37–40) where links are established between the Zimbabwean elite's 'propensity for acquisitiveness' and a 'regression to coercion and brazen expropriation and extortion of property in clear violation of existing law and practice' in the post-2000 period. This concept could be extended to encompass the war of liberation and the violence between the parties and their predecessors in the 1960s to draw the lines historically and thematically. In the late 1950s and early 1960s, the trade unions and nascent nationalist parties engaged in much violence, as Scarnecchia (2008) documents and Sachikonye notes. Scarnecchia, however, puts the propensity for acquisitiveness – for largesse offered by American union federations and, later, by the American state – close to the centre of his story, but Sachikonye does not, at that stage. The link is severed almost completely in most analyses of the liberation war: the cause may have been just, but the means were not, so the ethics were sundered – but the record of the *material base* of the war is ignored other than with brief discussions of peasants happily feeding their 'boys', or the latter forcing their elders to feed them, or archives of thank you letters to donors all over the world. Yet a 'political economy' of the war's history is possible. A 1986 interview with Henry Hamadziripi mentions a sweet factory, from which the profits went to ZANU (Chivasa 1986). There must have been many more ways of buying arms and provisions other than relying on scientific socialists in the 'east', social democrats in the Scandinavian corners of the 'west', and Cold Warriors handing over arms to those moving away from the Soviet camp, and they deserve research. A later interview with Kombayi (2004), the former mayor of Gweru almost killed by ZANU PF vice-president Simon Muzenda's minions while campaigning for the 1990 election as a Zimbabwe Unity Movement candidate, points to the continuity of coercive accumulation in Zimbabwe's recent history.

Kombayi's hotel office was at the end of a hallway festooned with photographs. The first ones were celebratory: nationalists' weddings and rallies in the 1950s and 1960s. They came to an unhappy end with the aftermath of guerrilla leader Josiah Tongogara's deadly car accident, which occurred as he was driving to inform the guerrilla soldiers in Mozambique of the Lancaster House settlement. Further on, the striped backs and gashed buttocks of tortured Movement for Democratic Change supporters were displayed. As he recounted his days in the liberation war, Kombayi said that it was Rex Nhongo who taught ZANU PF that 'the gun means money'. Kombayi worked for the Rhodesian railway at the Lusaka end, and used his wages to establish a butcher-shop in Zambia's capital. When the Zimbabwean nationalist movements established themselves there, he became a devoted supplier of many of their mainstays (and chaired some of their controversial biennial war councils). In 1977 he joined the Zimbabwean African National Liberation Army (ZANLA – the armed wing of ZANU) in its Mozambican camps, as head of logistics, directly under ZANLA's second-in-command, Rex Nhongo (who on independence changed his name back to Solomon Mujuru, became head of the armed forces, retired to his farms – some taken in the post-2000 moment – and his shops, but remained a powerful politician until his August 2011 death in his burning house). Thousands of the camps' new residents were verging on starvation. Kombayi recollected that Nhongo asked Mozambican president Samora Machel permission to shoot a few elephants in the national parks so his charges could eat some protein-enriched stew. Machel agreed – a few elephants could not have meant too much to the man who had already agreed to imprison the ZIPA 'rebels' Nhongo had revealed to Mugabe (Mhanda 2011) – so many young Zimbabweans did not die of kwashiorkor. However, according to Kombayi, Nhongo did not stop there. He proceeded to kill rhinos. He took their horns to the Gulf States on his trips to the London banks for which he had ZANLA signing authority, in which he deposited the proceeds of his transactions in the Gulf.

Whether exact or not – the late Kombayi had a reputation for somewhat exaggerated stories – this narrative speaks to processes of violence and accumulation that make contemporary Zimbabwe's form of accumulation by vicious rent-seeking understandable historically. The farm invasions, the diamond-curse, and the *Chipangano* are not recent inventions: they arise from a long history of conquest and struggles against it in which the link between power and accumulation is forged by violence.

There may have been moments when that trajectory could have been altered: perhaps when in 1961 Joshua Nkomo signed an agreement with the British for a gradual increase in the franchise: this was rejected as 'docile' by the members of the National Democratic Party who later created ZANU (Mlambo 1972, 163; Martin and Johnson 1980, 68). Maybe further into the war of liberation, if successful, ZIPA's efforts to unify ZAPU and ZANU could have prevented *Gukurahundi* down the line – although Henry Kissinger's vision of ZIPA as a potential pawn of the Soviet Union along with Robert Mugabe's dislike of their challenges prevented that small window of possibility from opening beyond a crack (Scarnecchia, forthcoming).

Of course, whether or not this form of accumulation leads to 'progress' in the sense that its bloody proceeds eventually 'trickle down' to create real wealth – through the formation of surplus value producing classes – or they simply serve to enforce a form of conspicuous consumption that only trickles up to the 'crony capitalists' and out to those with whom they do business globally, is the perennial question about the fate of primitive accumulation in Africa and much of the rest of the 'Third World'. Analyses such as Thebe's in this collection contribute immensely to our understanding of how varied and blended modes of accumulation are manifested in the 'hidden transcripts' within the 'vernacular' modes of tenure in the small-scale agrarian and 'communal' side of Zimbabwe's forms of accumulation and survival.[5] Larger answers to these problems are formulated in different time frames: Marx's historical scope on primitive accumulation in Europe does not offer much immediate hope. Perhaps serfdom disappeared by the end of the fourteenth century, and by the last third of the fifteenth and first decade of the sixteenth the '*prelude* of the revolution that laid the foundation of the capitalist mode of production' had been established (Marx in Tucker 1972, 433). By the end of the seventeenth century 'the different moments of primitive accumulation had distributed themselves ... more or less in chronological order ... over Spain, Portugal, Holland, France, and England'. It was in the latter country where the 'systematical combination, embracing the colonies, the national debt, the modern mode of taxation, and the protectionist system' (Marx in Tucker 1972, 436) merged, hastened by the power of the state and colonialism. The proletariat's origins coincided with the accumulation of capital from the slave trade and the production via that form of labour – through the eighteenth century. These time frames are rarely considered when the 'progress' of Zimbabwe's 'inclusive government' is charted.

These are the sorts of *longue durees* of which Keynes said the only certainty was that many people would be dead at their end. To hasten a better short term, scholars can only measure Hoffman's interpretation of Hegel's slaughter benches (in this issue). In the absence of certainty about whether these benches seat a 'real' bourgeoisie and its nemesis, the proletariat it needs but does not want, some might suggest it is best to advocate the relative simplicities of deeper democracy and wider human rights. Even these truths are not so self-evident, however: their pursuit can entail more deaths and torture than any decent human being in a position to stop them could countenance. Thus the dilemmas of Zimbabwe's current political impasse – and Morgan Tsvangirai's mid-2008 decision to pull out of the deep end of democracy in the face of his supporters' continued deaths (Tsvangirai 2011, 479–84; cf. Chan 2011, 192–4) that brought on what might be a longer drawing out of the blend of accumulation, power and violence for which no end is in sight. We are not really any closer to untying the Gordian knot of human rights and political economy that half a decade ago Raftopoulos noted blights the Zimbabwean political, activist, and academic landscape (2006; also Moore 2004; cf. Howard-Hassmann 2010, prioritising human rights and the international 'responsibility to protect'). In that light, the scholarly contributions in the following pages, and the conference preceding them, can make only small contributions to 'progress'. They do, however, accumulate along with hundreds of other, far braver, ones, to maintain momentum.

Notes
1. The conference – of which this issue edition is a 'product' – was sponsored by the Open Society Initiative for Southern Africa, Interchurch Organisation for Development Cooperation, the Norwegian People's Aid and the Civil Society Monitoring Mechanism. Itai Zimunya must be thanked profusely for his long-term work as the OSISA 'point-man' in Zimbabwe, as must Eldred Masunungure's Mass Public Opinion Institute and especially Monica Munzwandi and her team for fine organisation and logistics. Showers Mawowa and Judith Todd deserve special appreciation too. Bulawayo Agenda assisted in its fair city. Patrick Bond emailed the proceedings to all and sundry, all over, every day. Kubatana's Amanda Atwood set up an audio and text archive, http://www.kubatana.net/html/archive/demgg/101108kub.asp?sector=DEMGG&year=0&range_start=1, and Edwina Spicer Productions filmed the event. Apparently about six scribes from Zimbabwe's Central Intelligence Organisation were also taking notes and discussing matters with the delegates. Finally but most gratefully, thanks to Norma Kriger and Brian Raftopoulos, who kept this boat afloat.
2. Not all of the larger plots of land went to ostensibly ZANU PF supporters; or not all recipients *stayed* ZANU PF supporters. Between February and June 2002 the state-run *Sunday Mail* published a list from the Ministry of Lands and Agriculture of those who received Model A-2 (Commercial Scheme) farms (Justice for Agriculture 2002). A Dr. Mtuli Ncube, then a lecturer at the London School of Economics, is listed as having received Sikumi Estate, nearly 8,400 hectares in size, near Hwange, Matabeleland North. As of late 2011 Ncube was Chief Economist and Vice President of the African Development Bank, after holding posts as Head of the Business School at the University of Witwatersrand in Johannesburg, and for a few months thereafter Dean of the Faculty of Commerce, Law and Management at Wits. Before that, however, he was chair of Barbican Bank, which lost its licence in the early 2000s, but by 2010 was apparently opening once again (Mpofu 2011). While in Johannesburg Professor Ncube was involved in the organisation of at least two well-advertised public appearances by the president of the MDC, Morgan Tsvangirai, and at a Wits University public seminar on the Zimbabwean situation advocated the establishment of private property rights as the *sine qua non* of Zimbabwean progress.
3. Rutherford's review essay in the form of a conference paper came to the editors as they were starting work on this edition. In spite and because of Kirk Helliker's previous review in these pages, we felt the debate deserved even more comprehensive treatment; thus we asked its author to elaborate some more.
4. Another problem with the idea of 'patriotic history' is that it can be made much too powerful, approaching the status of a *driver* of Zimbabwe's modern history and political economy, accelerated and steered by a small coterie of 'public intellectuals' (Tendi 2010).
5. Thebe's article was submitted to *JCAS* independently of the conference, but its fine texture promised to illuminate much of the present and future discussion about how small commodity producers work and will work in rural Zimbabwe.

Note on contributor
David Moore is Professor of Development Studies and head of that department at the University of Johannesburg. He has researched and written on Zimbabwean politics since 1984. His next output will be 'The ZIPA Moment in Zimbabwean History, 1975–1977:

Mugabe's Rise and Democracy's Demise' forthcoming in Carolyn Basset and Marlea Clarke, eds., *Legacies of Liberation: Post-colonial Struggles for a Democratic Southern Africa*, Toronto and Cape Town: Fernwood and HSRC. His most recent one was 'Bloody African Development: War and Accumulation on the Dark Continent', *New Political Economy*, 16, 1 (February 2011).

References

Ahluwalia, P., L. Bethlehem, and R. Ginio. 2007. Introduction: Unsettling violence. In *Violence and non-violence in Africa*, ed. P. Ahluwalia, L. Bethlehem, and R. Ginio, 1–11. London: Routledge.
Chan, S. 2011. *Old treacheries, new deceits: Insights into Southern African politics*. Johannesburg and New Haven: Jonathan Ball and Yale University Press.
Chivasa, M. 1986. Hamadziripi – War Veteran. *Parade*, February, 12 ff.
De Waal, V. 1990. *The politics of reconciliation: Zimbabwe's first decade*. London: Hurst.
Godwin, P. 2006. *When a crocodile eats the sun: A memoir of Africa*. Boston: Little Brown.
Gray, J. 2007. *Black mass: Apocalyptic religion and the death of Utopia*. Toronto: Doubleday.
Howard-Hassmann, R. 2010. Mugabe's Zimbabwe, 2000–2009: Massive human rights violations and the failure to protect. *Human Rights Quarterly* 32, no. 4: 898–920.
Justice for Agriculture. 2002. Confirmed VIP's allocations - The landless poor? http://www.swradioafrica.com/pages/farms.htm (accessed November 24, 2011).
Kilgore, J. 2009. *We are all Zimbabweans now*. Cape Town: Umuzi.
Kombayi, P. 2004. Interview with David Moore, Gweru: September.
Kriger, N. 1992. *Zimbabwe's Guerrilla war: Peasant voices*. Cambridge: Cambridge University Press.
Kriger, N. 2003. *Guerrilla violence in post-war Zimbabwe: Symbolic and violent politics 1980–1987*. Cambridge: Cambridge University Press.
Martin, D., and J. Johnson. 1981. *The struggle for Zimbabwe: The Chimurenga war*. Harare and London: Zimbabwe Publishing House and Faber.
Marx, K. (1867) 1972. Capital volume I – part VIII: The so-called primitive accumulation. In *The Marx-Engels Reader*, ed. R. Tucker, 2nd ed, 431–38. New York: Norton.
Mawowa, S., and A. Matongo. 2010. Inside Zimbabwe's roadside currency trade: The 'World Bank' of Bulawayo. *Journal of Southern African Studies* 36, no. 2: 319–37.
Mbeki, T. (2001) 2008. How will Zimbabwe defeat its enemies? A discussion document, African National Congress mimeograph July 10; reprinted with some alterations as 'The Mbeki-Mugabe Papers: A Discussion Document'. *New Agenda* 2nd Quarter: 56–75.
Mhanda, W. 2011. *Dzino: Memories of a freedom fighter*. Harare: Weaver.
Mlambo, E. 1972. *Rhodesia: The struggle for a birthright*. London: C. Hurst.
Moore, D. 2004. Marxism and Marxist intellectuals in schizophrenic Zimbabwe: How many rights for Zimbabwe's left? A comment. *Historical Materialism* 12, no. 4: 405–25.
Moore, D. 2009. Liberation movements and democracy in Africa: Beyond the easy answers. *Open Space* 2, no. 5: 56–61.
Moore, D. Forthcoming. The Zipa Moment in Zimbabwean History. In *Legacies of liberation: Post-colonial struggles for a Democratic Southern Africa*, ed. C. Basset and M. Clarke. Toronto and Cape Town: Fernwood and Human Sciences Research Council.
Moyo, J. 2011. Zanu-PF's militia feeds on extortion. *Mail and Guardian*, November 18–24.
Mpofu, N. 2011. Re-licensed Banks – Where can they fit in? *Financial Gazette*, April 28.
Ndlovu-Gatsheni, S. 2006. The Nativist Revolution and Development Conundrums in Zimbabwe. *Accord Occasional Paper Series* 1, no. 4: 3–40.
Ndlovu-Gatsheni, S. 2008. Reaping the bitter fruits of Stalinist tendencies in Zimbabwe. *Concerned African Scholars Bulletin* 79 (June): 21–31.
Ndlovu-Gatsheni, S. 2009a. *Do 'Zimbabweans' exist? Trajectories of nationalism, national identity formation and crisis in a postcolonial state*. Oxford: Peter Lang.
Ndlovu-Gatsheni, S. 2009b. Making sense of Mugabeism in local and global politics: 'So, Blair, keep your England and let me keep My Zimbabwe'. *Third World Quarterly* 30, no. 6: 1139–58.

Ndlovu-Gatsheni, S. 2011. The Zimbabwean nation-state project: A historical diagnosis of identity and power-based conflicts in a postcolonial state. *Discussion Paper 59*, Nordiska Afrikainstitutet.

Orner, P., and A. Holmes. 2011. *Don't listen to what I'm about to say: Voices of Zimbabwe*. Johannesburg: Jonathan Ball.

Raftopoulos, B. 2006. The Zimbabwean crisis and the challenges for the left. *Journal of Southern African Studies* 32, no. 2: 203–19.

Ranger, T. 1980. The changing of the old guard: Robert Mugabe and the revival of ZANU. *Journal of Southern African Studies* 7, no. 1: 71–90.

Sachikonye, L. 2011. *When a state turns on its citizens: 60 years of institutionalised violence in Zimbabwe*. Harare and Johannesburg: Weaver Press and Jacana.

Scarnecchia, T. 2008. *The urban roots of democracy and political violence in Zimbabwe: Harare and Highfield, 1940–1964*. Rochester: University of Rochester Press.

Scarnecchia, T. 2010. Imperialists and allies: Robert Mugabe's diplomacy with Americans and Africans at the Rhodesia Geneva Talks 1976, Cold War Cultures Conference, University of Texas at Austin, September 29–October 2.

Scoones, I., N. Marongwe, B. Mavedzenge, J. Mahenehene, F. Murimbarimba, and C. Sukume. 2010. *Zimbabwe's land reform: Myths and realities*. Oxford, Auckland Park, Harare: James Currey, Jacana and Weaver Press.

Shumba, R. 2006. Social identities in the National Youth Service of Zimbabwe. MA diss., Department of Sociology, University of Johannesburg.

Shumba, R. 2010. *Constructing youth identities in National Youth Service: An exploration of the National Youth Service of Zimbabwe*. Saarbrücken: LAP Lambert.

Sithole, M., and J. Makumbe. 1997. Elections in Zimbabwe: The ZANU (PF) hegemony and its incipient decline. *African Journal of Political Science* 2, no. 1: 122–39.

Staunton, I. 2009. *Damage: The personal costs of political change in Zimbabwe*. Harare: Weaver Press.

Tendi, B-M. 2010. *Making history in Mugabe's Zimbabwe: Politics, intellectuals and the media*. Oxford: Peter Lang.

Tsvangirai, M. (with Bango, W.) 2011. *Morgan Tsvangirai: At the deep end*. Johannesburg: Penguin.

ZANU PF politics under Zimbabwe's 'Power-Sharing' Government

Norma Kriger

Department of Anthropology and Development Studies, University of Johannesburg, Auckland Park, South Africa

> Using informal network analysis to understand ZANU PF politics, the key significance of the Inclusive Government (IG) is twofold. First, competition between ZANU PF and the 'opposition' parties in the IG helps informal networks to cohere sufficiently to run a parallel government that effectively sabotages the IG. Second, the parallel government itself operates to a significant degree through informal networks, further entrenching this form of politics. Informal networks that rely on violence and patronage – or consent and coercion – capture the dynamic shaping contemporary politics in Zimbabwe.

Introduction

After nearly 30 years of *de facto* one-party rule in Zimbabwe, ZANU PF became a reluctant participant of a power-sharing arrangement in February 2009, known as the Inclusive Government (IG). The impetus for power-sharing came from the AU and SADC following Mugabe's re-election as President in June 2008 in such a violent campaign that Morgan Tsvangirai, the leader of the larger Movement for Democratic Change formation (MDC-T), withdrew from the run-off election to stop the suffering being inflicted upon his supporters. Having won the first round of the presidential contest against Mugabe in March 2008, Tsvangirai expected his party to be the dominant power in the new government, if power had to be shared. However, he and Arthur Mutambara, the leader of the small MDC formation – at the table mainly because Mbeki wanted to use it to neutralise MDC-T's power – joined ZANU PF's leader, Mugabe, in signing the Global Political Agreement (GPA). The incorporation of 'opposition' parties in the government changed the political context but not ZANU PF's *de facto* rule through violence, intimidation, and repression against the 'opposition' in government and civil society opponents, patronage, and narrow nationalist appeals. However, ZANU PF's rule is increasingly through informal networks rather than institutions qua institutions.

This article brings to the fore the informalisation of politics – the prominence of informal networks in ZANU PF – under the IG. Informal networks, composed of individuals with positions in state institutions and the party and others outside these organisations, seek power within the party and against the 'opposition' in government through violence and patronage, themselves often interdependent processes. These informal networks blur the distinction between state and nonstate institutions, coercive and noncoercive institutions, and public and private organisations. From the perspective of an analysis grounded in informal networks, the key significance of the power-sharing government is two-fold. First, ZANU PF's competition with the 'opposition' parties in the IG helps informal networks to cohere sufficiently to run a parallel government that effectively sabotages the IG. Second, the parallel government itself operates to a significant degree through informal networks, further entrenching this form of politics. Informal networks that rely on violence and patronage – or consent and coercion – capture the dynamics shaping contemporary politics in Zimbabwe.

The notion of informal political networks is well-established in African politics, including as a crucial component in the concepts of 'warlordism', 'shadow states', the 'criminalization of the state', and the 'instrumentalisation of disorder' (Bayart, Ellis, and Hibou 1999; Reno 1998; Chabal and Daloz 1999). These concepts have been applied to many African countries characterised as having weak states, failed states, or collapsed states, and often also having armed opponents. For these and other reasons, this body of literature has not influenced the study of Zimbabwean politics. The concept of informal political networks used in this article shares with this literature chiefly its departure from the orthodox view of 'party' and 'state' as institutions. In contrast, the literature on politics in Zimbabwe, and more specifically on the GPA and the IG, remains embedded in conventional approaches to 'party' and 'state' as if they still function as institutions.

One approach to the power-sharing government is to measure its progress in implementing specific provisions of the GPA (e.g. Sokwanele 2011a; Idasa 2011). Leaving aside the problematic assumption that the agreement takes precedence over the parties' agendas, the inherent piecemeal nature of this approach is ill-suited to capture political dynamics. Another approach, whether downplaying or taking seriously the agreement, examines the political dynamic in the IG and its consequences for democratic reform envisaged in the GPA. For Cheeseman and Tendi (2010), the strength and intransigence of ZANU PF and the military are impediments to democratic reform because it would lead to loss of power. These authors therefore see a politics of continuity, despite the power-sharing government. Matyszak (2009) portrays the relationship between Tsvangirai and Mugabe in the IG as 'symbiotic': Tsvangirai and the MDC-T's deliberate policy of appeasing Mugabe actually plays into Mugabe's strategy of making full use of his state power to resist democratic reform. Raftopoulos (2010, 707) understands the GPA as 'a major aspect' of the 'passive revolution' in which 'a ruling party facing an organic political and economic crisis has used the space to reconfigure and renegotiate the terms of its existence with the opposition, civil society and the international community'. He emphasises ZANU PF's control of the state's 'coercive forces', the centre of the party, or 'the military' as the major obstacle to democratic reforms (Raftopoulos 2010, 712; 714). While recognising the GPA and the IG as providing a new context, he sees the ruling party's on-going reconfiguration of the state, society, and economy as a politics of continuity with the party's responses to the multiple crises from 1998 to 2008 (Raftopoulos 2009).

These analysts overstate the extent to which ZANU PF's power resides within state institutions qua institutions even as they, and others (e.g. ICG 2011b, 14 – fn 131), observe the continuing fragmentation and weakening of ZANU PF and the MDC formations under the IG. This article makes the fragmented character of ZANU PF politics the primary rather than the subordinate focus and posits both that informal alliances have been re-forming the party and that they are not necessarily weak. For ZANU PF, control of party and state institutions remains as critical as ever, but control is exercised increasingly by networks of individuals located in and outside institutions. These networks might include individuals at any level in the hierarchy of the security sector, the bureaucracy and the party, MPs, councillors, traditional leaders, youth militia, unemployed youth, national entrepreneurs, and, though not the focus here, also regional and global actors. Some speculate that MDC elites will be co-opted into these informal networks, if indeed the process has not already begun.

The growing prominence of informal alliance politics in ZANU PF seems to overlap with the period (1998–2008), widely identified as one of multiple crises. Tracing when and why powerful personal networks of violence and patronage emerged is important but not the focus of this article. Broadly, though, several factors have spawned and strengthened this type of politics: the economic opportunities that the military and political elite had access to in the DRC from 1998; the party's allocation of unlawfully expropriated land (and other economic assets such as mines) to the ruling elite along with the privatisation of violence through war veterans, youth militia, and party youth and the operation of militia bases on occupied private white-owned farms, mainly from 2000; the long-running succession battle within ZANU PF to replace Mugabe as party leader and President; and most recently, the creation of a 'parallel' government under the IG. It is unsurprising, therefore, that a few scholars began searching for concepts beyond conventional understandings of 'state' and 'party' to come to grips with the challenges of governance in Zimbabwe from 1998 (e.g. Maclean 2002; Moore 2003).

The article is divided into two sections. The first section shows that the different factions in ZANU PF are held together chiefly by a shared vested interest in preventing the 'opposition' parties in the IG, and in particular, the MDC-T, from coming to power as a result of democratising reforms. This fragile unity has made it possible for ZANU PF to establish a parallel government – itself both a symptom of the privatisation of party and state politics and also a factor intensifying the phenomenon. The second section illustrates in greater detail the existence of competing personalised networks of power to highlight how the use of violence and patronage affects not only ZANU PF politics *vis-à-vis* the 'opposition' parties in government but also the character of competition among networks within ZANU PF. Both sections share a narrative about the prominence of informal alliances operating across the formal and informal institutions and seeking power through violence and patronage. Violence and patronage, rather than being independent, are often interdependent mechanisms of creating and building power. Identifying personal networks is obviously extremely difficult. What follows is inevitably sketchy and meant to be chiefly suggestive of a conceptual approach to understanding the dynamics by which ZANU PF rules in contemporary Zimbabwe.

Inclusive government: holding informal networks of power together

The IG has provided ZANU PF with a common goal that has helped to contain entrenched factional feuding over access to power and resources. The goal is to prevent the introduction of democratising reforms and the holding of free and fair elections that would lead to regime change and victory for the MDC-T. The repercussions for ZANU PF elites and their associates could then be prosecution for economic and political crimes and loss of access to patronage. The very favourable terms of the GPA together with Mugabe's skilful manipulation of the few GPA provisions where ZANU PF did make small concessions have enabled ZANU PF to maintain its formal control of state institutions, a prerequisite for the creation of a parallel government to undermine the IG and marginalise the 'opposition' parties.[1] The creation of a parallel government is both a symptom and an aggravating cause of the informalisation of politics. The parallel government holds together the competing informal networks in the party by ensuring that they share power through violence and access to resources.

The GPA and the IG: ZANU PF's advantages

The GPA, which was the basis for creating a power-sharing government, barely dented the power of President Mugabe and ZANU PF. The lack of implementation mechanisms provided for in the agreement led Derek Matyszak (2008, 3) to remark that '[T]he bulk of the 15 page Agreement comprises pious statements devoid of any practical consequence and which are little more than political posturing'. The core of the agreement is Article XX, Framework for A New Government, the only provision to be incorporated into the amended constitution. The GPA and the amended constitution state that the Prime Minister, Morgan Tsvangirai, is to share executive authority with the President but 'the nature of this executive authority is no where (sic) indicated in the agreement or constitution' (Matyszak 2009, 3).

In contrast, President Mugabe retains almost all of his executive authority. For example, he controls the police, the security forces, and the intelligence agencies; signs all bills passed by the parliament before they can become law; chairs and chooses the cabinet; and can decide which Ministers are responsible for specific Acts of Parliament. He also has the power to proclaim martial law and public emergencies and can grant pardons. Reflecting its preservation of the *status quo*, the GPA did not require judicial and security sector reform, the disbandment of militia, and the repeal or even amendment of repressive laws – all cornerstones of ZANU PF power prior to the formation of the IG (Ero and Varney 2008; Matyszak 2009; GPA 2008).

Where Mugabe was required by the GPA and the amended constitution to concede some power, he flouted the requirements. Permitted to appoint 31 ministers, of which 16 were to be nominated by the MDC formations (3 by the MDC-M and 13 by the MDC-T) (GPA Article 20.1.6(5)), Mugabe appointed 41 ministers – 21 nominated by ZANU PF, 15 by MDC-T, and 4 by MDC-M – to be able to better manage the patronage demands in his party (ICG 2009, 3). Moreover, Mugabe allocated nearly all the ministerial posts unilaterally in November 2008, ensuring that ZANU PF got its pick of portfolios, including Defence, Foreign Affairs, Local Government and Housing, and Home Affairs, while the MDC formations were allocated '"empty" portfolios, junior portfolios or portfolios related to infrastructure or service delivery' (Matyszak 2009, 4). The latter ministries – including health, water, energy, and education – were close to total collapse and would depend on foreign donor funding for recovery. The MDC-T was later allocated the Ministry of Finance and, after intense bargaining, nominated a Minister to share Home Affairs with the ZANU PF Minister.

Under the GPA and the amended constitution, Mugabe also had to make key appointments 'in terms of the constitution or under any legislation' with the consent of the Prime Minister (Matyszak 2009, 2–3). Instead, Mugabe made unilateral appointments of permanent secretaries and ambassadors (ICG 2010, 5; Matyszak 2009, 12). Earlier, Mugabe unilaterally reappointed provincial governors and the Reserve Bank governor, and appointed a new Attorney-General while the parties were negotiating the GPA and in the period before the formation of the IG (ICG 2008, 3; ICG 2009, 3). These unilateral appointments violated the spirit of the July 2008 agreement by ZANU PF and the two MDC formations not to take decisions or measures that would have a bearing on the formation of a new government (MOU 2008, Article 9). In August 2010, Mugabe unilaterally reappointed provincial governors when their terms expired (ICG 2011a, 6). Yet in spite of the importance that Mugabe and ZANU PF attached to maintaining state control, it should not be the basis for deducing that the party rules chiefly through these institutions as opposed to networks that operate within and outside them.

ZANU PF's parallel government

ZANU PF's parallel government has held the party together while deliberately disrupting and marginalising the IG. The foundations of the unofficial government continue to be the use of violence, intimidation, and repressive laws against the 'opposition' parties and opposition civil society organisations and patronage for loyalists. Informal networks are important in the operation of the parallel government. Three examples illustrate how ZANU PF has sabotaged the IG while propping up its own support base using violence and/or patronage. First, ZANU PF has prevented civil service restructuring that would harm important party bases of violence and patronage and redound to the favour of the 'opposition' in government. Second, it has used state companies to deny mining resources to the Treasury in order to retain important levers of patronage and starve the government of much-needed budget resources. Third, it has continued to allow personalised networks of violence and patronage to operate against the opposition in rural areas.

Preventing the removal of irregularly hired civil servants

The Civil Service Skills and Audit, requested by the Minister of Public Service (MDC-T) and conducted despite enormous resistance from the Public Services Commission (PSC)(ZANU-PF-controlled), identified 75,000 civil servants as suspect and in need of further investigation (Biti 2011, 81). Currently, almost 40% of civil servants are youth militia hired irregularly by the ZANU PF government in 2008 to provide intelligence and engage in other partisan activities, including participation in violence orchestrated by rural bases.[2] Of these, some 10,000 were hired in the Ministry of Youth as 'youth development officers' or 'ward officers' (The Anatomy of Terror 2011). Others are in service delivery ministries where they lack the required skills to perform the technical tasks for which they were hired. The cabinet, a centre of ZANU PF power, has blocked publication of the report and therefore its implementation (Sibanda 2011b). Removing these workers from the payroll would save the Treasury an estimated $20 million in wages per month (Chifera, Dube, and Rusere 2011). Not only does keeping these youth militia on the payroll deny the official government much-needed revenue but it also positions them to be the eyes and ears of the party in the civil service, schools, and health-care facilities and to continue to be rewarded as they engage in violence as members of informal networks. Since the completion of the audit, there have been reports that ZANU PF has recruited more youth militia into the police and army through its control of recruitment into the civil service and the security sector (ICG 2011a, 9 – fn 65).

The blocking of civil service reform by ZANU PF involved the PSC, a body appointed by the President under the constitution (Matyszak 2008, 9), the ZANU PF-controlled cabinet, and the ZANU PF permanent secretary in the Ministry of Public Service. These blocking mechanisms demonstrate the importance of Mugabe's control of appointments to state posts. Networks outside the state appear not to have been necessary to impede civil service restructuring.

Using mining revenue to pay civil servants

ZANU PF has privatised control over the diamond mining sector to run an unofficial Finance Ministry parallel to the official Finance Ministry. The Ministry of Mines and Mining Development is headed by Obert Mpofu (ZANU PF) while the Finance Minister is Tendai Biti, Secretary-General of the MDC-T. In his 2011 midterm fiscal policy review, Minister Biti lamented that 'there is no connection between Zimbabwe's income from diamonds, its output and international prices..... Despite the huge production at Marange in 2011, no payment has been received by Treasury for income earned between 1 January and 30 June 2011' (Biti 2011, 32). According to Southern Africa Report, an estimated 90% of diamond revenue was still unaccounted for in November 2011 and allegedly benefitting 'the security forces, ZANU-PF and a range of politically linked individuals' (ICG 2011b, 14 – fn 127).

The diamond revenues that do not enter the treasury are also used to promote ZANU PF competition with the MDC. Two examples help to make this point clear: the use of diamond revenues to pay civil servants and to finance arms and other defence-related deals. First, ZANU PF used its control of diamond revenues to thwart the MDC-T's budget-balancing efforts and win favour with civil servants by demonstrating that its patronage resources were being used to pay for their salary increases. In July 2011, the ZANU PF-controlled state company, Zimbabwe Mining Development Corporation, paid $40 million in civil servant salary increases – one-third of the Treasury's monthly wage bill (US$120 million) for civil servants. Biti had opposed a civil servants' salary hike on the grounds that the government could not afford it and that civil servants' wages already consumed more than 63% of the annual government budget (Bloch 2011). Second, after Minister Biti blocked official arms purchases, 'there have been several reports of military commanders personally securing diamonds-for-guns deals with Chinese officials', whether for use in winning an election, as in the presidential run-off election in 2008, or in a coup, or in factional struggles over succession (PAC 2010, 17).[3]

The importance of informal networks in the generation and allocation of Marange mining revenues undergirds the ability of the parallel government to pay civil servants as if it were the official government. The broad contours of these networks are brought into sharper focus later in the discussion of network competition.

Maintaining control in rural areas

Like the ZANU PF government during the crisis, the parallel government relies on personalised networks of violence and patronage to benefit its supporters and victimise and deny benefits to opposition supporters. The Anatomy of Terror (2011) report published anonymously to protect the civic activists and field researchers and their informants from ZANU PF retribution, provides the first attempt to provide details of how ZANU PF organised violence, including the names, functions, and organisational affiliations of those involved. The study covered 15 constituencies in five provinces and focused on the organisation of violence during the presidential run-off election in 2008 and violence since the formation of the IG, mostly spurred by the constitutional outreach program and announcements that elections would occur soon. The report provides data that are a powerful testimony to the vitality of personalised networks of power and the often inextricable links between violence and patronage. Focused on the constituency level, however, the ways in which grassroots networks are linked at the highest level are not always clear.

The organisation of violence in each constituency varies considerably but two important generalities emerge. First, those involved in organised rural violence include serving and retired military personnel (from the rank of sergeant to generals), police, Central Intelligence Organisation (CIO) agents, Members of Parliament (or in two cases, parliamentary candidates who lost in the 2008 election), Cabinet Ministers, war veterans, youth militia, rural district councillors, national and local party officials (from district level to the Politburo and Central Committee), provincial governors and district administrators, civil servants, and traditional leaders. In the 15 constituencies studied, three ZANU PF cabinet ministers were named as being involved in the coordination of base operations (Vice President Mujuru and Minister Savior Kasukuwere, MPs for Mt. Darwin West and South, respectively, and Transport Minister Nicholas Goche), three members of the Joint Operation Command (Prisons Service Commissioner, Retired Major General Paradzai Zimondi, Police Commissioner-General Augustine Chihuri, Reserve Bank Governor Gideon Gono), and top military men (Brigadier General Nyikayaramba, Brigadiers Milaso and Kamonera, and Major General George Kafesu.)

Second, the organisers of rural violence have been engaged in an intricate web of patronage that persists under the power-sharing government. Perpetrators of violence often already have government or parastatal jobs or receive them as rewards for violence. They may also be given permission to engage in illegal gold panning in their local area or be granted access to market stalls; receive cash, credit, and food from individuals involved in the networks of violence, some of whom have local businesses and farms occupied during the land invasions; obtain access to diverted international donor aid; and enjoy opportunities to extort and loot resources (money, livestock, etc.) from opposition members. Meanwhile, ZANU PF supporters more generally may be rewarded with government-provided food aid and farm inputs while these resources are denied to opposition supporters. Opposition members may also be displaced from their constituencies by violence and threats from the ZANU PF networks of violence.

The organisation of one constituency, Maramba Pfungwe, a communal land in Mashonaland East province, provides a specific case of how named individuals, working within and outside the state organised violence in 2008, benefited from patronage. The constituency is a staunch ZANU PF stronghold. All nine wards in the constituency were won by ZANU PF in the 2008 election and the MP, Washington Musvaire, belongs to ZANU-PF. Bases were created by ward councillors, ZANU-PF district party structures, and the militia. Army colonels Mudzimba and Charamba were the commanders of all the bases in Maramba Pfungwe. They gave orders to army Captain Pfidze and the MP to organise violence and liaised directly with the member in charge, Inspector Nekati, at Mutawatawa police station and a police sergeant at Police Internal Security Intelligence section to prevent the arrest of perpetrators of violence. The two army colonels and captain and the MP formulated strategies of violence against MDC activists. Captain Pfidze commanded seven named war veterans and three named soldiers who had been involved in Operation Maguta, an army-controlled distribution of agricultural inputs to ZANU PF loyalists. The MP and the army captain worked with Chief Chinyerere and Chief Chiutsi, who transmitted information to village and kraal heads. The traditional leaders, elected ward councillors, and ZANU PF district party structures then identified potential victims. The youth militia implemented the violence. The councillors were also instructed by the MP to control the operations of all NGOs in their wards. Councillors controlled activities at the bases in their wards. No perpetrators of violence had been arrested.

Of the 15 bases operating in the constituency during the presidential election run-off in 2008, four had been activated in mid-2010 soon after President Mugabe and PM Tsvangirai had announced possible elections in 2011. All youths were reportedly forced to go for training (usually Friday and Saturday evenings) at bases where sexual abuse occurred. Reports provided the names of trainers and their positions. Some village headmen were said to have been stripped of their office because of MDC political affiliations and replaced by siblings (Crisis Coalition of Zimbabwe 2010). While most of the dormant bases had been at public schools, the four active bases were in an open space at a business centre, at two Apostolic churches that met under trees, and at a third near a primary school. The church bases attracted 200 to 300 people when services were held. Influential base leaders included church leaders, one a war veteran and the other a war collaborator (the postindependence name given to the youth who provided logistical support to the guerrillas during the liberation war).

The food aid provided by two NGOs, Catholic Relief Services and Christian Care, was captured by councillors and traditional leaders who were responsible for its distribution, and like the parastatal Grain Marketing Board's food aid, was directed to ZANU PF supporters, youth militia, and other activists. Several ZANU PF activists and supporters benefited from agricultural inputs provided under the army's Operation Maguta. The GMB and NGOs employed ZANU PF youth. MDC supporters were not allowed to buy from local shops and shop owners who defied this ban were punished by the militia. The constituency is rich in gold and the militia was allocated illegal gold panning rights while these were denied to MDC supporters.

The violence against MDC supporters often resulted in the destruction of houses, livestock, food, and other property or looting of their food and property by the perpetrators of violence.

ZANU PF networks of violence and patronage in rural areas demonstrate how state institutions qua institutions have been undermined. The location of bases on private property (private homes, farms occupied during the land invasions, business centres, and churches) and in public institutions (public schools, police stations, rural district council community halls, and District Development Fund and Grain Marketing Depot offices) illustrates the blurring of public/private spheres. Similarly, the distinction between state and nonstate institutions and coercive and noncoercive state organisations have become blurred and lost significance as networks are comprised of individuals in all these institutions.

In sum, the parallel government demonstrates the relative powerlessness of the IG and the dominance of ZANU PF in its competition with the MDC. The power of the parallel government has been illustrated by its effective resistance to removing its clients – youth militia and other irregularly hired personnel – from the civil service, its ability to mobilise very substantial mining revenues and use some portion thereof to finance one-time wage increases for civil servants, and its capacity to organise rural bases that engage in violence and intimidation of the opposition. Informal networks of violence and patronage underpin the operation of the parallel government, even as some institutions, like the Public Service Commission, exercise institutional power. Beneath the appearance of ZANU PF unity against the opposition are networks of power that compete against each other and the MDC-T, the focus of the next section.

ZANU PF networks compete with each other and against MDC

If the shared desire for informal networks to run a parallel government helps to hold ZANU PF together, it does not conceal the operation of informal networks within the party competing with each other for power even as they compete against the MDC and its supporters. The networks compete with each other and against their MDC opponents with violence and patronage, including resources often forcibly taken from opponents. Two randomly selected arenas – urban politics and mining politics – help to illustrate how network competition is entangled with ZANU PF opposition to the MDC and its supporters.

Urban politics

Politics in Epworth, a periurban constituency about 10 miles from Harare, and Mbare, a high-density suburb of Harare, was not merely a power struggle between MDC-T and ZANU PF but was also inextricably linked to the competition between two top-ranking ZANU PF politicians, Amos Midzi and Hubert Nyanhongo. Amos Midzi lost the 2008 lower house election in Epworth to Eliah Jembere, the MDC-T candidate, and therefore lost his Minister of Mines and cabinet posts. He was elected Harare Province party chair over Nyanhongo in November 2009 with the support of retired General Solomon Mujuru while Nyanhongo had the backing of Defence Minister Mnangagwa. The post had been vacant for over a year because the two men's supporters had engaged in violent clashes at an earlier election held at party headquarters (The Zimbabwean 2009). Nyanhongo, a retired Lieutenant Colonel in the army, is the Deputy Minister of Energy and Power Development, a Central Committee member, the Harare South lower house MP elected in 2008, and the only ZANU PF MP to be elected in Harare Province (Sibanda 2011a). The two men reportedly both wanted to be appointed Harare Province governor, even before the death of the incumbent in March 2011, and they needed to demonstrate support in the capital to boost their bid for the governorship (SPT 2011, 36). During the presidential run-off election campaign, Midzi commanded all Epworth bases, for which Dhonoro/Masasa was the central base. Today Dhonoro/Masasa base is under Midzi's leadership, as are the three other active bases in Epworth. However, Nyanhongo is trying to wrest control of Dhonoro/Masasa base from Midzi. The base is actually located in Harare South, where Nyanhongo is the MP. Dhonoro-Masasa base is in a private house, as are the other three active bases (The Anatomy of Terror 2011).

Midzi, along with politburo member, Tendai Savanhu, who failed to win the Mbare constituency in the 2008 lower house election, encouraged *Chipangano* (Agreement) youth violence against the MDC-T in Mbare, according to Mbare's MDC-T MP (The Zimbabwean 2011; Zaba 2011). Midzi, once more assisted by Tendai Savanhu, reportedly continues to provision the bases he controls in Epworth (including Dhonoro) with money, weapons, food, vehicles, and payments in cash, marijuana, and beer to the youth. The tussle between the two ZANU PF heavyweights has divided ZANU PF youth involved in base activities against MDC-T supporters (The Anatomy of Terror 2011). Perhaps anticipating that he will not secure the Harare governorship, Nyanhongo is also vested in becoming the MP for Nyanga North in Manicaland province, a constituency won by MDC-T's Douglas Mwonzora in the 2008 election (Mukarati 2011). Nyanhongo is believed to command a base in this constituency. As a retired Lieutenant Colonel in the army, he instructs members of the army to supply the youth militia and war veterans in his team (The Anatomy of Terror 2011; Sibanda 2010; 2011a).

The violence and patronage governing competition among the elite are also the mechanisms by which the ZANU PF created youth organisations, *Chipangano* and *Upfumi Kuvadiki* (Wealth to the Youths), which seek to mobilise support for ZANU PF and dent the MDC-T's support in Mbare and Epworth. According to Solidarity Peace Trust, the youth violence in January and February 2011 was 'once more linked to access to resources – who gets to have vending and housing stands in Mbare' (SPT 2011, 36). More than 200 ZANU PF youths patrolled the area. The youth assaulted and evicted MDC-T supporters from their homes, destroyed the houses and possessions of the MDC-T councillor for the area, drove MDC supporters from their vending stalls, and looted their goods. The youths also damaged the MDC-T offices in Mbare and looted equipment. Police either took part in the violence and looting or watched passively. MDC-T supporters reported torture by police and CIO members in police cells and in Carter House, which *Chipangano* youth appropriated from the Harare municipal council and allegedly use as a base (*SPT* 2011, 36–7; Gumbo 2011). In October 2011, MDC-T Mbare MP, Piniel Denga said that all Mbare Musika market stalls had been purged of MDC supporters and allocated to ZANU PF loyalists and that the project to rehabilitate the Matapi flats had also been disrupted to prevent the MDC-T deriving political advantage (The Zimbabwean 2011). In November 2011, rather than lose the $5 million grant provided by the Bill and Melinda Gates Foundation because *Chipangano* youth prevented work on the housing project, the Harare municipal council announced the project would be moved to another Harare high-density suburb (Gumbo 2011).

In Epworth, ZANU PF also seeks to win support through violence and patronage in a solid MDC-T constituency. Most residents in Epworth's informal settlements were evicted from their homes in Harare's high-density suburbs during Operation Murambatsvina in 2005. ZANU PF threatens to deny them residential stands in the informal settlements unless they participate in ZANU PF activities. ZANU PF also allocates market stands in Mupedzanhamo near the central business district of Harare and in Siyaso market (The Anatomy of Terror 2011). In February 2011, youth militia destroyed flea market stalls that were being constructed under the Constituency Development Fund which would have been a source of patronage for the MDC-T MP who initiated the project (Maseko 2011).

Urban politics in Epworth and Mbare in Harare province, an MDC-T stronghold, are both driven by ZANU PF's informal networks of power. Violence and patronage have infused the competition between the networks of Midzi and Nyanhongo, with recurring violent clashes among the youth whom they reward for their activities. In the conflict with the MDC-T, ZANU PF perpetrators of violence and others who support the party reap rewards; known or suspected MDC-T supporters are punished by physical attacks and intimidation, evictions from their homes and market stalls, looting of their possessions, and denial of access to housing stands and vending stalls. The three MDC-T MPs elected in March 2008 – Eliah Jembere (Epworth), Piniel Denga (Mbare), and Douglas Mwonzora (Nyanga North) – have all been victims of repeated violence and intimidation (SPT 2008, 24; 2011, 29; Harding 2008; MMPZ 2011; Gonda 2010).

Diamond mining

Opportunities for accumulation by individuals linked to informal networks have been linked not only to 'the informalisation of production structures' that intensified during the crisis (1998–2008) (Raftopoulos 2009, 221–2) but also to the informalisation of politics, two interrelated processes. In the competition among elites for access to diamonds, 'the biggest winners are obviously the same clique of insiders and securocrats that have always benefitted from all illicit ZANU enterprises' (PAC 2010, 17) For some, the Joint Operations Command (JOC) is in charge of the Chiadza mines (PAC 2010, 4–5; 7). For others, such as a prison official in Mutare who spoke to a foreign journalist before the formation of the IG, top figures in the ruling ZANU PF party and security officials were running the illegal trade in diamonds mined at Chiadzwa, a district in Marange communal area in Manicaland, and the armed forces worked for the political heavyweights in ZANU PF.

The people in the police, prisons service, army, and CIO have got groups of people who are working for those lieutenants, known as 'syndicates', says the official. 'Usually these high-ranked officers in the armed forces are working for the ministers, governors and other ZANU-PF bigwigs' (Raftopoulos 2010, 221–2). Only companies with close connections to ZANU PF's political and security elite have obtained mining concessions at Marange. Since the formation of the IG, five companies have been granted licenses to mine at Marange: two Chinese companies, two South African private companies – Mbada and Canadile – and Pure Diamonds (Kadzere

2010; Veritas 2011). In July 2009, the Ministry of Mines accepted expressions of interest from companies willing to enter into joint ventures with the state company, ZMDC (PAC 2010, 5). ZMDC formed a wholly owned subsidiary, Marange Resources, to represent its interests in joint ventures, and became a 50% owner of two joint venture companies, Mbada and Canadile. Minister Mpofu played a prominent role in the nomination of the companies with which ZMDC formed Mbada and Canadile and the selection of ZMDC representatives on these companies' boards. Among the shareholders in the companies with which ZMDC formed joint ventures were a substantial number of retired members of the military (HRW 2010a, 6; Global Witness 2010, 15; PAC 2010, 5). The two Chinese companies seem to owe their concessions to personal relationships with the CIO chief, Happy Bonyongwe, and the chief of the Zimbabwe Defence Forces, Constance Chiwenga (Swain 2011).

The mining concessions only continue as long as the personal relationships that made them possible remain productive. The largest shareholder of the private company that joined ZMDC to form Canadile, retired Major Lovemore Kurotwi, a senior figure in the Fifth Brigade that operated ignominiously in Matabeleland in the 1980s, and reputedly a nephew of the former Commander of the Zimbabwe Defence Forces, Vitalis Zvinavashe, fell out with Mines Minister Mpofu (HRW 2010a, 6; PAC 2010, 5; Sokwanele 2011b, 20). The ZMDC took 100% control of Canadile, including its equipment and stockpiled gems. The government has charged Kurotwi with having obtained a mining license fraudulently, but Kurotwi alleges in a letter to parliament that Mpofu cancelled the license because he (Kurotwi) refused to pay Mpofu a $10 million bribe. Kurotwi's complaint that he was arrested at Mpofu's command and that some officials in the Ministry of Mines were turning away investors because of 'personal, selfish interests' highlights the personalised nature of this conflict and the way in which the actors are using the court and the parliament to resolve it. Meanwhile, press reports suggest that the ZMDC senior officials who were arrested with Kurotwi in 2010 but on separate charges may have had interests in Canadile (Daily News 2011; Zimbabwe Independent 2010; New Zimbabwe 2010; The Zimbabwean 2010).

Personalised struggles within the ZANU PF political and military elite for access to diamond mines have been intertwined with succession politics. Longstanding competitors to succeed President Mugabe, Emmerson Mnangagwa, Defence Minister and chair of the JOC, and the late retired General Solomon Mujuru, also fought to control the diamond mines. Mujuru had become a director of River Ranch mine in southwest Zimbabwe, along with ZANU PF Central Committee member, Trivanhu Mudariki, and a Saudi investor, who had effectively grabbed the mine from its legal owners in 2004 (PAC 2010, 8). According to PAC, Mujuru's ownership of River Ranch mine 'goes to the very heart of Mujuru's struggle for control of ZANU' (PAC 2010, 8) – presumably an allusion to the claim that Mujuru hoped to win the succession through control of ZANU PF structures and would need the patronage to win support (ICG 2010, 5; 8). Similarly, Mujuru's shareholding in African Consolidated Resources Ltd – widely held to be much larger than the 3% made public – is believed to be the reason that the ZMDC expropriated without compensation its mining concession and equipment in 2006 (PAC 2010, 4). Mnangagwa and the JOC wanted exclusive access to mining Marange diamonds. Mujuru's suspicious death in August 2011 and the death of his key diamond buyer,

Bothwell Hlahla, only a few days earlier in a car accident (Muleya and Zaba 2011), point to a likely link between diamonds, patronage, and succession politics.

Violence and patronage govern the operation of mining syndicates in Marange, which have been mining large parts of the fields illegally since 2007 (Global Witness 2010, 6). Individual soldiers and police form profit-sharing syndicates with civilians whom they recruit, often forcibly, to illegally dig for diamonds. If the workers demand too large a share of the profits or if they are caught mining for themselves, they are likely to become victims of violence (PAC 2010, 12; 20; Global Witness 2010, 6; 8; HRW 2010b, 5; 7). In August 2011, the BBC Panorama reported being informed by victims of two torture camps in Marange, at least three years in existence, where civilians who run afoul of their syndicate leaders are punished by police and military (BBC News Africa 2011; Andersson 2011). If the syndicates are raided by private security companies or the armed police support unit, 'the police or soldiers offer no protection to their syndicate' (PAC 2010, 12). Locals and mine workers are arbitrarily displaced if they live in areas where the mining operations of syndicates or joint venture companies occur (IDMC and NRC 2010, 56).

Conclusion

The informalisation of ZANU PF politics is firmly entrenched. Personal networks are the bases for building and maintaining power in the party and against the opposition, using violence and patronage, themselves often interconnected. The privatisation of politics, patronage, and violence by competing factions is easily concealed by focusing on the competition between ZANU PF and the 'opposition' parties in the IG and on ZANU PF's ability to maintain most of its state power under the IG. But informal politics suffuses the parallel government which ZANU PF has established to ensure there will be no regime change. When the IG no longer brings the competing factions together against the opposition or when Mugabe dies or retires, the privatised nature of ZANU PF's rule could well inaugurate a new type of undemocratic regime.

Acknowledgements

The author wishes to thank David Moore and Timothy Scarnecchia for their useful comments.

Notes

1. ZANU PF has been aided in its ability to establish a parallel government by the MDC formations' willingness to protest and then capitulate and the collusion or absence of serious resistance from the South African facilitators, the regional body, SADC, and the African Union.
2. The percentage of youth militia is calculated from 75,000 suspect civil servants identified in the audit and 29,000 youth militia in the government. The 29,000 militia figure is from press reports and is cited in Veritas, Bill Watch 13/2009, 5 April 2009.
3. Interestingly, Minister Biti signed a $98 million loan agreement between the Chinese and the Zimbabwean governments in which diamond mining revenues from the Chinese government's joint venture with the ZMDC will be used to repay the loan. The government is using the loan to build a National Defence College, also known as the Robert Mugabe School of Intelligence, in Mazowe. Press reports suggest that the college will be used to train youth militia and spy on opponents (Swain 2011).

Note on contributor

Norma Kriger is a Research Associate in the department of Anthropology and Development Studies at the University of Johannesburg. She is the author of *Guerrilla Veterans in Post-War Zimbabwe: Symbolic and Violent Politics, 1980–1987* (Cambridge University Press 2003) and *Zimbabwe's Guerrilla War: Peasant Voices* (Cambridge University Press 1992), and has written numerous articles on Zimbabwe elections and migration.

References

Andersson, H. 2011. Marange diamond field: Zimbabwe torture camp discovered. *BBC News*, August 8. http://www.bbc.co.uk/news/world-africa-14377215.
Bayart, J-F, S. Ellis, and B. Hibou. 1999. *The criminalization of the state in Africa*. London: James Currey.
BBC News. 2011. Marange diamonds: Zimbabwe denies 'torture camp', August 9. http://www.bbc.co.uk/news/world-africa-14468116.
Biti, T. 2011. *Riding the storm: Economics in the time of challenges. The 2011 mid-year Fiscal Policy Review*. Presented to Parliament by Hon. T. Biti; MP Minister of Finance, July 26. http://www.zimtreasury.org/downloads/Mid-Year-Fiscal-Policy-Review.pdf.
Block, E. 2011. The good, the bad, and the ugly. *The Independent*, 1 December.
Chabal, P., and J-P. Daloz. 1999. *Africa works: Disorder and political instrument*. Oxford: James Currey.
Cheeseman, N., and B-M. Tendi. 2010. Power-sharing in comparative perspective: The dynamics of 'unity government' in Kenya and Zimbabwe. *Journal of Modern African Studies* 48, no. 2: 203–29.
Chifera, I., G. Dube, and P. Rusere. 2011. Zimbabwe Finance Minister Biti tries to curb costly official foreign travel. *VOA*, Feb 14.
Crisis Coalition of Zimbabwe. 2010. 'Talk' of 2011 elections sparks violence. *The Daily Catalyst*, May 6.
Daily News. 2011. Mpofu faces Parly grilling, November 7. http://www.dailynews.co.zw/index.php/news/34-news/5176-mpofu-faces-parly-grilling.html.
Ero, C., and H. Varney. 2008. Zimbabwe: Victims get short shrift in power-sharing deal, allAfrica.com September 19. http://ictj.org/en/news/coverage/article/1995.html?printer_friendly=1.
General Political Agreement (GPA). 2008. *Agreement between the Zimbabwe African National Union-Patriotic Front (ZANU-PF) and the two Movement for Democratic Change (MDC) formations, on resolving the challenges facing Zimbabwe*, September 15, 2008. Harare. http://www.kubatana.net/html/archive/demgg/080915agreement.asp?sector=DEMGG&year=0&range_start=1#download.
Global Witness. 2010. *Return of the blood diamond. The deadly race to control Zimbabwe's new-found diamond wealth*, June 14. London: Global Witness.
Gonda, V. 2010. Zimbabwe: Diamond watchdog charged, plus two MDC MPs in custody. *SW Radio Africa*, June 7. http://allafrica.com/stories/201006071843.html.
Gumbo, T. 2011. Youth gang forces Harare to relocate gates-funded housing project. *VOA*, November 8. http://www.voanews.com/zimbabwe/news/Youth-Gang-Forces-Harare-City-Council-To-Relocate-Donor-Housing-Funded-Project--133466008.html.
Harding, A. 2008. Zimbabwe opposition MPs in hiding. *BBC News*, July 21. Harare. http://news.bbc.co.uk/2/hi/7517431.stm.
Human Rights Watch (HRW). 2010a. *Deliberate chaos. Ongoing human rights abuses in the Marange diamond fields of Zimbabwe*, June 2010. New York: Human Rights Watch.
Human Rights Watch (HRW). 2010b. *Kimberley process: Demand end to abuses in diamond trade*, November 1. http://www.hrw.org/print/news/2010/10/29/kimberley-process-demand-end-abuses-diamond-trade.
Idasa. 2011. States in transition observatory. Idasa. *GNU Watch*, January 2011. http://idasa.krazyboyz.co.za/media/uploads/outputs/files/gnu_watch_january_20111.pdf.

Internal Displacement Monitoring Center (IDMC) and Norwegian Refugee Council. 2010. *Internal displacement. Global overview of trends and developments in 2010*. Zimbabwe, March 2011.

International Crisis Group (ICG). 2008. *Ending Zimbabwe's nightmare: A possible way forward*. Africa Briefing No. 56, December 16. Pretoria/Brussels.

International Crisis Group (ICG). 2009. *Zimbabwe: Engaging the Inclusive Government*. Africa Briefing No. 59, April 20. Harare/Pretoria/Nairobi/Brussels.

International Crisis Group (ICG). 2010. *Zimbabwe: Political and security challenges to the transition*. Africa Briefing No. 70, March 3. Harare/Pretoria/Nairobi/Brussels.

International Crisis Group (ICG). 2011a. *Zimbabwe: The road to reform or another dead end?* Africa Report No. 173, April 27. Harare/Johannesburg/Nairobi/Brussels.

International Crisis Group (ICG). 2011b. *Resistance and denial: Zimbabwe's stalled reform agenda*. Africa Briefing No. 82, November 16. Johannesburg/South Africa.

Kadzere, M. 2010. Zimbabwe: Three new diamond miners licensed. *The Herald*, November 9.

Maclean, S.J. 2002. Mugabe at war: The political economy of conflict in Zimbabwe. *Third World Quarterly* 23, no. 3: 513–28.

Maseko, N. 2011. Zimbabwe political violence likely to continue closer to elections. *The Zimbabwe Telegraph*, February 9.

Matyszak, D. 2008. *Losing focus: Zimbabwe's 'Power-Sharing' agreement*. Research and Advocacy Unit, October 23. Zimbabwe.

Matyszak, D. 2009. *Power dynamics in Zimbabwe's Inclusive Government*. Research and Advocacy Unit, September 15. Zimbabwe.

Media Monitoring Project of Zimbabwe (MMPZ). 2011. *Weekly Media Review*, 2011–6, February 7–13, 2011.

Memorandum of Understanding (MOU) between Zimbabwe African National Union (Patriotic Front) and the two Movement for Democratic Change Formations, July 21, 2008. http://www.thepresidency.gov.za/pebble.asp?relid=1748.

Moore, D. 2003. Review of Zimbabwe's Presidential elections 2002: Evidence, lessons and implications by Henning Melber (2002). Discussion Paper 14, Uppsala: Nordiska Afrikainstitutet. *Transformation* 51: 145–9.

Mukarati, L. 2011. Jostling over Harare Governor post. *Financial Gazette*, July 22. http://eu.financialgazette.co.zw/top-stories/9149-jostling-over-harare-governor-post.html.

Muleya, D., and F. Zaba. 2011. Zimbabwe: Mujuru allies cry 'Murder Most Foul'. *Zimbabwe Independent*, August 19. http://www.theindependent.co.zw/local/32126-mujuru-allies-cry-murder-most-foul.html.

New Zimbabwe. 2010. 6 held over $2bn Marange fraud, November 4. http://www.newzimbabwe.com/news/news.aspx?newsID=3720.

Partnership Africa Canada (PAC). 2010. *Diamonds and clubs: The militarized control of diamonds and power in Zimbabwe*. Ottawa: PAC.

Raftopoulos, B. 2009. The crisis in Zimbabwe, 1998–2008. In *Becoming Zimbabwe*, ed. B. Raftopoulos and A. Mlambo, 201–32. Harare: Weaver Press.

Raftopoulos, B. 2010. The global political agreement as a 'Passive Revolution': Notes on contemporary politics in Zimbabwe. The Round Table 99, no. 411: 705–18. http://dx.doi.org/10.1080/00358533.2010.530414.

Reno, W. 1998. *Warlord politics and African states*. Boulder, CO: Lynne Rienner.

Sibanda, T. 2010. Wave of new violence erupts in Chimanimani district. *SW Radio Africa*, August 17. http://www.swradioafrica.com/news170810/wave170810.htm.

Sibanda, T. 2011a. ZANU PF arming its militia in Nyanga North. *SW Radio Africa*, March 4. http://www.swradioafrica.com/news170810/wave170810.htm.

Sibanda, T. 2011b. Failure to release civil service audit report is ZANU PF plot. *SW Radio Africa*, September 5.

Sokwanele. 2011a. *Zimbabwe Inclusive Government watch:* Issue 33, November 2011. http://www.sokwanele.com/zigwatch.

Sokwanele. 2011b. *The Marange diamond fields of Zimbabwe: An overview*, November 2, Sokwanele.

Solidarity People's Trust (SPT). 2008. *Desperately seeking sanity: What prospects for a new beginning in Zimbabwe?*, July 29. Durban: SPT.

Solidarity People's Trust (SPT). 2011. *The Hard road to reform*, April 13. Johannesburg: SPT.
Swain, J. 2011. ZANU in shadow of elusive magnate, March 12. http://www.businesslive.co.za.
The Anatomy of Terror. 2011. Sokwanele, June 9. http://www.sokwanele.com/node/2333.
The Zimbabwean. 2009. Loser claims votes rigged in Zanu election, November 11. http://www.thezimbabwean.co.uk/news/26493/loser-claims-votes-rigged-in-zanu-election.html.
The Zimbabwean. 2010. Canadile official spills the beans, November 20. http://www.thezimbabwean.co.uk/news/35693/canadile-official-spills-the-beans.html.
The Zimbabwean. 2011. Security forces intensify violence against MDC, October 26. http://www.thezimbabwean.co.uk/.
Veritas. 2009. *Bill Watch*, 13/2009, April 5.
Veritas. 2011. *Bill Watch*, 13/2011, June 6.
Zaba, F. 2011. Savanhu linked to *Chipangano*. *Zimbabwe Independent*, November 11. http://www.theindependent.co.zw/local/33114-savanhu-linked-to-chipangano.html.
Zimbabwe Independent. 2010. Zimbabwe: Mpofu accused of asking for bribes in diamonds saga, November 11. http://www.theindependent.co.zw/local/28745-mpofu-accused-of-asking-for-bribes-in-diamonds-saga.html.

Narratives of progress: Zimbabwean historiography and the end of history

Ian Phimister

Department of History, University of Sheffield, UK and University of Pretoria, South Africa

The tradition of all dead generations weighs like a nightmare on the brains of the living (Karl Marx, *Eighteenth Brumaire of Louis Bonaparte*).

> This brief commentary takes its inspiration from the opening address delivered by John Hoffman, and printed in these pages; that is, progress is usefully understood as a contradictory, contested and ambiguous process. But rather than attempt a comprehensive survey of the past 40 or so years of academic analyses of Zimbabwe's pasts, what follows has as its focus the emergence of 'patriotic history' and particularly its nationalist antecedents. These are critically examined. Although not concerned with the generality of recent studies that are neither nationalist nor materialist in orientation, this paper sketches in outline the rise, fall and rise of radical accounts. It ends by suggesting how such analyses might be taken forward.

Patriotic history

According to Melber (2011, 89), the seizure of power by Southern Africa's national liberation movements 'signals in their understanding something similar to what Francis Fukuyama dubbed as the end of history'. From this perspective, national liberation is a just and historically necessary conclusion to the struggle between 'the' people and the forces of racism and colonialism. From this, two conclusions follow: the region's national liberation movements are progressive, and their coming to power marks the end of a process. For them to be overthrown would constitute a counter-revolutionary victory for reactionary forces.[1] These are the assumptions underpinning 'patriotic history', even if the precise moment of its articulation has turned on the intensification of particular political struggles.

In the Zimbabwean case, this is an interpretation framed by many of Robert Mugabe's more recent speeches and pronouncements (Mugabe 2001). As understood by Sabelo Ndlovu-Gatsheni, the defining characteristics of 'patriotic history' are the central roles ascribed to land and race, circumscribed by loyalty to the liberation movement in the shape of ZANLA/ZANU. A further dimension has been the affirmation of Zimbabwe's sovereignty against external interference, especially where the latter has taken the form of selective Western support for human rights.² For Blessing-Miles Tendi (2010a, 4), the essence of 'patriotic history' boils down to 'ZANU-PF as the alpha and omega of Zimbabwe's past, present and future'. To all intents and purposes, Zimbabwean history is reduced to a succession of *chimurengas*–never, it might be noted in passing, *umvukelas*–in which the present ruling dispensation is the only legitimate heir to the Nehanda and Kaguvi spirit mediums (Tendi 2010a, see also Tendi 2008, Tendi 2010b).

That this celebration of a violent past is narrowly self-serving has been easy enough to expose, and several important books and articles have done just that (Ndlovu-Gatsheni 2009, 234–98 and Tendi 2010b, see also Kriger 2006). But if indeed this particular political project by ZANU-PF does seek to mark the 'end of history', then the historiographical roots of the turn to 'patriotic history' merit closer scrutiny than they have so far received. Those who now piously enjoin us to distinguish between nationalist historians ('bad') and historians of nationalism ('good'), are themselves guilty of special pleading (Ranger 2004, 2005). They pass too lightly over political and intellectual sympathies manifest in the 1960s and 1970s and which endured until very recently. Although the behaviour of the child long since grown to adulthood is now an embarrassment to be shunned, the long-term responsibility of the parent should be acknowledged, particularly when parent and offspring have so much in common. These include the flattening of difference; the privileging of certain voices over others; and the identification of hegemonic nationalism as the bearer of improvement and progress.

Nationalist history: from voices to silence

Nowhere in Zimbabwean historiography is this tendency better exemplified than in the work of Terence Ranger. Some early studies aside (Ranger 1964, 1967a), his books and articles have exercised a generally pernicious nationalist influence for over a generation. From the fanciful extrapolations and factual misrepresentations in *Revolt in Southern Rhodesia* (Ranger 1967b); through the gloss applied in *Peasant Consciousness and Guerrilla War* (Ranger 1985), to the vicious excesses of the second chimurenga waged by ZANLA; by way of the tin ear first displayed in *The African Voice* (Ranger 1970) and again evidenced by *Voices from the Rocks* (Ranger 1999); to the celebration of the silence of the grave in 'Matabeleland Today' (Ranger 1989),³ these invariably provided usable pasts for an authoritarian nationalism under construction from the mid-1950s onwards.⁴ While each of these examples could be examined at length, constraints of time oblige this paper to look briefly at only two particular cases.

Ranger's *Revolt in Southern Rhodesia* (1967b) is the foundation on which much nationalist and 'patriotic' historiography rests. Yet for all that this book was much praised at the time, research conducted in the 1970s and early 1980s demonstrated beyond doubt that *Revolt* had got it spectacularly wrong in every important respect, even to the extent of misquoting crucial documents. Its crude nationalist underpinnings were first exposed by Julian Cobbing's scholarly account of the Ndebele Rising. The Ndebele *umvukela*, Cobbing concluded, did not witness 'the emergence of a leadership which was charismatic and revolutionary', as Ranger claimed. As the Ndebele had not been divorced from their 'traditional' leadership by the mid-1890s, the leading role ascribed by Ranger to religious leaders was quite simply wrong. They certainly did not co-ordinate a united Ndebele-Shona resistance against the whites. Nothing like the 'first act of "Zimbabwean" nationalism', the Ndebele Rising was rather 'the last act of the independent Ndebele state' (Cobbing 1977, 18 and Cobbing 1976).

If Cobbing's demolition of Ranger's explanation of the Ndebele Rising was not enough, it very soon became apparent that *Revolt's* chapters on the Shona rising were equally unreliable. In a series of closely argued articles and essay reviews, David Beach subjected Ranger's work to forensic scrutiny. The results demonstrated that Ranger's findings were unedifying, to say the least. Acknowledging that no assessment of *Revolt* could be complete 'without some reference to the political context in which it was written', Beach explained to his readers that at a time when the settler counter-revolution of UDI appeared to be going from strength to strength in the face of African disunity, Ranger's interpretation of the Risings seemingly offered hope for the future. With past divisions overcome under their new religious leadership, in Ranger's version the Ndebele and the Shona 'achieved almost complete tactical surprise, with a preconcerted, coordinated, almost simultaneous rising in each zone in March and June 1896'. In short, wrote Beach, '*Revolt* served as a "charter for Zimbabwe as a focus for present-day political action"'. But in serving the interests of 1960s nationalism, it certainly wasn't good history. For Beach, Ranger's book turned far too much on inference, analogy and assertion, and too little on what the documents actually said. Contrary evidence had sometimes been omitted. On Beach's meticulous reading of every available file, there was nothing about the Shona rising, or risings, as he preferred to see them, to support Ranger's usable past. In neither Mashonaland nor Matabeleland had events come anywhere near to approximating 'the Rangerian model of a tightly-knit Ndebele-Shona religious high command organizing a pre-planned, simultaneous rising' (Beach 1979, 20 and Beach 1980).[5] But precisely because it purported to reveal a history of united struggle against settler colonialism, a past shorn of ambiguity and complexity, *Revolt* was perfectly attuned to the needs of the new Jacobins.

Given that this article was conceived for a conference in Bulawayo, it is fitting that the focus of the second case study should be Matabeleland.[6] Published in 1989, Ranger's article purported to describe the situation in the west of the country in the second half of the decade (Ranger 1989, 161–2 and 172).[7] Without once mentioning the murderous activities of the Fifth Brigade, his egregious account of Matabeleland instead emphasised Mugabe's generosity and courage. Although the author professed to be 'in no doubt about the scale of... the brutalities of 1983 and 1985', he wrote as if the 'balance of terror' was weighted most heavily on the side of the dissidents. Underpinned by the belief that there was 'almost no suspicion of me as a historian sympathetic to ZANU/PF', and seemingly oblivious to the possibility that informants located with the help of 'a guide provided for me by the District Administrator' might not be entirely forthcoming about state-sponsored mass violence in the very recent past, Ranger's article noted that there had been 'too many collapses of discipline, too many rapes, too many killings', but only on the part of dissidents. Beneficiaries of Mugabe's offer of an amnesty, the people of Matabeleland South's Matobo district had apparently, of their own accord, reached a general opinion: 'a condemnation of dissident violence' (Beach 1979, 20, 1980, 1986, Ch 5; Tsomondo 1977). That this prudent expression of opinion might have been influenced by popular memory of Bhalagwe Camp, the huge detention centre in the south of the district where thousands of villagers were detained and tortured by the Fifth Brigade (The Catholic Commission for Justice and Peace in Zimbabwe 2007, 223-31), was nowhere considered in this myopic view of Matabeleland's recent past.

Alternative histories: radical history

For all that 'patriotic history' and its nationalist antecedents were so manifestly wanting, alternative accounts, some initial successes notwithstanding, ultimately found it difficult to establish themselves within and without Zimbabwe. To begin with, it is not as if radical scholars were particularly slow off the mark after 1980. Despite the widespread tendency at Independence and afterwards, noted by Hoffman in his opening conference address, to see ZANU-PF as the embodiment of progressive politics, a number of notably critical voices were raised early on. Both Saul (1980) and Astrow (1983), for example, anticipated ZANU-PF's 'betrayal' of the revolutionary possibilities of the overthrow of colonialism, as did David Moore's close inspection of liberation struggle ideologies (1988, 1991). Over the course of that first decade, others followed suit, particularly Lionel Cliffe and Colin Stoneman, and the various contributors to the two volumes edited by the latter (Stoneman 1981, 1988; Stoneman and Cliffe 1989). Notable contributions by Zimbabwean scholars in much the same period were brought together in *Zimbabwe. The Political Economy of Transition, 1980-1986* (Mandaza 1986). Edited by Ibbo Mandaza, its examination of the pattern of events since Independence was framed by an opening chapter by Mandaza himself. As the Second Chimurenga never 'encompassed within it even the idea of a socialist revolution', the postcolonial state was 'an apparent mediator between capital and labour...inclined towards controlling...popular demands' (Mandaza 1986).

Where scepticism was voiced about the so-called 'national democratic stage' of the revolution during the 1980s, however, it tended to bemoan the entrenchment of capitalism rather than lament the absence of democracy. Criticism was doubtless also muted by a reluctance to attack Zimbabwe's new rulers in a period of intensifying anti-apartheid struggle, but more damaging to the hard won 1970s gains of political economy (Phimister 1979) were the conservative consequences of the emergence of postmodernism and postcolonial studies in the northern hemisphere. While these latter developments questioned all grand narratives, subsequent intellectual convulsions affected radical analyses more than most, at least for a time, especially in the immediate aftermath of the collapse of the Soviet Union and so-called 'actually existing socialism'.

But although more and more historiographical space was occupied by nationalism's praise singers,[8] it was never uncontested. Norma Kriger (1992) and Steven Robins (1996) exposed the glaring weaknesses of what the latter termed nationalism's 'praise texts'. Inside the country itself, the Economic History Department of the University of Zimbabwe, and latterly the Institute of Development Studies of the same institution, as well as a handful of individuals in other Departments and independent organisations, found continuing inspiration from historical materialism broadly conceived. To take the most prominent example, one of the first studies to explore the contextual limitations of democracy as practised by the region's militarist liberation movements was another collection of essays edited by Mandaza, this time together with Lloyd Sachikonye (1991).

Labour history remained a key bastion of radical analysis. Research in this field by Brian Raftopoulos in particular (Raftopoulos 1995b; Raftopoulos and Phimister 1997; Raftopoulos and Yoshikuni 1999; Raftopoulos and Phimister 2000; Raftopoulos and Sachikonye 2001),[9] served as a springboard for what was to become over the course of the 1990s and beyond, a series of wide-ranging and thorough-going critiques of authoritarian nationalism (Raftopoulos 2003; Raftopoulos and Savage 2005). Infused with political and intellectual urgency, these interventions were themselves hotly debated as academics on the Left struggled to understand the dynamics driving the post-2000 crisis in terms of rights versus redistribution (Yeros 2002; Moore 2004; Raftopoulos 2006; Moyo and Yeros 2007),[10] a dispute which lost momentum once they were acknowledged as not necessarily mutually exclusive. They were anyway revised and taken up by a younger generation of scholars guided by Raftopoulos and Alois Mlambo, and published in 2009 as *Becoming Zimbabwe* (Raftopoulos and Mlambo 2009).

Conclusion: becoming history

This tightly edited and well-received collection marked not only a significant resurgence of radical scholarship, but also nicely exemplifies Hoffman's insistence that notions of progress are most usefully understood as complex and contested processes. More than this, it may also be that such processes are best approached through the interplay of local, national, regional and international contexts. In this way, for example, what Raftopoulos has memorably termed the 'discourse and destructive party accumulation project of ZANU-PF' (Raftopoulos 2010) would resonate beyond the region if located within the wider regimes of accumulation by dispossession identified by David Harvey (2003) as cited in Callincos 2009, 14). It is a point that was developed with particular force by John Saul when commenting on Hoffman's paper. Notions of progress, insisted Saul, are essentially political, not philosophical questions. The best studies of Zimbabwe's pasts have always understood this, foregrounding relations of power and exploitation, even as they placed them in historical context. With fluffy social histories entirely devoid of any understanding of political economy continuing to appear (Ranger 2010), only a renewed emphasis on contradictions and classes is likely to produce accounts of the past free of the nightmares of the present.

Acknowledgements

I am most grateful to David Moore and to an anonymous reviewer for their comments and suggestions.

Notes

1. For further discussion, see variously, Good (2002), Melber (2003) and Southall (2003).
2. The outstanding study in this regard is S. Ndlovu-Gatsheni, *Do 'Zimbabweans' Exist? Trajectories of Nationalism, National Identity Formation and Crisis in a Postcolonial State* (Bern 2009).
3. For pointed criticisms of these books and articles, see amongst others, Beach (1979), Cobbing (1977), Cross (1972), Kriger (1992), Robins (1996) and Phimister (2003).

4. See especially Raftopoulos (1995), and Scarnecchia (2008). For a notably prescient analysis, see Slater (1975).
5. Both criticisms are discussed further in chapter five of Beach (1986). See also Tsomondo (1977, 13).
6. What follows is taken in part from Phimister (2008).
7. See also Ranger (2006), where it is claimed that 'human rights organisations did not publically condemn Zimbabwe in the 1980s'. This is contradicted by Lindgren (2005).
8. Amongst others, see Martin and Johnson (1981), Frederickse (1983), Lan (1985), Maxwell (1999), Ranger (1995, 1999).
9. Important materialist analyses written in this period on non-labour topics include Bond (1998), Bond and Manyanya (2002) and Mlambo (1997).
10. See also Moyo and Yeros (2005), Mamdani (2008), Chung (2006).

Note on contributor

Ian Phimister is currently Professor of International History at the University of Sheffield. He has held positions at the Universities of Zambia, Cape Town and Oxford. His research and publications cover Central and Southern Africa, as well as patterns of overseas investment associated with the City of London.

References

Astrow, A. 1983. *Zimbabwe: A revolution that lost its way?*. London: Zed Press.
Beach, D. 1979. Chimurenga: The Shona rising of 1896-7. *Journal of African History* 20: 395–420.
Beach, D. 1980. Essay review. *International Journal of African Historical Studies* 13, no. 1: 103–108.
Beach, D. 1986. *War and politics in Zimbabwe 1840-1900*. Gweru: Mambo.
Bond, P. 1998. *Uneven Zimbabwe. A study of finance, development, and underdevelopment*. Trenton: Africa World Press Inc.
Bond, P., and M. Manyanya. 2002. *Zimbabwe's plunge. Exhausted nationalism, neoliberalism and the search for social justice*. Harare: Weaver Press.
Callincos, A. 2009. *Imperialism and global political economy*. Cambridge: Polity Press.
Chung, F. 2006. *Re-living the second Chimurenga*. Uppsala: Nordic Africa Institute and Harare: Weaver Press.
Cobbing, J. 1976. The Ndebele under the Khumalos, 1820 96. PhD thesis, University of Lancaster.
Cobbing, J. 1977. The absent priesthood: Another look at the Rhodesian risings of 1896-1897. *Journal of African History* 18.
Cross, S. 1972. Protest in Rhodesia. *Transafrican Journal of History* 5: 61–84.
Frederickse, J. 1983. *None but ourselves*. London: Penguin.
Good, K. 2002. *The liberal model and Africa. Elites against democracy*. Basingstoke: Palgrave.
Harvey, D. 2003. *The new imperialism*. Oxford: Oxford University Press.
Kriger, N. 1992. *Zimbabwe's Guerrilla war*. Cambridge: Cambridge University Press.
Kriger, N. 2006. From patriotic memories to patriotic history in Zimbabwe, 1990-2005. *Third World Quarterly* 27: 1151–69.
Lan, D. 1985. *Guns and rain. Guerrillas and spirit mediums in Zimbabwe*. London: James Currey.
Lindgren, B. 2005. Memories of violence: Recreation of ethnicity in post-colonial Zimbabwe. In *No peace no war: An anthology of contemporary armed conflicts*, ed. P. Richards, 158–64. Athens and Oxford: Ohio University Press and James Currey.
Mamdani, M. 2006. Lessons of Zimbabwe. *London Review of Books* 30: 17–21.
Mandaza, I., ed. 1986. *Zimbabwe. The political economy of transition, 1980-1986*. Dakar: CODESRIA.
Mandaza, I., and L. Sachikonye, ed. 1991. *The one party state and democracy. The Zimbabwe debate*. Harare: SAPES books.

Martin, D., and P. Johnson. 1981. *The struggle for Zimbabwe: The Chimurenga war*. Harare: Zimbabwe Publishing House.

Maxwell, D. 1999. *Christians and chiefs in Zimbabwe. A social history of the Hwesa People c. 1870s – 1990s*. Edinburgh: Edinburgh University Press.

Melber, H. 2003. *Limits to liberation in southern Africa. The unfinished business of democratic consolidation*. Cape Town: HSRC Press.

Melber, H. 2011. Liberation movements as governments in Southern Africa–On the limits to emancipation. *Strategic Review for Southern Africa* 33: 78–102.

Mlambo, A. 1997. *The economic structural adjustment programme: The case of Zimbabwe, 1990-1995*. Harare: University of Zimbabwe Publications.

Moore, D. 1988. The Zimbabwean 'organic intellectuals' in transition. *Journal of Southern African Studies* 15: 96–105.

Moore, D. 1991. The Ideological Formation of the Zimbabwean Ruling Class, *Journal of Southern African Studies* 17: 472–95.

Moore, D. 2004. Marxism and Marxist intellectuals in schizophrenic Zimbabwe: How many rights for Zimbabwe's left? A comment. *Historical Materialism* 12: 405–25.

Moyo, S., and P. Yeros, ed. 2005. Land occupations and land reform in Zimbabwe: Towards the national democratic revolution. In *Reclaiming the land: The resurgence of rural movements in Africa, Asia and Latin America*, 165–209. London: Zed Books.

Moyo, S., and P. Yeros. 2007. Intervention: The Zimbabwe question and the two lefts, *Historical Materialism* 15: 171–204.

Mugabe, R. 2001. *Inside the third Chimurenga*. Harare: Government of Zimbabwe.

Ndlovu-Gatsheni, S. 2009. *Do 'Zimbabweans' exist? trajectories of nationalism, national identity formation and crisis in a postcolonial state*. Bern: Peter Lang.

Phimister, I. 1979. Zimbabwean economic and social historiography since 1970. *African Affairs* 78: 253–68.

Phimister, I. 2003. Doing violence to the past: Zimbabwe's new old history, *Kronos. Journal of Cape History* 29: 210–15.

Phimister, I. 2008. The making and meanings of the massacres in Matabeleland. *Development Dialogue* 50: 197–214.

Raftopoulos, B. 1995a. Gender, nationalist politics and the fight for the city: Harare 1940-1950s. *Southern African Feminist Review* 1: 30–45.

Raftopoulos, B. 1995b. Nationalism and labour in Salisbury 1953-1965, *Journal of Southern African Studies* 21: 79–95.

Raftopoulos, B. 2003. The state in crisis. Authoritarian nationalism, selective citizenship and distortions of democracy in Zimbabwe. In *Zimbabwe's unfinished business: Rethinking land, state and nation in the context of crisis*, ed. A. Hammar, B. Raftopoulos, and S. Jensen. Harare: Weaver Press.

Raftopoulos, B. 2006. The Zimbabwean crisis and the challenges for the left. *Journal of Southern African Studies* 32: 203–19.

Raftopoulos, B. 2010. The global political agreement as a "passive revolution": Notes on contemporary politics in Zimbabwe. *The Round Table* 99: 705–18.

Raftopoulos, B., and A. Mlambo, ed. 2009. *Becoming Zimbabwe*. Harare: Weaver Press.

Raftopoulos, B., and I. Phimister, ed. 1997. *Keep on knocking: A history of the labour movement in Zimbabwe: 1900-97*. Harare: Baobab Books.

Raftopoulos, B., and I. Phimister. 2000.Kana Sora ratswa ngaritswe": African nationalists and black workers – The 1948 general strike in colonial Zimbabwe. *Journal of Historical Sociology* 13: 289–323.

Raftopoulos, B., and L. Sachikonye, ed. 2001. *Striking back: The labour movement and the post-colonial state in Zimbabwe 1980-2000*. Harare: Weaver Press.

Raftopoulos, B., and T. Savage, ed. 2005. *Zimbabwe: Injustice and political reconciliation*. Cape Town: Institute for Justice and Reconciliation.

Raftopoulos, B., and T. Yoshikuni, ed. 1999. *Sites of struggle: Essays in Zimbabwe's urban history*. Harare: Weaver Press.

Ranger, T. 1964. The last word on Rhodes? *Past and Present* no. 28: 116–27.

Ranger, T. 1967a. The rewriting of African history during the scramble: The Matabele dominance in Mashonaland. *African Social Research* no. 4: 271–82.

Ranger, T. 1967b. *Revolt in Southern Rhodesia 1896-7. A study in African resistance.* London: Heineman.
Ranger, T. 1970. *The African voice in Southern Rhodesia 1898-1930.* London: Northwestern University Press.
Ranger, T. 1985. *Peasant consciousness and Guerrilla war.* London: James Currey.
Ranger, T. 1989. Matabeleland since the Amnesty. *African Affairs* 88: 215–34.
Ranger, T. 1995. *Are we also not men? The Samkange family and African politics in Zimbabwe 1920-64.* London: James Currey.
Ranger, T. 1999. *Voices from the rocks. Nature, culture and history in the Matopos Hills of Zimbabwe.* Oxford: James Currey.
Ranger, T. 2004. Nationalist historiography, patriotic history and the history of the nation: The struggle over the past in Zimbabwe, *Journal of Southern African Studies* 30.
Ranger, T. 2005. Rule by historiography: The struggle over the past in contemporary Zimbabwe. In *Versions of Zimbabwe: New approaches to literature and culture*, ed. R. Muponde and R. Primorac. Harare: Weaver Press.
Ranger, T. 2006. Narrative and responses: The Zimbabwean case. Unpublished Paper, University of Connecticut.
Ranger, T. 2010. *Bulawayo burning. The social history of a Southern African city 1893-1960.* Woodbridge: Boydell and Brewer.
Robins, S. 1996. Heroes, heretics and historians of the Zimbabwe revolution. *Zambezia* 23: 73–93.
Saul, J. 1980. Zimbabwe: The next round. *Socialist Register* 17: 170–202.
Scarnecchia, T. 2008. *The urban roots of democracy and political violence in Zimbabwe: Harare and Highfield, 1940-1964.* New York: University of Rochester Press.
Slater, H. 1975. The politics of frustration: The ZAPU-ZANU split in historical perspective. *Kenya Historical Review* 3: 261–86.
Southall, R. 2003. Democracy in Southern Africa: Moving beyond a difficult legacy, *Review of African Political Economy* 30: 255–72.
Stoneman, C., ed. 1981. *Zimbabwe's inheritance.* London: Macmillan.
Stoneman, C. 1988. *Zimbabwe's prospects.* Basingstoke: Macmillan.
Stoneman, C., and L. Cliffe. 1989. *Zimbabwe: Politics, economics and society.* London: Pinter.
Tendi, B-M. 2008. Patriotic history and public intellectuals critical of power. *Journal of Southern African Studies* 43: 379–96.
Tendi, B-M. 2010a. *Making history in Mugabe's Zimbabwe. Politics, intellectuals and the media.* Oxford: Peter Lang.
Tendi, B-M. 2010b. *Zimbabwean history in context: A comparison of the history book with existent history curriculum and teaching.* http://www.weaverpresszimbabwe.com/latest-reviews/59-becoming-zimbabwe/317-review-of-becoming-zimbabwe-tendai-rtp.html
The Catholic Commission for Justice and Peace in Zimbabwe. 2007. *Gukurahundi in Zimbabwe. A report on the disturbances in Matabeleland and the Midlands 1980–1988.* New York: Columbia University Press.
Tsomondo, M. 1977. Shona reaction and resistance to the European colonisation of Zimbabwe, 1890-98. *Journal of Southern African Affairs* 2: 11–31.
Yeros, P. 2002. Zimbabwe and the dilemmas of the left. *Historical Materialism* 10: 3–15.

Civil society and state-centred struggles

Kirk Helliker

Department of Sociology, Rhodes University, South Africa

>This article is about civil society and state-centred struggles in contemporary Zimbabwe. I first identify and outline three current understandings of civil society. Two understandings (one Liberal, one Radical) are state-centric and exist firmly within the logic of state discourses and state politics. A third understanding, also Radical, is society-centric and speaks about politics existing at a distance from the state and possibly beyond the boundaries of civil society. This civil society-state discussion frames the second section of the article, which looks specifically at Zimbabwe. It details civil society as contested terrain (from the late 1990s onwards) within the context of a scholarly debate about agrarian transformation and political change. This debate, which reproduces (in theoretical garb) the key political society (or party) fault-lines within Zimbabwean society, has taken place primarily within the restricted confines of state-centred discourses.

Introduction

This article is about civil society and state-centred struggles in contemporary Zimbabwe. Globally, the notion of civil society is a highly contested one and it has been cleansed of some of its more radical discursive history. At times it has been, quite problematically, reduced to the 'NGO sector'. The term 'progress', which was the main theme for the conference out of which this article arose, has a Euro-centric ring to it. Nevertheless, if understand dialectically, it has a certain universality that speaks to present-day Zimbabwean contestations.

The article is divided into two main sections. First of all, I identify and outline three current understandings of civil society and by necessity raise the vexed question of the state. Two understandings (one Liberal, one Radical) are state-centric and exist firmly within the logic of state discourses and state politics. A third understanding, also Radical, is society-centric and speaks about politics existing at a distance from the state and possibly beyond the boundaries of civil society. All three understandings normally describe civil society in terms of its institutional make-up (and concomitant political content) and not as a social space marked by civil liberties and voluntary-contractual relations.

This civil society-state discussion frames the second section of the article, which looks specifically at Zimbabwe. It details civil society as contested terrain (from the late 1990s onwards) within the context of a scholarly debate about agrarian transformation and political change. This debate, which reproduces (in theoretical garb) the key political society (or party) fault-lines within Zimbabwean society, has taken place primarily within the restricted confines of state-centred discourses. As a result, intellectual work on Zimbabwe is in large part disengaged from Radical society-centred conceptions of civil society which may offer a sounder basis for authentic social progress.

I conclude the article by tentatively questioning the applicability of the notion of civil society–understood as a particular kind of social space and not in terms of its institutional makeup–to a capitalist society in which the hallmarks of liberal state democracy are severely compromised (such as Zimbabwe).

Civil society

This section considers three prevailing conceptions of civil society and civil society-state linkages: a Liberal conception, and state-centric and society-centric Radical conceptions.

The liberal version of civil society

The dominant understanding of civil society in Africa is a Liberal one. 'Civil society', in current Liberal thought, forms part of a conceptual couplet: both a civil society-state couplet and a civil society-communitarian couplet. These couplets assert that civil society (seen as a progressive social force) struggles against the modern state (with its democratic deficits and often authoritarian rule in the case of Africa) and against pre-modern communitarian sociality (often lodged in rural areas where civil society is said to be incipient and undeveloped). State and communitarian relations both entail totalising compulsions contrary to the voluntary and contractual civility of 'civil society'.

The first couplet depicts civil society as a universalising logic that opposes the particularistic interests of the state, and it becomes the driving force behind processes of democratic modernity. Civil society is defined in relation to the nation-state and, generally, this relationship is portrayed as antagonistic throughout Africa, with civil society as progressive and the state as regressive. A universalising civil society wages war against a particularistic and centralising state and is supposed to recover for society a range of powers and activities that states have usurped in previous decades. This argument makes problematic the Hegelian notion that the state and not civil society represents the general interest (although it is an argument made with specific reference to un-democratic states), as well as the Marxist claim (such as articulated by Antonio Gramsci) that civil society is a regressive site marked by domination and conflict (Baker 2002).

In terms of the second couplet, the concept of civil society is compared, in typical modernisation language, to communitarian forms of social organisation that continue to structure (in particular) agrarian social realities. In a real sense, this is consistent with Mamdani's (1996) well-known distinction between citizens (within civil society) and subjects (of traditional rule). Communitarian relations (for example, chiefdoms and customary tenure) are said to be regressive particulars that result in democratic and development deficiencies. From the Liberal perspective, these relations undermine the unequivocally progressive and universalising content of civil society and its modernist endeavours vis-à-vis the (un-democratic) nation-state.

Despite the recent flourishing of actual civil society in Africa under anti-statist neo-liberal conditions, the Liberal interpretation of the concept is statist or at least state-centric. In the end, the Liberal position entails an instrumentalist view of civil society (understood organisationally) as a formidable weapon for democratising the nation-state. At one level, then, civil society is defined in opposition to (or against) the (un-democratic) state. On another level, though, the *modus operandi* of civil society is contained with the rationalities of liberal democratic state politics. Any antagonism between state and civil society occurs within a broad state-civil society consensual framework (based on the rule of law) through which the liberal state delimits and structures what is acceptable (i.e. civil society) politics. Ultimately, civil society is supportive specifically of the liberal democratic state form, leading to state-civil society collaborative and partnership arrangements that facilitate overall social domination. Politics beyond this consensual domain are viewed by both state and civil society as outside the realm of authentic politics and hence as illegitimate politics if not outright criminal. For this reason, the Liberal notion of civil society is highly exclusionary, as Fernandes (2010) strikingly highlights in the case of contemporary Venezuela.

Conceptually, Non-Governmental Organisations (NGOs)–as professionalised entities–fall within liberal civil society as the critical institutional force. Hence, NGOs are often portrayed as constituting civil society or at least are viewed as the most 'civil' arm of civil society. Development NGOs, it is argued, play a particularly important role vis-à-vis building rural civil sociality. At the same time, NGOs in Africa (both foreign and indigenous) are regularly appraised critically as mere instruments of global donors that seek to challenge states deemed undemocratic. As part of a global 'conscious conspiracy' (Manji and O'Coill 2002, 579), NGOs are said to have a 'hidden agenda' (Monga 1996, 156). As Crewe and Harrison (1998, 89) note: 'Donors [and their NGO 'creations'] are sometimes portrayed as strategically wielding the control they have over recipients for their own ends in a coordinated way to uphold the present capitalist system'. In this way, NGOs fit neatly into the liberal civil society mould in trying to bring about democratic transition and consolidation. At the same time, there is some global evidence which suggests that at times specific NGOs move outside the liberal state consensus (Borras Jr. 2008).

Radical civil society (state-centric and society-centric)

Unlike the NGO-ish Liberal view of civil society, the two Radical notions depict progressive civil society (understood in terms of its institutional make-up) as social movement-based. The state-centric position (which, traditionally, is associated with a large body of classical-mainstream Marxist and Nationalist thinking) speaks about political strategies directed at the state and proclaims the possibility of transformation in, through and by means of the state. Society-centred radical change is more in line with Anarchist and Radical Libertarian thought that speaks not of acquiring or capturing state power (either through evolutionary or revolutionary means) but of developing counter-power (or, perhaps more apt, anti-power) inside the bowels of civil society without and despite the state.

The society-centric perspective argues that social (including class) domination is embodied within the very form of the state; in other words, domination within capitalism is tied up inextricably with (and within) the very fabric and texture of the modern state. State-centred theorists, such as Wainwright (2005, 52), while not denying that state institutions controlled by even Left (or Centre-Left) political parties regularly–as a pronounced trajectory–'lord it over the people', nevertheless claim that 'the pull of the state away from the people is not inscribed in the state's character [in a law-like fashion] but is historically produced and subject to historical transformations'. This implies that transformation in and through the state cannot be ruled out *a priori* and is contingent on the balance of social forces.

For society-centric theorists, authentic politics is 'autonomous' politics unbound from the logic and rationalities of the state (that is, politics not on the state's terrain or terms), whether this logic derives from the liberal state/civil society consensus or from–supposedly–radical state-driven projects of transformation (as per the Radical state-centric notion). Liberal democratic and radicalised (i.e. 'Left-leaning' but regularly authoritarian) states, in their own ways, constantly seek to transform non-state spaces into state spaces–understood not institutionally but subjectively as social fields defined, categorised, made legible to and controlled by the state. This takes on different and shifting forms: consensually (through the NGO form), via compulsive local patronage politics but also coercively. Radical society-centred politics often goes against the grain of state and NGO rationalities; hence autonomous sites of struggle prove difficult to nurture and sustain. Chatterjee (2002, 70) notes though in relation to India that the 'squalor, ugliness and violence of popular life' (and popular struggles) cannot be imprisoned 'within the sanitised fortress of civil society'. In this sense, an un-civil space outside civil society may form the basis of genuine social progress (Neocosmos 2011).

This discussion of Liberal and Radical versions of civil society frames the following critical overview of civil society in Zimbabwe.

Zimbabwe

Initially, in the early years of Zimbabwean independence, the ruling Zimbabwe African National Union-Patriotic Front (ZANU-PF) party inhibited the growth of autonomous trade unions and social movements, and effectively took them under its organisational wing. Independent trade unions and urban civic groups emerged in the 1990s, but they were increasingly met with a degree of repression by the party through the organs of the state (Nhema 2002). The exact relationship between ZANU-PF and the land movement (starting in the year 2000) remains controversial. Critics of fast track (Hammar, Raftopoulos, and Jensen 2003) claim that the land movement was simply an electoral ploy of ZANU-PF and that it was initiated and stage-managed by the ruling party. Others (Moyo and Yeros 2005) argue that the land movement cannot be reduced neatly to the party and that the movement had (at least originally) a degree of autonomy from the party-state. In this section I examine the main debate that has been present in some form within Zimbabwean studies over the past decade, and I discuss its relevance to critical questions about Zimbabwean civil society.

A good entry point into the debate is certain claims made by Moyo and Yeros (2005). They refer to the land occupations underpinning fast track land reform as 'the most important [recent] challenge to the neocolonial state in Africa' (Moyo and Yeros 2005, 165), with fast track having a 'fundamentally progressive nature' (Moyo and Yeros 2005, 188). The Zimbabwean state, in large part because of its anti-imperialist stance and anti-colonial restructuring, is labelled as a 'radicalised state' (Moyo and Yeros 2007). Other scholars, such as Raftopoulos and Phimister (2004) and Marongwe (2008) make substantially different arguments in highlighting the regressive nature of political changes in Zimbabwe over the past decade.

Critics of Moyo and Yeros claim that the latter's statements about fast track entail almost perverse value judgements made by 'patriotic agrarianists' (Moore 2004, 409) or 'left-nationalists' (Bond and Manyanya 2003, 78) who fail to conceptualise analytically or even highlight empirically the repressive character of state nationalism in contemporary Zimbabwe, designated as an 'exclusionary' nationalism (Hammar, Raftopoulos, and Jensen 2003), an 'exhausted' nationalism (Bond and Manyanya 2003) or an 'authoritarian populist anti-imperialism' (Moore 2003, 8). Raftopoulos and Phimister (2004) argue that this authoritarianism involves an 'internal reconfiguration of Zimbabwean state politics' (Raftopoulos and Phimister 2004, 377) and amounts to 'domestic tyranny' (Raftopoulos and Phimister 2004, 356), and they speak about a 'number of African intellectuals on the Left' (including Moyo and Yeros, but also Ibbo Mandaza) who 'leapt to the defence of ZANU PF' (Raftopoulos and Phimister 2004, 376) and its re-distributive economic policies.

For their part, Moyo and Yeros claim that their critics (who they call neo-liberal apologists for imperialism or 'civic/post-nationalists') demote the significance of national self-determination and the agrarian question in Zimbabwe as expressed in the land movement by focusing on the movement's excessive violence and eventual co-option by the ruling party and state. They therefore argue that it is essential to conceptualise the land occupations in the context of a re-radicalised (and revitalised) state nationalism and the ongoing movement of the National Democratic Revolution (NDR) under post-colonial conditions.

The debate involves fundamentally different conceptions of the Zimbabwean crisis. On the one hand, there is a radical nationalist discourse that speaks of a land crisis and that stresses national sovereignty and re-distributive policies. In terms of this discourse, Raftopoulos (2006) says that land 'became the sole central signifier of national redress, constructed through a series of discursive exclusions' (Raftopoulos 2006, 212). This process of exclusion entails sidelining and undercutting sub-national counter-narratives found in what the state would label as the more 'marginal' spaces of Zimbabwean society, including rural Matabeleland and the urban trade union movement (Alexander, McGregor, and Ranger 2000, Raftopoulos 2001). On the other hand, there is a liberal democratic discourse that refers to a governance crisis and that emphasises human rights and political democratisation (Hammar, Raftopoulos, and Jensen 2003, Sachikonye 2002), and that involves a 'managerial, modernising nationalism' (Rutherford 2002, 1).

The first discourse focuses on the external (imperialist) determinants of the crisis and the latter on its internal (nation-state) determinants (Freeman 2005). However, both discourses seem to have roots in the notion of the NDR, with the former prioritising the 'national' (in struggling against imperialism) and the latter the 'democratic' (in struggling against an authoritarian state) (Moore 2004). For example, Mandaza (with links to the ruling party), says that during the late 1990s post-nationalist forces in alliance with foreign elements were engaged in a subterranean 'social crisis strategy' that sought to make Zimbabwe ungovernable, and that the (supposedly radical) intellectual representatives of these forces sought to prioritise issues of governance and democracy 'at the expense of addressing the National Question' (The 'Scrutator' in *The Zimbabwe Mirror*, 28 April to 4 May 2000). Thus, the civic nationalism propagated by these theorists (such as Raftopoulos) is portrayed as 'progressive' urban civil groups warring against the state, and this entails seeking to undermine economic (re-distributive) nationalism rightly articulated (according to Mandaza) by a beleaguered nation-state under the onslaught of imperialism in the capitalist periphery.

This literature has been marked sometimes by crude objectifications and dualisms (not unlike the rhetoric of the political parties–ZANU-PF and the opposition Movement for Democratic Change, MDC). For instance, war veterans that led and drove the land occupations of White commercial farms are seen as the storm-troopers of an authoritarian government and political elite with intentions of economic accumulation. The land movement, as an internally differentiated social movement with a fluidity and vibrancy of its own, is reduced to the machinations of a corrupt political party. On the other side of the political spectrum, the argument goes that urban civics are anti-land reform and are mere local instruments of global capital and donors pursuing crafty imperialist agendas. Urban civics, involving diverse and complex organisational forms responsive to a range of global and local pressures, are treated homogeneously as 'black boxes' devoid of agency, simply existing to respond to the tunes of the pied piper.

The debate in many ways captures the main political schisms and discourses that exist in Zimbabwean society, therefore articulating party-political conflicts in theoretical clothing. The conflict is state-centric (changing the state or defending the state) and, ultimately, the debate reproduces state rationalities and subjectivities. In this regard, the Liberal notion of civil society (laid out by the 'civic nationalists') clearly dominates in relation to academic commentary on Zimbabwe, and it is exemplified in the many writings of Kagoro (2003, 2005) as chairperson of the Crisis in Zimbabwe Coalition (CZC). The Liberal notion involves highlighting the institutional make-up or 'organisations of civil society' (Laakso 1996, 218) (in the form of urban civics or NGOs) and its progressive character (Magure 2009). Civil society as a bounded socio-political space constituted in and through civil liberties is rarely discussed. Intriguingly, the 'radical nationalists' do not dispute this institutional delimitation of civil society but rather challenge civil society's supposed progressive status.[1] Likewise, the state-aligned dominant faction of the war veteran movement would find it extremely repugnant to be labelled as part of 'civil society' (McCandless 2011).

The 'civic nationalists' speak about the progressive nature of civil society and the regressive nature of the Zimbabwean state. The range of intellectuals aligned to this position includes both Liberals and Leftists, as witnessed by the list of intellectuals that voiced their concerns about an article written by Mamdani (2008) in the *London Review of Books* which purportedly supported ZANU-PF. This aligning of Liberals and Radicals in 'proclaiming civil society as the most viable alternative to the failed state' was noted nearly two decades ago by Jonathan Moyo (1993, 4), now of ZANU-PF fame. In the face of an authoritarian Zimbabwean state, the contemporary civic nationalists regularly glorify and romanticise civil society in building democracy, reducing the latter to urban civic bodies (for example, the National Constitutional Assembly, NCA and the CZC) and middle-class NGOs. Development NGOs in Zimbabwe, notably international NGOs such as World Vision, are effectively locked into the liberal civil society paradigm in seeking to modernise agriculture in customary areas (Helliker 2008). Likewise, many foreign-funded local NGOs (such as Kunzwana Women's Association) doing 'development' work amongst farm labourers on commercial farms (in a self-declared civilising mission) seek to build civil association on these farms; in doing so, they fail to recognise the existence of more indigenous forms of rural civility (Rutherford 2004). This all leads to a cleansed, exclusionary and hollowed out notion of civil society, and fails to recognise that antagonisms over the past decade have not occurred in a neat and tidy dichotomous civil society/state fashion. For instance, under pressure from 'occupiers' on commercial farm property, the Zimbabwean state abandoned its long-term alliance with White agricultural capital (arguably part of an economic-rooted civil society) and forged a fresh alliance with the 'occupiers' (arguably on the edge of a rule-of-law civil society).

The point is that this argument downplays tensions that occur within civil society and focuses on tensions between 'progressive' civil society and the 'regressive' state (or, more aptly, the argument at times displaces the former tensions onto the latter). The work by Ncube (2010), in highlighting the tensions within Zimbabwean civil society, is an excellent corrective in this regard; in particular, he speaks of a hegemonic civil society linked to ZANU-PF and a counter-hegemonic civil society aligned to MDC, and of the struggles between them. In the case of fast track, and the wider political struggles that emerged around it, considerable conflict took place within civil society–including between commercial landholders and farm workers and between urban-based NGOs (including the NCA) and the Zimbabwe National Liberation War Veterans Association (ZNLWVA). But, as McCandless (2011) documents, such conflicts also occurred between (and within urban civics), notably between the NCA and CZC. In addition, as part of civil society, land-holding commercial farmers (admittedly known for their quasi-authoritarian agrarian rule) played a particularly regressive role in seeking to uphold racialised rural spaces in Zimbabwean society against a state that was undercutting 'domestic government' (to use Rutherford's–2001–Foucauldian notion).

This Liberal civil society argument also fails to do justice to the varied kinds and textures of sociability in rural fast track Zimbabwe. When civilities amongst rural petty commodity producers are acknowledged, it is normally in relation to their involvement in market-oriented forms of farmer production, distribution and consumption. The mobilisation and organisation that occurred during the land movement is regularly labelled as 'uncivil' because it undermined private property regimes and the prevailing market-based land transactions. Some ethnographic accounts of the mobilisation strategies and the forms of organisation that existed on the occupied farms even at the height of the land movement in the years 2000 and 2001 show that they often took on an easily recognisable civil form and content, as did the links between the farm structures on the one hand and the district and provincial war veteran associations on the other (Sadomba 2011). Research on older resettlement areas in Zimbabwe (from the 1980s) indicates that the redistribution of large-scale farms may in fact lead to the development of 'civil social activities' (Barr 2004), at least in comparison to the customary areas, as resettled farmers forge social relationships in the absence of traditional authorities. However, the seeming imposition of chieftainship systems in the newly resettled (fast track) farms may counter the diverse forms of civil associations that have painstakingly emerged over the past ten years (Murisa 2011).

At the same time, civil groups are regularly and 'sadly undemocratic' (Makumbe 1998, 311). An ethnography of urban-based civic NGOs in Zimbabwe (notably human rights organisations) shows that their internal processes are often characterised by un-constitutional (and un-civil) procedures (Rich-Dorman 2001). More recently, the conflict within the NCA and the subsequent formation of the CZC led to serious self-reflection even within 'urban civil society'. For instance, Brilliant Mhlanga (2008) a human rights activist, wrote in 2008 that Zimbabwean 'civil society is showing double standards' and that it 'has internalised the image of the ruling party, its tactics and general guidelines, and is therefore fearful of freedom of any meaningful change' (see also Tendi 2008). Even those Zimbabwean academics who have long idealised urban civics as the site for transformation recently acknowledge the factionalised and troublesome nature of the civic movement (Saunders 2010).

Overall, the aim of Zimbabwean civil society is to democratise the state because, in the end, the state is the guarantor of democracy. The NCA and aligned urban groups have therefore sought to defend and advance political and civil liberties (i.e. to build civil society, as a rule-of-law social space) as well as to achieve power through the MDC in the contest for state hegemony. Civil society, as a set of organisations, is treated instrumentally and the state is perceived as the ultimate emancipator of society. The opposing side in the Zimbabwean debate, which I now discuss, loosely adopts the Radical state-centric argument and also posits the state as the critical site for social transformation.

Moyo and Yeros (2005, 2007), and Mandaza in a series of commentaries in *The Zimbabwe Mirror* from the year 2000 to 2002, overplay the prospects of genuine agrarian transformation by means of the Zimbabwean state. This is despite the fact that at times they, first of all, privilege autonomous rural action (the land occupations, which they label as 'uncivil' but not in any negative sense) in resolving lingering land questions; and, secondly, recognise that the state co-opted and subdued what was initially an autonomous movement. Their ultimate state fixation arises mainly because of a pre-conceived and fixed understanding of political change, most notably in terms of the National Democratic Revolution (NDR).

For instance, the land movement, starting in the year 2000, is said to represent a 'climax' of constant and consistent struggles over land by semi-proletarians (Moyo 2001, 314)–the ordained historical subjects of change–that seek to dramatically address both the agrarian and national questions and thereby the unfinished business of the NDR. In doing so, 'left-nationalists' bring to the fore the functionality of the state in legitimising and strengthening the land movement in the direction of the NDR.[2] State bureaucrats, aspiring black capitalists and ruling party leaders were able to develop hegemony over the movement, and they claimed ownership over the land revolution based on their liberation and indigenisation credentials. The worker-peasant basis of the agrarian reform process was soon in danger of a 'full reversal' (Moyo and Yeros 2005, 194) because of the comprador aspirations of the black bourgeoisie.

Moyo and Yeros go on to assert though that the process 'did not go far enough *within* the ruling party and the state to safeguard the peasant-worker character of the movement or to prepare the semi-proletariat organizationally against the reassertion of the black bourgeoisie' (Moyo and Yeros 2005, 193 their emphasis). It could in fact be argued that the opposite is the case, and that the agrarian change strategy went *too far* within the state and was thereby captured by what Raftopoulos (2006, 216) labels as the state 'commandism' of ZANU-PF. Despite the significance they often give to movement autonomy, the arguments by Moyo and Yeros seem to be part of a more general state-centred theory of change, such that movement un-civility 'obtained radical land reform *through the state* and *against imperialism*' (Moyo and Yeros 2005, 179 their emphasis). It may be claimed that, unlike the other position in the debate that puts civil society on a pedestal, Moyo and Yeros are mesmerised by the state–which they prefer to label as a radicalised state and not as an authoritarian state–as a source for breaking with the civility of capital and for apparently post-imperialist transformation.

It is the politically progressive aspect of the land movement that is the most contentious argument made by Moyo and Yeros. They note that land redistribution over the past few years has undone racial property rights in rural areas and has redressed historical injustices by giving significant number of worker-peasants access to land. In so doing, it has undermined the racial manifestation of the class struggle in Zimbabwe thus laying the basis for the next–and presumably more class-based– phase of the NDR. Mandaza argues in a similar vein: on the one hand, the emergent African bourgeoisie is bound to benefit most from the land reform process, yet this will simultaneously open up the struggle 'tomorrow between the black bourgeoisie and the underclass of society' (*The Zimbabwe Mirror*, 14 July to 20 July 2002). This is largely a teleological depiction of Zimbabwean society and history, and part of a grand narrative of social change (not unlike the grand narrative of civil society-led democratic transition and consolidation propagated by the civil-nationalists).

What the critics of Moyo and Yeros roundly denounce is their underestimation (or underplaying) of state violence. Thus, Moyo (2001, 325–30) argues that the short-term pain of uncivil and violent practices during the occupations must be weighed against the longer-term benefits for democratisation in advancing the NDR. Mandaza likewise argues that it is a 'politically reactionary position ... to deny the principle of land redistribution simply because the methods being employed are said to be bad' (*The Zimbabwe Mirror*, 27 October to 2 November 2000). In other words, the Revolution is to be defended at all costs, particularly given the penetration of the enemy within, in the form of civil society. For Raftopoulos and Phimister (2004, 376), this implies a crude stage-ist notion of change in that 'democratic questions will be dealt with at a later stage, once the economic kingdom has been conquered' (see also Moore 2003).

Oddly enough, during the 1990s, Mandaza (1994) raised significant doubts about the Zimbabwean state as a candidate for social transformation. He argued then that 'the principle of the sole and authentic liberation movement [ZANU] provided the rationale, and indeed the licence, whereby the party in post-independence period can ride rough-shod–in the interests of the masses!–over the interests of the very people it purports to serve' (Mandaza 1994, 195). This state logic is perhaps consistent with the subduing of the land movement by the Zimbabwean state through the fast track land reform programme, and relates to the Radical society-centric critique of the state. Indeed, top-down agrarian restructuring has been a marked feature of the Zimbabwean landscape over the past 10 years, such that both urban civil society and the state (in their own particular ways) sought to undercut an autonomous land movement. 'Left-nationalists' would claim (and quite rightly) that the Zimbabwean state is a critical site of struggle and tension which embodies both progressive and regressive moments (and not purely the latter as asserted by civic-nationalists), and that these contradictory moments became manifested in its fluctuating response to the land movement. In this sense, their position is consistent with the Radical state-centric view of transformation, although the land movement is said to fall outside the realm of the civil. Labelling the land movement as 'uncivil' is on the whole done to distinguish it from imperialist civil society, but this claim does speak to the understanding of civil society as rule-of-law based social space.

Conclusion

The two positions in the Zimbabwean debate both provide partial stories. In doing so, they simultaneously identify and emphasise specific opposing trajectories (or internally related contradictory moments) that mark tension-riddled Zimbabwean society. Sensitivity to these trajectories is necessary to start thinking about the prospects for progress (understood as a contradictory, open-ended and invariably unfinished process) in Zimbabwe. But the trajectories identified are ultimately subsumed under grand narratives that fall within a common statist framework and valorise state politics (as different sides of the same state-centric coin), by conceptually capturing the social struggles in Zimbabwe as centred on the state. This involves a narrative about defending civil liberties against an authoritarian state and advancing towards a liberal democratic state, or a narrative about using the commanding heights of the state to advance distorted processes of transformation. These were the stories that were constantly being told about Zimbabwe during the first decade of this century. The stories dovetail into the contestation over a specific state form (notably about regime change) but the state form itself is never queried. Deploying a Radical society-centred conception of transformation may lead to different stories that open up new vistas of understanding about what animated the urban civics and land occupations.

Underlying the debates about civil society, democratic change and agrarian transformation in Zimbabwe has been a deathly silence on whether civil society in fact exists in post-2000 Zimbabwe. It may be convincingly argued that traditionally, the notion of civil society is linked specifically and exclusively to liberal democratic capitalist societies and that societies marked by compulsive forms of rule (authoritarianism and traditionalism) are devoid of civil societies. Hence, colonial settler societies in Africa, in which chieftainships dominated agrarian spaces and colonised subjects in urban spaces were racially oppressed, were characterised only by 'White' civil society. Post-colonial Zimbabwe, where rural chiefdoms remain and repressive modes of state rule prevail throughout the country, may likewise be largely devoid of a rule-of-law civil society (despite the marked prevalence of NGOs). In this light, debates about the pros and cons of (an existing) civil society in contemporary Zimbabwe would be misplaced.

Notes

1. In a rare collaborative work (Moyo, Makumbe, and Raftopoulos 2000), Moyo (a radical nationalist) and Raftopoulos and Makumbe (civil nationalists) use civil society 'loosely'

(2000, xii) as equivalent to NGOs, understood though as both intermediary donor-funded organisations and community-based organisations. The point is that this is an institutionally based definition of civil society.
2. Interestingly, prior to the 'wave' of democratisation throughout Africa during the 1990s, Shivji (1989) theorised about the NDR and human rights, and argued (unlike Moyo and Yeros) that the furtherance of the NDR necessitated a distinctive anti-authoritarian (and thus democratic) thrust that privileged the right of the popular classes to organise independent of the repressive nation-state. In this respect, Neocosmos (1993) repeatedly emphasises the critical link between 'democratisation from below' (1993, 8) and agrarian reform, and he argues that democratic struggles are 'the primary issue' (1993, 15) in ensuring progressive reform.

Note on contributor

Dr Helliker currently lectures in the Department of Sociology, Rhodes University, Grahamstown, South Africa. His current research interests are agrarian and land reform, social movements, and the politics of emancipation. He has recently co-edited two books on land reform and civil society, one on Southern Africa in general and one specifically on Zimbabwe: Helliker, Kirk and Tendai Murisa, eds (2011), *Land Struggles and Civil Society in Southern Africa*, New Jersey: Africa World Press; and Moyo, Sam, Helliker, Kirk and Tendai Murisa, eds (2008), *Contested Terrain: Land Reform and Civil Society*, Pietermaritzburg: SS Publishers. His email address is k.helliker@ru.ac.za

References

Alexander, J., J. McGregor, and T. Ranger. 2000. *Violence and memory: One hundred years in the 'Dark Forests' of Matabeleland*. Cape Town: David Philip.
Baker, G. 2002. *Civil society and democratic theory: Alternative voices*. London: Routledge.
Barr, A. 2004. Forging effective new communities: The evolution of civil society in Zimbabwean resettlement villages. *World Development* 32, no. 10: 1753–66.
Bond, P., and M. Manyanya. 2003. *Zimbabwe's plunge: Exhausted nationalism, neoliberalism and the search for social justice*. Harare: Weaver Press.
Borras Jr., S. 2008. Re-examining the 'Agrarian Movement-NGO' solidarity relations discourse. *Dialectical Anthropology* 32: 203–9.
Chatterjee, P. 2002. The rights of the governed. *Identity, Culture and Politics* 3, no. 2: 51–72.
Crewe, E., and E. Harrison. 1998. *Whose development?: An ethnography of aid*. London: Zed Books.
Fernandes, S. 2010. *Who can stop the drums? Urban social movements in Chavez's Venezuela*. London: Duke University Press.
Freeman, L. 2005. Contradictory constructions of the crisis in Zimbabwe. *Historia Journal of the South African Historical Association* 50, no. 2: 287–310.
Hammar, A., B. Raftopoulos, and S. Jensen, ed. 2003. *Zimbabwe's unfinished business: Rethinking land, state and nation in the context of crisis*. Harare: Weaver Press.
Helliker, K. 2008. Dancing on the same spot: NGOs". In *Contested terrain: Land reform and civil society in contemporary Zimbabwe*, ed. S. Moyo, K. Helliker, and T. Murisa, 239–74. Pietermaritzburg: S & S.
Kagoro, B. 2003. The opposition and civil society. In *Zimbabwe's turmoil: Problems and prospects*, ed. R. Cornwell, 7–25. Pretoria: Institute of Security Studies.
Kagoro, B. 2005. The prisoners of hope: Civil society and the opposition in Zimbabwe. *African Security Review* 14, no. 3: 19–29.
Laakso, L. 1996. Relationship between the state and civil society in the Zimbabwean elections 1995. *Journal of Commonwealth and Comparative Politics* 34, no. 3: 218–34.
Magure, B. 2009. Civil society's quest for democracy in Zimbabwe: Origins, barriers and prospects, 1900-2008. PhD Department of Political and International Studies, Rhodes University.
Makumbe, J. 1998. Is there a civil society in Africa? *International Affairs* 74, no. 2: 305–17.

Mamdani, M. 1996. *Citizen and subject: Contemporary Africa and the legacy of late colonialism*. Cape Town: David Philip.

Mamdani, M. 2008. Lessons of Zimbabwe. *London Review of Books* 30, no. 23:17–21.

Mandaza, I. 1994. The state and democracy in Southern Africa: Towards a conceptual framework. In Between state and civil society in Africa: Perspectives on development, ed. E. Osaghae, 190–210. Dakar: CODESRIA.

Manji, F., and C. O'Coill. 2002. The missionary position: NGOs and development in Africa. *International Affairs* 78, no. 3: 567–83.

Marongwe, N. 2008. Interrogating Zimbabwe's fast track land reform and resettlement programme: A focus on beneficiary selection. PhD. PLAAS, University of Western Cape.

McCandless, E. 2011. *Polarisation and transformation in Zimbabwe*. Lanham: Lexington Books.

Mhlanga, B. 2008. Civil society's double standards inimical to change in Zimbabwe. http://www.kubatana.net (accessed July 17, 2011).

Monga, C. 1996. *The anthropology of anger: Civil society and democracy in Africa*. Boulder, CO: Lynne Rienner.

Moore, D. 2003. Zimbabwe's triple crisis: Primitive accumulation, nation-state formation and democratization in the age of neo-liberal globalization. *African Studies Quarterly* 7, nos. 2&3: [online]. http://web.africa.ufl.edu/asq/v7/v7i2a2.htm

Moore, D. 2004. Marxism and Marxist intellectuals in schizophrenic Zimbabwe: How many rights for Zimbabwe's left? A comment. *Historical Materialism* 12, no. 4: 405–25.

Moyo, J. 1993. Civil society in Zimbabwe. *Zambezia* XX, no, 1: 1–13.

Moyo, S. 2001. The land occupation movement and democratisation in Zimbabwe: Contradictions of neoliberalism. *Millennium: Journal of International Studies* 30, no. 2: 311–30.

Moyo, S., J. Makumbe, and B. Raftopoulos. 2000. *NGOs, the state and politics in Zimbabwe*. Harare: SAPES Books.

Moyo, S., and P. Yeros. 2005. Land occupations and land reform in Zimbabwe: Towards the national democratic revolution. In *Reclaiming the land: The resurgence of rural movements in Africa, Asia and Latin America*, ed. S. Moyo and P. Yeros, 118–41. London: ZED Books.

Moyo, S., and P. Yeros. 2007. The radicalised state: Zimbabwe's interrupted revolution. *Review of African Political Economy* 34, no. 111: 103–21.

Murisa, T. 2011. Lacuna in rural agency: The case of Zimbabwe's agrarian reforms. In *Land struggles and civil society in Southern Africa*, ed. K. Helliker and T. Murisa, 113–54. Trenton, NJ: Africa World Press.

Ncube, C. 2010. Contesting hegemony: Civil society and the struggle for social change in Zimbabwe, 2000-2008. PhD International Development Department, University of Birmingham.

Neocosmos, M. 1993. The agrarian question in Southern Africa and 'accumulation from below' (Research Report No. 93) Uppsala: The Scandinavian Institute of African Studies.

Neocosmos, M. 2011. Transition, human rights and violence: Rethinking a liberal political relationship in the African neo-colony. Paper presented at Critical Studies Seminar Series, Rhodes University.

Nhema, A. 2002. *Democracy in Zimbabwe: From liberation to liberalization*. Harare: University of Zimbabwe Publications.

Raftopoulos, B. 2001. The labour movement and the emergence of opposition politics in Zimbabwe. In *Striking back: The labour movement and the post-colonial state in Zimbabwe 1980-2000*, ed. B. Raftopoulos and L. Sachikonye, 1–24. Harare: Weaver Press.

Raftopoulos, B. 2006. The Zimbabwean crisis and the challenges for the left. *Journal of Southern African Studies* 32, no. 2: 203–19.

Raftopoulos, B., and I. Phimister. 2004. Zimbabwe now: The political economy of crisis and coercion. *Historical Materialism* 12, no. 4: 355–82.

Rich-Dorman, S. 2001. Inclusion and exclusion: NGOs and politics in Zimbabwe. PhD thesis, Department of Politics and International Relations, University of Oxford.

Rutherford, B. 2001. *Working on the margins–black workers, white farmers in postcolonial Zimbabwe*. Harare: Weaver Press.

Rutherford, B. 2002. Zimbabwe: The politics of land and the political landscape. *Green Left Weekly*, 487. http://www.greenleft.org.au

Rutherford, B. 2004. Desired publics, domestic government, and entangled fears: On the anthropology of civil society, farm workers, and white farmers in Zimbabwe. *Cultural Anthropology* 19, no. 1: 122–53.

Sachikonye, L. 2002. Whither Zimbabwe? Crisis and democratisation. *Review of African Political Economy* 29, no. 91: 13–20.

Sadomba, Z.W. 2011. *War veterans in Zimbabwe's revolution*. Oxford: James Currey.

Saunders, R. 2010. Zimbabwe: Liberation nationalism, old and born again. http://www.africafiles.org (accessed July 20, 2011).

Shivji, I. 1989. *The concept of human rights in Africa*. London: CODESRIA Book Series.

Tendi, B.-M. 2008. Patriotic history and public intellectuals critical of power. *Journal of Southern African Studies* 34, no. 2: 379–96.

Wainwright, H. 2005. Response to John Holloway. In *Change the world without taking power? ... or ... take power to change the world?* ed. Amsterdam: IIRE, 49–55. International Institute for Research and Education.

Anti-developmental patrimonialism in Zimbabwe[1]

Martin Dawson[a] and Tim Kelsall[b]

[a]*Associate, Africa Power and Politics Programme, Research Programme Consortium, London, UK;* [b]*Visiting Fellow of the War Crimes Studies Centre, University of California at Berkeley, USA*

> Research on investment climates and economic growth in developing countries is shifting from institutional 'best practices' towards ways in which developmentally successful regimes make use of economic rents. After discussing rent flows in Zimbabwe's history, the paper concludes that the country exhibits a pattern of centralised, short-term rent utilisation, with disastrous results, showing that the centralisation of rent-management by itself does not indicate a 'developmental patrimonialism'.

Introduction

Conventional wisdom on promoting poverty-reducing growth in African countries recommends strengthening investment climates by importing best practices from the West. Africa should have sound macro-economic management, transparent public finances, free-and-fair elections, well-defined property rights, the rule of law, and an arm's length relationship between business and the State. Such institutions are thought necessary to combat the damaging syndrome of anti-developmental governance often termed 'neo-patrimonialism'. In contrast to Western best-practice, African neo-patrimonialism is said to involve a lack of transparency surrounding public finance, poorly defined or politicised property rights, authoritarian/personalistic political systems, pervasive rent-seeking, and cronyist or clientelistic relations between business and the State.

A growing body of evidence suggests however that 'best-practice' policies, promoted as part of the governance agenda, have had little impact. Those African States that are growing quickly appear not to be doing so on the basis of such practices, while the vast majority of countries seem a long way from launching a growth-promoting capitalist transformation, even if they are growing moderately well. None of the recently successful Asian economies, or Western economies at their point of capitalist take-off, enjoyed institutions compatible with today's 'best-practice' advice (Chang 2003; Khan 2006, 2009). Instead, successful developers operated under political regimes able to transfer economic rents into productive

---

* The Africa Power and Politics Programme is a consortium research programme funded by the UK Department for International Development (DFID) and Irish Aid for the benefit of developing countries. The views expressed in this publication are those of the author and not necessarily those of DFID, Irish Aid or the Programme as a whole.
Corresponding author. Email: martindawson1985@gmail.com

hands and to placate potential threats to growth, often accompanied by corruption, cronyism, and clientelism. What characterised developmental regimes was not so much the presence or even the magnitude of these phenomena so much as the desire and ability to constrain or steer them to growth-promoting ends. Leaders in developmental countries realised that they stood to maximise their own welfare over the long run by encouraging the economy and associated rents to grow (Khan 2000b).

Rents are excess incomes that accrue to factors of production in uncompetitive markets, for example, the rents that accrue to a government-created monopoly, or to economic actors in pre-capitalist settings. In neo-classical economic analyses, rents and the effort expended on securing them (rent-seeking) are regarded as unproductive and inefficient. Partly in consequence, the term 'rent' has acquired a generally pejorative connotation in development circles.

But, as Khan has shown, this note may be false. The neo-classical analysis is based on impossible assumptions about perfectly competitive markets and static comparative advantage. In the real world, rents abound – some are growth-enhancing, others growth retarding. Managing development involves a balancing act between growth enhancing and retarding rents. A successful developmental government is likely to assign rents in the form of rights over natural resources to those with the potential to use them productively or to create some monopoly trading rights that protect new industries from competition. Because the creation and distribution of these rents may be contentious, a developmental government is also likely to have to transfer some not directly productive rents to troublesome groups in the interests of maintaining political stability (Khan 2000a, 2000b). Because most developing countries have rudimentary fiscal bases and administrations, this distribution is likely to occur along personalistic, clientelistic, or patrimonial lines, and may involve corruption (Khan 2000a, 2000b). Africa's 'developmental patrimonial' regimes are developmental precisely because they managed the balance between growth-enhancing and growth-retarding rents more or less adequately, even though they were, with the notable exception of Kagame's Rwanda, far from free of unproductive rent-seeking and corruption (Kelsall et al. 2010).

Khan's findings resonate with a growing body of unorthodox evidence on the investment climate and economic growth. Moore and Schmitz (2008), and Abdel-Latif and Schmitz (2009), for example, argue that growth coalitions are often relationship-based, not rules-based; Rodrik (2007) has argued that a variety of institutional forms can fulfil the function of promoting economic growth; Grindle (2004) has written about the need for 'good enough' rather than 'good' governance; North, Wallis, and Weingast (2009) explain the enduring importance of economic rents in transitional economies; while Levy (2010) has described the 'best practice' agenda as 'bankrupt'.

The most successful developers in Africa all qualify as neo-patrimonial regimes. These 'developmental patrimonial' regimes have centralised rent-management with long-term horizons, typically involving a strong dominant party, a visionary leader, and a competent and confident economic technocracy. By contrast, the less developmental regimes all show either a failure to centralise rents, or a short-term perspective (Cammack and Kelsall 2010; Kelsall et al. 2010).

If Rwanda, with its centralised, long-horizon rent-management provides an example of developmental patrimonialism, and Tanzania, with its decentralised, short-horizon rent-management, a case of developmentally disappointing patrimonialism, Zimbabwe represents a third type. A strongly neo-patrimonial State once thought to have much economic promise, Zimbabwe is regarded today as an archetypal 'basket-case' economy. In spite of rent-management being quite tightly centralised by the ruling party, it is being used for anti-developmental purposes.

A brief history of rents in Zimbabwe

Present-day Zimbabwe has its origins in the territory carved out in 1890 by Cecil Rhodes' British South Africa Company (BSAC), which ran the colony until 1923. The BSAC enticed new settlers with generous grants of land, confiscated (without compensation) from the indigenous inhabitants, initially through armed dispossession and later through a 'legal' process. A range of laws from the Land Apportionment Act (1930) to various Industrial Conciliation Acts drew clear boundaries between white citizen and black subject and established whites, and, in particular, white rural capital, clearly in the ascendancy. After 1923, competition for rents between the domestic political elite and the capitalist class (e.g. urban industrialists, rural agro-capitalists)[2] was stabilised through a system of State marketing boards and protective tariffs, mediated through a range of sectoral representative associations (Selby 2006, 51).

From the late 1940s, an urban and rural black middle class emerged, extracting a few economic concessions from the State but failing to obtain significant political concessions that would have brought redistributive power. In the face of international condemnation, the Rhodesian regime declared unilateral independence in 1965. International sanctions from 1966 and the State's import substitution programme led to the development of a diversified economy. The Land Tenure Act of 1969 consolidated primitive accumulation by whites, allocating approximately half the agricultural land to 6000 white farmers and the rest to 4 million black mostly peasant farmers.

The failure of the State to accommodate black demands promoted the rise of more militant voices and the armed conflict that ushered in Zimbabwe. The transitional arrangements negotiated at Lancaster House protected white economic interests, particularly their land holdings. Robert Mugabe's ZANU party assumed power, subsequently consolidating its power through a reign of terror in the ZAPU stronghold of Matabeleland. Zimbabwe became a *de facto* one-party state when ZAPU and ZANU merged in 1987 to form ZANU-PF, with ZAPU leader Joshua Nkomo taking the vice-presidency.

At Independence in 1980 Zimbabwe had a relatively well-developed and diverse market economy, albeit highly regulated, and an under-developed peasant-based economy. The market economy was predicated upon large-scale commercial agriculture and mining, supported by manufacturing and industrial sectors serviced by a relatively well-developed financial sector. ZANU abandoned its pre-independence revolutionary promises of fundamental structural change (while retaining the rhetoric) in favour of a pragmatic accommodation of the capitalist sector, at the same time implementing a welfarist social policy and boosting the peasant economy with subsidies and infrastructural development. The main outlines of the system for managing rents in this period are shown in Figure 1.

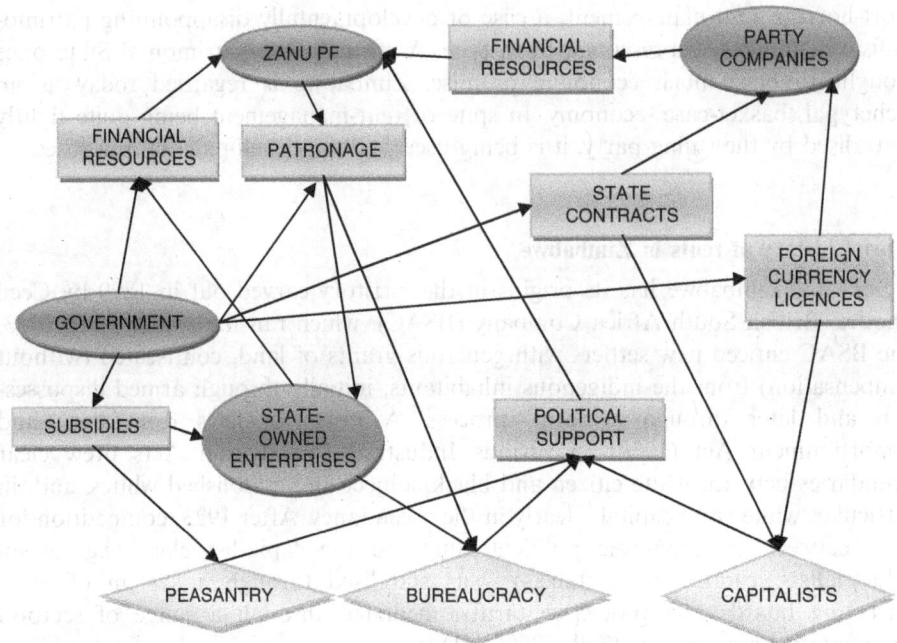

Figure 1. Rent flows in Zimbabwe – the 1980s.

The government provided agricultural subsidies to its key rural support base, the peasantry, while using state power to support state-owned enterprises and to favour companies owned by ZANU-PF. State contracts were also awarded to ZANU-PF companies, and both party companies and private capital returned resources and political support to ZANU-PF. The redistributive transfers to the peasant sector were intended to secure a political hegemony in the rural areas that, in ZANU-PF's heartland, was unchallenged until March 2008. The pricing structure adopted for maize and other agricultural commodities undoubtedly had a developmental dimension, though bureaucratic delays in fixing prices and making payments sometimes adversely affected farmers.

The State attempted to establish a new business class by issuing foreign currency licences to aspiring black business people. However, anyone obtaining licences could charge a massive premium merely by 'selling' them to established businesses – with no costs of production or other business risks. A class of 'briefcase businessmen' developed, hustling for the best bidder and reaping enormous returns. There were occasional prosecutions of some rent takers but no systemic clamp down.

ZANU's accommodation of the former beneficiaries of colonialism was rooted in the geo-political realities of the time with encouragement from the presidents of the 'Frontline States' which had suffered a wholesale flight of capital and skills after decolonisation. These considerations, coupled with the need to consolidate political power, led to a strategic alliance with white capital that preserved and promoted privilege, setting the stage for an elite cooption process (Brand 1981)[3] and, more ominously, preserving the bogey of racist politics to be played out much later.

The non-agricultural economy continued to be dominated by large foreign corporations. In 1980 perhaps two-thirds of the economy could be loosely termed 'foreign-owned' (Stoneman 1981).[4] A process of cooption saw appointments of well-connected or politically powerful individuals to the boards of many companies. There was a growing coincidence of elite class interests and a lessening of racial divisions in businesses, at least at board level, and Zimbabwe saw the growth of a new 'bureaucratic-financial *comprador* elite' (Bond and Manyanya 2003). New foreign direct investment was very limited and while investment in health and education was substantial, economic stagnation meant few jobs were created to absorb the educated.[5]

A significant share of the economy was in the hands of SOEs which increasingly changed from production and marketing mechanisms into sites of political patronage as the State appointed boards based less on technical competence than on clientelism. After a major corruption scandal in 1988,[6] patronage politics became the norm. By 2005 SOEs would be ordered to erect stands and pay rentals at the ZANU-PF congress.[7] The abuse of SOEs for political advantage at the expense of economic growth inevitably resulted in institutions that became less and less efficient. Since the SOEs operated as short-horizon and centralised sites of rent-seeking, the cost of maintaining these grew substantially as profitability declined, leading the state to look at ways to restore their usefulness.[8]

The 1980s appears to be a period in which the growth functions of economic rents, while not completely ignored, played second fiddle to the political imperatives of post-conflict redistribution, patronage, and self-enrichment. ZANU-PF failed to confront and control burgeoning corruption: a 'Leadership Code' issued by the party in 1984 acknowledged the problem but did not curb short-term unproductive rent-seeking. When politicians were convicted of corruption, ZANU-PF's responses sent a clear message – corruption was acceptable as long as one was in favour with the party.[9]

ZANU-PF's readiness to extract rents from business through regulatory predation increased insecurity for capital, raising costs, and it became increasingly profitable not to produce but to trade, seeking arbitrage on everything from foreign currency to fuel. In such an environment, a productive capitalist sector could not develop. Instead, an elite of political businessmen and outright 'robber barons' emerged, whose positions and profits depended not on productivity but on connections to the Party (Otieno 2009).

The economy, built upon import substitution during UDI and maintained by the post-independence government, reached a crisis point in the late 1980s. A structural adjustment programme (ESAP) shifted the economic orientation of the state to an export-driven model. From 1992 import controls were eased and by January 1994 the lucrative arbitrage for briefcase businessmen disappeared (Robertson 2010).[10] Davies (2004, 29) suggests that by 1990

> ...the limits of the state as a site for personal wealth acquisition were being reached. The fiscal constraints on state expenditures limited the scope for patronage, rent seeking and other forms of personal wealth acquisition. The scope of arenas such as abuse of foreign exchange administration was also shrinking as low economic growth limited the spoils.

ZANU-PF's move from a centralist capitalist welfarist model to a globally oriented market economy saw a widening gulf between the 'haves' and the 'have-

Table 1. Zimbabwe – Economic indicators 1980–2006.

	1980–1990	1991–2000	2001–2006
Average annual GDP growth (%)	4.30	0.90	−5.70
Employment growth (%)	1.90	0.40	−7.50
Formal employment (% of pop.)	12.20	10.90	7.00
Manufacturing (% of GDP)	20.35	17.7	15.00

Source: UNDP (2008).

nots'. Popular discontent led to riots in 1995, 1998 and 2000. By 2004 the population below the poverty line increased to 68% while the Gini coefficient worsened from 0.53 in 1995 to 0.61 in 2003. Real earnings declined to less than 10% of their 1982 peak (UNDP 2008 – See Table 1).

The 'informal' sector expanded rapidly after ESAP as formal employment declined. 'Peoples' Markets', as well as both illegal and licenced vending became ubiquitous. Even here, ZANU-PF was able to utilise access rights to distribute resources to its supporters. While this may be construed as the state decentralising or partially losing control of rent-management, it is more likely simply a process of extending access to rents into the lower echelons of the party.

ESAP did lead to some sectoral growth in the 1990s, particularly in export-oriented sectors,[11] but overall GDP growth rates were unimpressive, averaging 1.2% annually from 1991 to 1995 (Bond and Manyanya 2003). The elimination of forex rents may have discomfited the rentiers but the liberalisation of the economy greatly increased the opportunities for old and new traders, especially in luxury goods, and there was a proliferation of trade outlets from 'flea' markets to established stores. In 2006, manufacturing had declined to less than 15% of GDP.

For most would-be businessmen, the route to success lay within supplicatory organisations such as the Indigenous Business Development Centre (IBDC), established in 1991 with Mugabe as its patron and Strive Masiyiwa as Secretary-General. By 1994 IBDC had extracted some access rights from the state such as a quota for building contracts but its internal dynamics gave rise to a more militant group, the Affirmative Action Group (AAG), chaired by Philip Chiyangwa, although the lines between the two groups were blurred as individuals belonged to both and the two groups set up a joint venture, Empowerment Corporation.[12] The state funded both organisations although it later complained about accountability.[13] A number of party-linked businessmen emerged through these organisations – such as Roger Boka, Enock Kamushinda, Philip Chiyangwa, Supa Mandiwanzira, Strive Masiyiwa, Peter Pamire, and Chemist Siziba. They used their access to the state to develop significant business interests, although Masiyiwa faced major obstacles when he tried to establish Econet, a mobile phone company. For a detailed account of Econet saga, see Velamuri (2003).

The Boka Scandal is perhaps the most egregious example of state-sanctioned cronyism. Roger Boka was issued with a commercial bank licence in May 1995 and established the United Merchant Bank (UMB) which collapsed three years later. UMB lavished its political cronies with unsecured 'loans'. The then-Mayor of Harare, Solomon Tawengwa, a member of ZANU-PF's Politburo, received over a million dollars as a kickback for turning a blind eye to the flouting of urban planning laws.[14] Boka also engaged in direct fraud, issuing over Z$1.2 billion of counterfeit bonds after the commercialisation of an SOE, the Cold Storage Commission. A government-appointed inquiry was appointed but Boka died in February 1999 and the investigation appears to have been interred with him.[15]

During this period, land was also a source of rents which the state used for patronage. In 2000, independent Member of Parliament Margaret Dongo released a list of senior government and party officials who had been allocated favourable leases for vast tracts of state land. Little came of such reports, which were largely ignored by the State and its promises to curb multiple farm ownership were not implemented.[16]

The relationship of 'elite accommodation' between white financial power (especially rural) and black political power which operated after 1980 had maintained land tenure inequalities in exchange for economic productivity and white political acquiescence. This began to crumble in the late nineties in the face of a growing political challenge to the ZANU leadership, both from its own supporters and from a new political party.

ESAP had reduced State economic and political control, and it no longer had a relatively simple set of clients to manage but faced demands from several groups, some former clients which now became independent and militant. At one end of the spectrum was the Zimbabwe National Liberation War Veterans Association (ZNLWVA) which emerged by 1997 as the most powerful independent voice 'within' ZANU-PF, able to extract significant rents from the State. In late 1997 Mugabe was forced by its members to hand out unbudgeted cash payments and increase monthly pension payments. The ZNLWVA was emboldened by the War Victims Compensation Fund scandal and by overt support from comrades in high office. The payouts precipitated a major collapse in the Zimbabwean dollar and 'Black Friday' on 14 November 1997 is often regarded as marking the start of the current economic crisis.

At the other end of the spectrum, a challenge to the regime coalesced around the Zimbabwe Congress of Trade Unions (ZCTU). Created in 1980 by the State, the ZCTU was essentially a department of ZANU headed by Mugabe's brother but by 1989, it had achieved some independence with Morgan Tsvangirai as its General Secretary. The ZCTU became instrumental in the formation of the National Constitutional Assembly in 1997 and then the Movement for Democratic Change (MDC) in 1999. The MDC was able to aggregate a disparate range of forces opposed to ZANU-PF – workers, students, middle-class urbanites, white commercial farmers – and, combining the financial resources of both urban black and rural white capital with the numerical strength of the working class, mounted a significant challenge to the monopoly on power that ZANU-PF had enjoyed for 20 years.

The growing pressure upon the state to engage in radical redistributive policies by an increasingly vocal and effective conglomeration of 'war veterans' and peasants resulted in an attempt to address the land issue, initially through constitutional methods, but, after the humiliating defeat in a constitutional referendum in February 2000, through violent and extra-legal means.[17] ZANU-PF destroyed the LSCF sector, appropriating farms and re-distributing these to its supporters. It also increased political repression of its opponents, and began the militarisation of the State. This period saw a flight of capital and disinvestment (touted as indigenisation by State spin-doctors). Anglo-American Corporation disposed of most of its assets, while Heinz sold off Olivine. These de-industrialising pressures were exacerbated in urban areas by factory invasions in 2001 which further unsettled business, increasing the emigration of both owners and workers. The effect upon the economy was calamitous: GDP per capita between 1998 and 2005 dropped 46%.[18]

With the economy collapsing, ZANU-PF began to implement increasingly arbitrary and erratic 'policies'. Rent allocation became a free-for-all, descending into predatory asset-stripping as *chefs*, 'war vets', bureaucrats and ordinary citizens scrambled to secure land and its resources.[19] The 'alliance' between the black political elite and white rural capitalists that had begun to disintegrate in late 1997 was over. In the uncertain terrain that arose, a new rural elite developed owing its loyalty unequivocally to the ruling party, whose largesse could be retracted at any moment. Insecurity of tenure coupled with inadequate financial and agricultural extension support removed any incentive to engage in productive farming. With the short-term horizon that resulted, asset stripping of both natural resources and farm improvements was inevitable. In a sign of growing loss of control of rent-management, the rentiers are frequently involved in conflicts over the spoils.[20]

Not even the informal sector was immune: in 2005 the regime unleashed 'Operation Restore Order' which demolished and criminalised the entire informal sector. An attitude of supra-economic omnipotence reached its height in 2007–2008 during the State's 'Operation Reduce Prices' when it issued *dictats* to reduce prices by 50% and unleashed the 'Crack Unit on Price Controls', forcing shopkeepers to mark down prices irrespective of either original or replacement costs. The goods would then invariably be 'purchased' by the same enforcers and their supporters – and apparently a few free-lance privateers.[21] This pillage provided enormous patronage, supplying goods to rank-and-file members of ZANU-PF and sending out a populist message, whilst condemning and arresting businessmen for seeking 'excessive profits'.[22] While the ZANU-PF elite's own businesses were usually exempted, some were caught up: a minister's husband, Peter Nyoni, was arrested for overcharging.[23] In Bulawayo, riot police fought off suspected police officers who were trying to loot a major wholesaler while soldiers invaded a police station to 'recover' looted items that had previously been confiscated.[24] Goods disappeared from supermarket shelves into hidden warehouses where they could only be purchased in US dollars.

The regime's disregard for basic economics was exposed by its 'management' of foreign currency. After 1994, a largely unregulated forex market existed which might have been expected to result in a more rational utilisation of the country's capacity to import. However forex was used not to sustain medium or long-term productive activities but to import consumer and luxury goods. The Zimbabwean dollar dropped from 0.65Z$ to 1US$ in 1980, to 11:1 in mid-1997 and to 40:1 by the end of 1998. In 1999 the government set a fixed rate, immediately creating a new rent source. By 2008, the official rate was a fraction of the street value and the informal economy abandoned the Zimbabwean dollar altogether. The state itself was one of the largest customers in the forex street trade: buyers were issued with newly printed 'bearer cheques' by the Reserve Bank to purchase forex at street markets. On at least one occasion, new denomination notes were in circulation at forex markets before they had been officially released by the RBZ. Fortunes were made by State-sanctioned 'cash barons' before the process crashed under the burden of hyperinflation and in February 2009, the State abandoned the Zimbabwean dollar.[25]

In 2006 a major new rent source developed in the diamond fields of Chiadzwa. For a comprehensive analysis see, for example, Partnership Africa Canada (2010). The concession, owned by De Beers but never developed, passed in April 2006 to Africa Consolidated Resources (ACR), whose shareholders apparently included General Mujuru (who was also a shareholder in diamond miners, River Ranch) and former ZANU-PF leader Dumiso Dabengwa.[26] ACR announced a major discovery and overnight thousands rushed to the fields to make their fortunes before the police declared war on 'illegal' miners in Operation *Mari Wakaiwanepi*? ('Where did you get all that money from?'),[27] positioning themselves as gatekeepers, renting access to the fields.[28] In 2008 after reports of gun battles, the army was deployed to secure the area.[29] The State has since established two joint ventures, Mbada Mining and Canadile Miners, with foreign mining groups. Mbada Mining is chaired by Mugabe's former helicopter pilot, Robert Mhlanga, who emerged from Zimbabwe's adventure in the Democratic Republic of Congo (DRC) as a millionaire while Mugabe's second wife, Grace, is a shareholder.[30]

ZANU-PF's commercial empire

ZANU-PF developed an extensive commercial empire and this study seeks to identify not only the businesses and holdings but to unravel the byzantine network of individuals who operate these on behalf of the party, to 'disaggregate the State' (Nest 2001) and explain the 'forging of clientage networks' (Raftopoulos 2005).

Prior to independence, ZANU-PF had political and business networks with individuals such as 'Tiny' Rowland of Lonrho[31] and businessman Jayant Joshi. Joshi was based in Britain in the 1970s and allegedly assisted ZANU members.[32] After 1980, ZANU-PF further developed its business interests within the country, forging significant economic power both within and without the State. Its main investment arm, M & S Syndicate (created in 1979) was primarily focused on agriculture, property management and investments, with shares in Fibrolite, G North, Jongwe Printing & Publishing, Ottawa, Star Travel, Treasure Holdings, and Treger Holdings as well as ZANU-PF's other main holding company, ZIDCO Holdings, which was established in 1984 with Chandra Patel (Joshi's uncle) who owned 45% through his UK company, Unicorn Exports & Imports. Zidco Holdings in turn held shares in Woolworth & Co Zimbabwe (until 1991), Oryx Natural Resources, Zidlee Enterprises, Eagle Investments, Zidco Imports & Exports, Catercraft, Jongwe Printing, Mike Appel, National Blankets, Oporto Investments, Treger Holdings, and Zidco Motors. Several companies – Segmented Investments, Sovereign, Hustonville, Tescrom, Amelia, Ryobi, Printfit, Smoothnest and M & S Investments – were allegedly created to circumvent targeted 'sanctions' imposed by western countries after 2003 (Anonymous 2010).

In 1992 ZIDCO claimed to employ almost 10,000 people with an annual turnover of Z$350 million. It was involved in a range of economic activities including 'government contracts, army tenders, supplies of textbooks,...imports of tobacco, liquor and a range of trinkets, builders' hardware, fridges and stoves, farm management, international consultancy and property investment' (Horizon 1992).

Total contributions to ZANU-PF are unknown but in 2003, corporate contributions including donations were the primary source of official party funding, providing Z$1.2 billion or 84% of its revenues. Accounts tabled at ZANU-PF's

2003 congress show receipts from a number of individuals and organisations including Tregers (Z$250 million), Catercraft (Z$20 million), National Discount House (Z$200 million) and Commercial Bank of Zimbabwe (Z$450 million). It also received $127,500,000 from the State under the Political Parties Finance Act. In contrast, the 2003 national revised budget was over Z$1100 billion.

In 2005, reported dividends were Z$5.8 million while for the nine months to 30 September 2006, ZANU-PF received payments from FBC Holdings (Z$3.5m), Mike Appel (Z$3.1m), Catercraft (Z$6.2m),and Zidlee (Z$1.2m).[33] The companies also offered patronage opportunities, such as directorships, employment, and supply contracts.

In 2004 an internal investigation of the party's empire, chaired by David Karimanzira, the then Secretary of Finance for the party, led to the flight of several directors of ZANU-PF companies but the report failed to implicate the chairperson of M & S, Emmerson Mnangagwa, despite calling for criminal investigations into the companies.[34] It appears that the investigations were the result of factional struggles between General Mujuru and Mnangagwa as well as Mugabe's concerns about Mnangagwa's presidential aspirations.[35] The results of two further investigations, by auditors Kudenga & Co and in 2006, by Didymus Mutasa, are also unavailable.[36] ZANU-PF's business empire is both opaque and keenly contested by factions within the party. This contestation may be a sign of a process of decentralising rent-seeking although the role of Mnangagwa indicates a centralised control, close to Mugabe. M & S is currently chaired by Gertrude Chikwava who also represents the Zimbabwe Mining Development Corporation (ZMDC) on the board of Canadile Miners.

Following the 2000 general election, Mugabe began a programme of State militarisation, appointing nominally retired officers to SOEs, Commissions, Boards and Authorities (Zimbabwe Institute 2008). Military men ran and controlled all elections in the country after 2000. Zimbabwe is, according to some, run by a military cabal, the Joint Operations Command (JOC), who benefit from their positions to accumulate farms and business opportunities, especially during the DRC war (United Nations 2001).[37] Interestingly, this militarisation does not extend into the ruling party – the late General Solomon Mujuru was the only soldier in the Politburo: Mugabe has been careful to preserve control over the party while meeting the rent expectations of his generals elsewhere (for example, the DRC, SOEs, farms and the Chiadzwa diamonds).

In 1996 Zimbabwe assisted Laurent Kabila to power in the DRC. Zimbabwe Defence Industries (ZDI), a private company owned by the Zimbabwe Defence Force (ZDF), awarded a contract to General Zvinavashe's transport company to ferry supplies to the DRC (Global Witness 2002; Dietrich 2000).[38] By the end of 1998, deals included the creation of a trading company, Congo-Duka, a joint venture between ZDI and Congolese SOE, General Strategic Reserves, and the appointment of Billy Rautenbach (see below) as head of Gecamines, the State-owned cobalt mine (Goredema 2003).[39] In 1998 over 10,000 Zimbabwean troops helped consolidate Kabila's power and to defend mining areas. Congo Duka was replaced by a new company, Operation Sovereign Legitimacy (OSLEG)[40] with a host of military men on its board. Osleg in turn created a joint venture company, Cosleg, with Kabila's Comiex-Congo. Despite the withdrawal of most Zimbabwean troops in 2002, commercial and military activity continued.[41]

Despite the anti-white rhetoric of ZANU-PF,[42] it continues to maintain a number of alliances with white businessmen.[43] John Bredenkamp and 'Billy' Rautenbach were allegedly embroiled in DRC investments while Nicholas 'van' Hoogstraten has allegedly assisted ZANU-PF leaders avoid sanctions while bankrolling the party (Africa Confidential 2008). These three 'crony capitalists' are the most egregious examples of a sub-class of capital that includes not only overt enthusiasts for Mugabe and his rule but also those who claim that they 'are only businessmen' and those, especially amongst the LSCF sector, who 'cut a deal' with the powerful (Godwin 2010, 246).

In summary, rents have been centralised by a leadership cabal straddling the Joint Operations Command, ZANU-PF, Government, party companies, and SOEs. It controls access to rents from land, foreign currency, diamonds, the DRC, and farm equipment, which are distributed primarily to members of the defence forces and to 'war veterans', with pro-ZANU-PF peasants, civil servants, and pro-regime capitalists being secondary beneficiaries. These groups provide the political support, and coercive power to maintain the regime in office. It is not yet clear how far power-sharing with the MDC has affected these arrangements – although the fact that the JOC continues to operate, and that the MDC used patronage politics to get the Finance Bill through parliament recently, suggests that changes have been negligible.

Land and mine invasions, unauthorised looting, and factional struggles for lower-level rents suggest that centralisation of rent-management is somewhat precarious. It seems clear that rent-management is focused on maximum enrichment and regime survival over the short-term. It is difficult to imagine a less propitious environment for long-term investment and growth. Regime supporters may currently be able to profit through consumption of natural resource rents, monopoly trading rights and black-marketeering but these income flows are not sustainable, let alone expanding. Figure 2 illustrates some of the rent flows in this period.

Zimbabwe in comparative perspective

Having identified the rent-management system, it is useful to ask why economic management has taken such a calamitous turn, and whether alternative paths might have been possible. Khan has argued that generalised violence in a country ends when the most powerful groups come to a political settlement whereby formal and informal institutions facilitate a distribution of benefits consistent with their relative power (Khan 2010, 20), for example, through the establishment of power-sharing 'unity governments' as in Kenya and Zimbabwe. Different political settlements have different implications for this 'growth-stability' trade-off which will be influenced by a number of variables, including the strength of elite groups outside the ruling coalition, the leadership strength of the ruling coalition *vis à vis* its own supporters, and the nature of the capitalist class. Generally speaking, the stronger the leadership and the more capable the capitalist class, the more scope the regime has for allocating rents to growth-promoting actors.

At Independence, much (brutal) energy was devoted to subduing and co-opting ZAPU, instead of facilitating growth. The Lancaster House settlement prevented the large-scale redistribution of land, the main source of natural resource rents, so it is no surprise that the leadership chose to deflect challenges by permitting lower-level leaders, those with the potential to organise opposition to their rule, to enrich

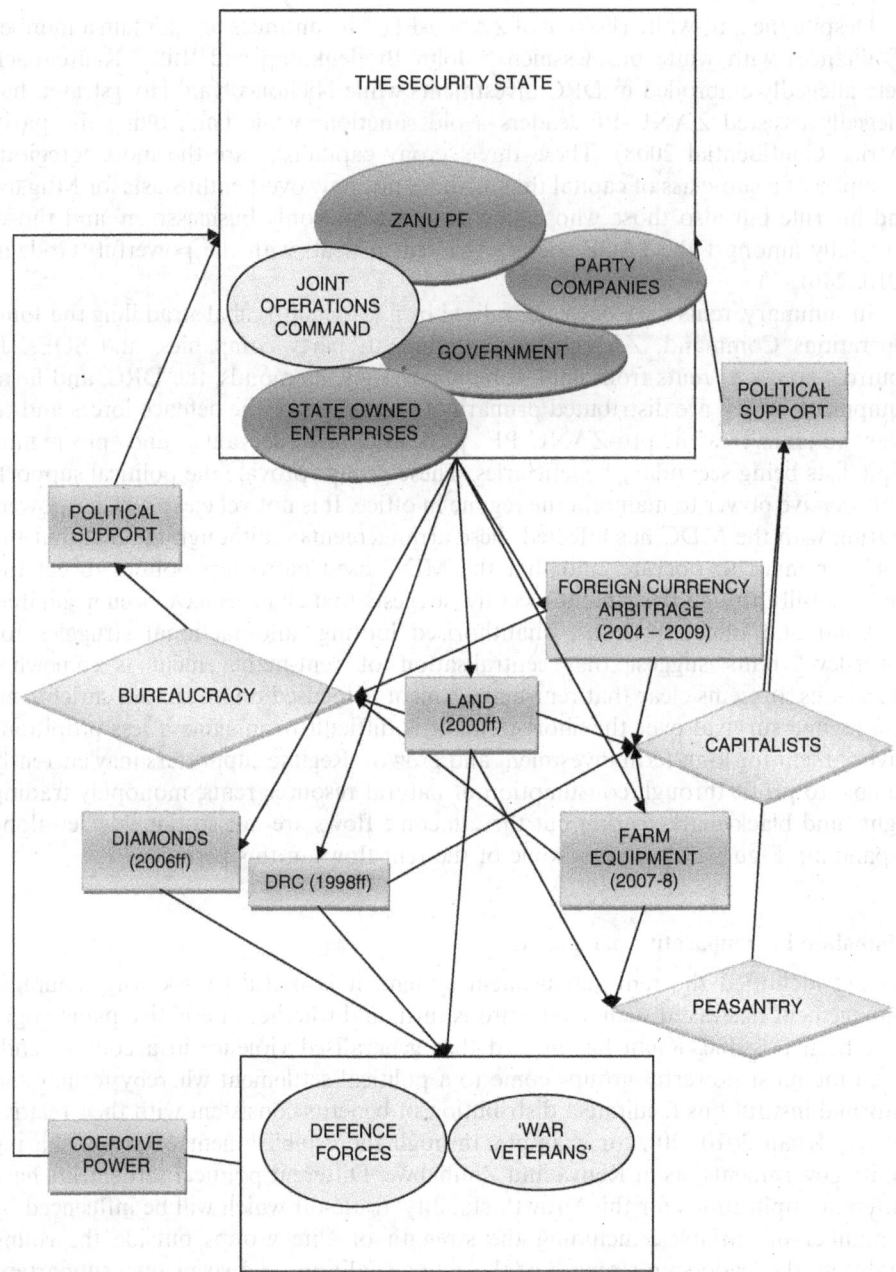

Figure 2. Changing alliances – rent flows in the new millennium.

themselves. The capitalist class, being overwhelmingly white, was politically weak and unable to resist petty predations or to press for pro-capital policies. There were therefore understandable strategic reasons why the ruling party emphasised a redistributive clientelist strategy rather than a generalised redistributive strategy or a vigorous pro-growth policy.

We should add to this, aspects of political culture and what might be called 'cognitive failure'. Culturally, the post-1980 regime had experienced racial oppression and a war against white rule and politically, it would have been difficult to embrace a development strategy with white capital at its core. The problems of relying on a protected industrial sector were perhaps not yet apparent in 1980 but by the late-1990s, this should have been obvious, and the cognitive failure and cultural aspects of the regime's choices must weigh more strongly. Furthermore, ZANU-PF is essentially a rural party that sees cities as alien creations where people become deracinated or 'totemless'. Cities are places for accumulation, the proceeds of which are re-invested *kumusha*,[44] the only legitimate sphere of human endeavour. This dichotomous construct is hardly a reflection of reality but of aspiration that informs both policy and action. Certainly, few older 'indigenous' Zimbabweans regard the cities as 'home' and this has slowed the development of specifically urban classes, whether these are working, intermediate or capitalist.

Like Tanzania, Zimbabwe's capitalist sector at independence was dominated by a non-African minority and its nationalist movement also had a broadly socialist ideology. It is not surprising then that like Tanzania, it has failed to consistently support a pro-growth strategy. In fact, Zimbabwe was arguably even less likely to pursue such a strategy than Tanzania. Although ZANU, like TANU, established itself as a dominant party soon after independence, it nevertheless faced stronger pressures for redistribution. This is not to justify ZANU's choices, and especially not the catastrophic reapportioning of land rents, but merely to restate that there were significant forces pushing the regime in this direction, while closing off others.

Rwanda provides a different perspective. Like ZANU, the RPF is a dominant party, and it faces serious external and probably internal challenges. Indeed, it is arguable that the RPF regime faces a much more difficult political situation than ZANU ever did. One would expect, therefore, that the ZANU regime would have had more room for manoeuvre when it came to promoting a growth strategy than the RPF does. If this is the case, it suggests that a pro-growth strategy would not have been impossible in Zimbabwe. Why then did the regime not pursue such a course? One possibility is that with a relatively developed capitalist sector, the regime had a source of rents on which to prey, and did not feel impelled to create them, as in Rwanda, from the ground up. Other reasons have already been discussed, namely the history of racial oppression suffered by the party and its supporters, and the influence of socialist and African nationalist ideologies.

In Rwanda, the RPF holding company has been a formidable vehicle for centralising rents, funding the party, and permitting a strong anti-corruption stance with the administration. ZANU-PF's holding companies, they have been important (though to a lesser degree) in centralising rents and channelling funds to the ruling party. However, those rents appear to have been short-term, parasitic or predatory, and thus growth-retarding, in contrast to the rents created by Tri-Star which are mostly learning rents that appear to be growth-promoting. Clearly, the holding company model can be used for good or ill, depending on the nature of the regime.

Conclusions

This paper has examined the structure of rent-management in Zimbabwe from Independence to the present day, describing how the Lancaster House Constitution prevented any wholesale redistribution of natural resource rents in the 1980s, and how the regime focused instead on channelling forex rents, parastatal jobs, and business sinecures to its supporters, while crushing its opponents militarily. Structural adjustment in the 1990s removed some patronage resources but created others. Facing increased pressure from a reconstituted political opposition, from its own popular base, and with the withdrawal of donor support, the regime's response was a catastrophic policy of reallocating white land at home, while pursuing natural resource rents abroad. Domestic investment and production all but collapsed, and inflation ran out of control.

We have argued that underpinning this dismal record has been a centralised structure of rent-management with a short-term orientation, demonstrating that while centralised rent-management may be a necessary precondition for economic growth under African conditions, it is not sufficient. Indeed, in the hands of a regime that is not growth-oriented, rent-centralisation may be more damaging than decentralisation.

There is nothing intrinsically developmental about party-holding companies. While potentially effective vehicles for centralising rent-management, their developmental impact depends on the orientation of the regimes. From a theoretical standpoint, single-factor institutional explanations are insufficient for differentiating between more and less developmental regimes. The implications of institutions cannot be divorced from the contexts in which they are embedded and the decision-logics of their controllers.

Does this analysis offer any pointers for the future in Zimbabwe? Recently, a richly detailed account of post-Independence Zimbabwean politics uses concepts of structure and agency to assess the country's potential to embark on a new path of good governance, democracy, and development (Bratton and Masunungure 2011). While noting that political transitions offer unique opportunities for structural change, the analysis remarks on the challenges posed by party fragmentation, survival politics, a culture of distributive clientelism, and an unpredictable military. The authors' hopes for better governance repose upon on 'democracy' and a more active citizenry (Bratton and Masunungure 2011, 47) but in our view this is naïve, not least because of the collective action problems involved in transferring mass desires for better governance into actual reform.

More likely, the most powerful elite groups will realise that the old ways are unsustainable, and will seek to forge new institutional vehicles for consolidating and expanding rents with the assistance of an improved investment climate and re-professionalised bureaucracy. Importantly, this would not necessarily imply stripping elites of their ill-gotten gains, or expecting individuals who have grown rich on plunder to become paragons of virtue. It would simply involve strengthening the technocratic aspects of the core economic agencies, tightening informal regulation of unproductive rent-seeking, while steering a greater proportion of rent-earning opportunities to sectors likely to be growth-promoting over the long-term.

Notes

1. This is an abridged version of M. Dawson and T. Kelsall (2011) Anti-developmental Patrimonialism in Zimbabwe. Working Paper 19: Africa Power and Politics Programme. The unabridged version of the paper is now available online at: http://www.institutions-af

rica.org/filestream/20111110-appp-working-paper-19-anti-developmental-patrimonialism-in-zimbabwe-dawson-and-kelsall-nov-11
2. Far from being a homogenous group, white commercial farmers were diverse and by no means united in their class interests and aspirations; see Selby (2006) for a comprehensive disaggregation which gives a rare insight into the internal political processes of this group.
3. 'The danger is that the Zimbabwean leadership might be possessed by [the social and economic structures], rather than adapting them to the needs of the people' (Brand 1981, 55).
4. In fact very similar to pre-UDI figures, when foreign interests were dominated by British (60%) and South African (30%) (Stoneman 1981, 118).
5. Some 200,000 school-leavers entered the market each year yet 'Employment creation has averaged a mere 10,000 jobs per annum over the 10 years of independence, far short of the planned target of 144,000 per annum' (Robert Mugabe speaking in 1990, cited in Brett 2005).
6. The 'Willowgate' Scandal involved leading politicians sourcing vehicles at controlled prices from and re-selling these for substantial profits.
7. See 'ZANU-PF Raids Parastatals', *Independent,* 9 September 2005, Paul Nyakazeya.
8. 'For the period 1986–1991 subsidies and advances to some 12 parastatals and government companies exceeded $2 billion. State support for parastatals at an average of Z$429.9 million during the period 1986/1987–1989/1990 was very high as compared to an increase of public enterprises losses by 48% in 1988/1989 compared to 1985/1986 levels' (Tambudzai 2003, 12). See 'A Framework for Economic Reform (FER) 1991-95', Government of Zimbabwe.
9. One minister, Frederick Shava, convicted and briefly imprisoned before being pardoned by Mugabe, continued in a senior post within the party, chairing ZIDCO until 1998. Geof Nyarota's (2006) autobiography, Against the Grain, gives an insight into the 'Willowgate' scandal.
10. John Robertson, a leading economist and commentator, maintains that the elimination of this rent market resulted in disaffection of those affected, who then cast about for new opportunities. The rise of the AAG and IBDC lend weight to this claim.
11. For a detailed analysis of the effects of ESAP in agriculture, see Makamure, Jowa, and Muzuva (2001).
12. The initial shareholding in the EC included the Zimbabwe Farmers' Union, the Affirmative Action Group, the Zimbabwe National Liberation War Veterans Association, the Indigenous Business Women's Organisation and the Small Scale Miners Association of Zimbabwe, with 9% each; Integrated Engineering Group, owned by Leo Mugabe, 10%; James Makamba's Kestrel Corporation, 15%. The Zimbabwe Farmers' Union, Affirmative Action Group, and Zimbabwe National Liberation War Veterans Association subsequently sold their shares to Kestrel. See 'Telecel Dogfight Escalates', *Independent,* 22 July 2010.
13. See 'World Bank Chihombori and Mawere', *Zimbabwe Times,* 21 September 2009, Geoffrey Nyarota, at http://www.thezimbabwetimes.com/?p=22907.
14. See 'The Executive Summary Report of the Investigating Team into the State of Governance and General Administration of the City of Harare' (1998).
15. For a summary see 'Case Study 3: The United Merchant Bank and Boka Group of Companies cases' in Goredema (2003).
16. See for example, 'Government to Undertake Yet Another Land Audit, the Eighth', *Financial Gazette,* 20 December 2006. Reports include the unpublished Buka Report (2003), the Utete Report (2004) which named 13 cabinet ministers and four provincial governors as multiple farm holders, the Nkomo Report (2004), the Chiwewe Report (2005), a Ministry of Lands Report, and the Mutasa Report (2009) whose author, Didymus Mutasa, is alleged to possess at least 10 farms. See 'Mutasa Owns 10 Farms', *Zimbabwean,* 18 June 2009.
17. See Selby (2006) and Utete (2003).
18. For example, 'Weeds and Wasted Lives on the Farm Run by UN's Rural Kingpin', *Times,* 27 June 2007. Note: GDP figures for 2004–2009 are very difficult to compare because of hyperinflation.

19. For a selection of chefs who received farms, see Justice for Agriculture (2002).
20. The shifting sands of who is 'in' and who is 'out' continue to entertain Zimbabweans; see for example, 'Chiwewe Weeps Over Chop', *Radio VOP*, 28 August 2008', Chiwewe to Expose Officials with 10 farms', *Zimbabwe Times*, 16 September 2009, 'Mliswa Case Shakes ZANU-PF to the Core', *Zimbabwe Standard*, 11 July 2010.
21. For example, 'Top Cops in Massive Looting Spree', *Financial Gazette*, 9 August 2007.
22. For example, 'Police Zero in on Forex Barons', *Sunday Mail*, 8 July 2007.
23. For example, 'Double Standards as Elite Gain from Price Controls', *SWRA*, 18 July 2007; 'As Business Plans Audit', *Zimbabwe Standard*, 15 July 2007.
24. See 'As Business Plans Audit', *Zimbabwe Standard*, 15 July 2007; 'Soldiers Storm Police Station to Recover Looted Food Items', *Zim Online*, 13 August 2007.
25. For example, 'Money for Nothing', *IRIN*, 4 January 2008; 'Zimbabwe Central Bank Adviser Off Hook', *Zim Online*, 29 December 2007.
26. 'Report exposes Mnangagwa and Mujuru involvement in Marange', SWRA, 14 June 2010.
27. For example, 'Marange Diamond Rush, the Race that Brought Instant Riches', *Mirror*, 8 January 2007; 'Diamonds are Mutare's Best Friends', *IRIN*, 6 August 2008.
28. See 'Police Officers Arrested over Diamond Bribes in Zimbabwe', *Monsters and Critics DPA*, 31 August 2007.
29. 'Chiadzwa – Army Sent in to Quell Gun Battles', *Financial Gazette*, 6 November 2008.
30. See 'Grace Mugabe Fingered in Diamonds Looting', *Radio VOP*, 30 July 2010.
31. These links were somewhat tenuous prior to Independence since Rowland favoured Nkomo's ZAPU –while funding Muzorewa and Sithole as well but after 1980, they were useful, for instance, in squashing reporting of the 5th Brigade massacres in Matabeleland. See Hall (1987) and Nkomo (1984).
32. The Joshi family were pivotal after 1980 until early 2004 when they fled Zimbabwe in the face of an internal investigation into ZANU-PF businesses. See 'Directors flee as ZANU-PF probes own companies' Sunday Mirror, 4 April 2004.
33. 'ZANU-PF pockets $10.5 mln dividends from associate firms, Financial Gazette, 4 January 2007.
34. The committee included Karimanzira, Solomon Mujuru, Obert Mpofu (then Matabeleland North Governor) and Thoko Mathuthu (then ZANU-PF deputy secretary for transport and welfare). 'ZANU-PF Probe Turns Ugly', *Financial Gazette*, 13 August 2004; 'Mnangagwa Emerges Unscathed', *Financial Gazette*, 9 September 2004.
35. See 'Mnangagwa Elbowed Out of Race', *Independent*, 12 June 2004.
36. 'Succession Stirs ZANU-PF Probe', *Independent*, 13 October 2006.
37. 'Mugabe's Generals', *Newsweek*, 22 July 2008.
38. 'Zanu P F Kabila in secret deal', *Financial Gazette*, 30 August 2001.
39. Also 'Fight over mineral wealth shifts from battlefields to boardrooms', *Business Report*, 22 July 2007.
40. Board members included Lieutenant-General Vitalis Zvinavashe, Job Whabira, Permanent Secretary, Ministry of Defence, Onesimo Moyo, Director, Minerals Marketing Corporation of Zimbabwe, and Isaiah Ruzengwe, General Manager, ZMDC. General Zvinavashe's brother, Colonel Francis Zvinavashe, retired Major-General Dauramanzi and Brigadier Moyo represented Osleg in the Congo.
41. 'Payback time for uncle Bob', *Zimbabwean*, 18 January 2007; 'Zimbabwe Troops in Action in the Congo', *Zimbabwe Today*, 18 November 2008; 'MDC Criticises Deployment of Soldiers to DRC', *Zimbabwean*, 15 December 2008; 'Ebola Kills 2 Zim Soldiers in DRC', *Zim Daily*, 2 January 2009.
42. 'Our party must continue to strike fear in the heart of the white man. They must tremble. They think because they are white they have a divine right to our resources. Not here. The white man is not indigenous to Africa. Africa is for Africans', Mugabe, 2000 ZANU-PF Congress; 'White Ally Scorned by Mugabe', *Observer*, 17 December 2010.
43. For example, Uncovering how Zimbabwean Tycoon Takes Advantage of Political Crisis', *Afrikcom*, 3 August 2008.
44. Literally 'at home' but signifying far more than a situational reference.

Notes on contributors

Tim Kelsall holds a PhD from the University of London (SOAS), has taught politics at the Universities of Oxford and Newcastle, and is a former editor of *African Affairs*, the world's highest impact Africanist journal. He is the author of several articles in international peer-reviewed journals, an edited collection with Carolina Academic Press, and research monographs with the Nordic African Institute and Cambridge University Press. He is currently a Visiting Fellow of the War Crimes Studies Centre, University of California at Berkeley, and a resource person for the Partnership for African Social and Governance Research, as well as leading APPP's Developmental Patrimonialism research stream.

Martin Dawson holds a degree in politics from the University of Cape Town and is an independent researcher on Zimbabwean issues, particularly around culpability, accountability and change. He is currently working with the Africa, Power and Politics Programme. The APPP is funded by the UK's DFID and Irish Aid for the benefit of developing countries. The views expressed in its outputs are those of the authors.

References

Abdel-Latif, A., and H. Schmitz 2009. State-business relations and investment in Egypt. *Research Report 61*. Brighton: Institute of Development Studies, Centre for the Future State.
Africa Confidential. 2008. ZANU-PF stashes the cash. http://www.africa-confidential.com/article/id/2707/ZANU-PF-stashes-the-cash (accessed August 18, 2010).
Anonymous 2010. Interview. Harare.
Bond, P., and M. Manyanya. 2003. *Zimbabwe's plunge: Exhausted nationalism, neoliberalism and the search for social justice*. Harare, Pietermaritzburg and London: Weaver Press, University of KwaZulu-Natal Press and Merlin Press.
Brand, C. 1981. The anatomy of an unequal society. Stoneman, C., ed. 1981. Zimbabwe's inheritance. London: Macmillan, 36–57.
Bratton, M., and E. Masunungure. 2011. *The anatomy of political predation: Leaders, elites and coalitions in Zimbabwe, 1980-2010. Developmental Leadership Program*. West Perth: DLP.
Brett, E.A. 2005. *From corporatism to liberalisation in Zimbabwe economic policy regimes and political crisis (1980-1997)*. Working Paper 58 (Series 1). London: Crisis States Research Centre.
Cammack, D., and T. Kelsall. 2010. *Developmental patrimonialism? The case of Malawi*. APPP Working Paper 12. London: Africa Power and Politics Programme.
Chang, H.-J. 2003. *Kicking away the ladder: Development strategy in historical perspective*. London: Anthem Press.
Davies, R. 2004. Memories of underdevelopment: A personal interpretation of Zimbabwe's economic decline. In *Zimbabwe: Injustice and political reconciliation*, ed. B. Raftopoulos and T. Savage, 19–41. Cape Town: Institute for Justice and Reconciliation.
Dietrich, C. 2000. The commercialisation of military deployment in Africa. *African Security Review* 9, no. 1. Accessed at http://www.iss.co.za/pubs/asr/9no1/Commerciallisation.html
Global Witness. 2002. *Branching out: Zimbabwe's resource colonialism in Democratic Republic of Congo*. London: Global Witness.
Godwin, P. 2010. *The fear*. London: Picador.
Goredema, C. 2003. Zimbabwe. In *Penetrating state and business organised crime in Southern Africa*, ed. P. Gastrow. London: Institute for Strategic Studies. Accessed 26 July 2010 at http://www.iss.co.za/pubs/Monographs/No89/Chap1.htm.
Grindle, M. 2004. Good enough governance: Poverty reduction and reform in developing countries. *Governance* 17, no. 4: 525–48.
Hall, R. 1987. *My life with Tiny: A biography of Tiny Rowland*. London and Boston: Faber & Faber.
Horizon 1992. *How Zanu (PF) built a capitalist empire*. Harare: Horizon Magazine.
Justice for Agriculture. 2002. *Confirmed VIPs allocations*. Harare: JAG. http://www.zimbabwesituation.com/VIP_farm_allocations.pdf (accessed September 2, 2010).

Kelsall, T., D. Booth, D. Cammack, and F. Golooba-Mutebi. 2010. *Developmental patrimonialism? Questioning the orthodoxy on political governance and economic progress in Africa*. APPP Working Paper 9. London: Africa Power and Politics Programme.

Khan, M.H. 2000a. Rent-seeking as process. In *Rents, rent-seeking and economic development: Theory and evidence in Asia*, ed. M.H. Khan and K.S. Jomo, 70–144. Cambridge: Cambridge University Press.

Khan, M.H. 2000b. Rents, efficiency and growth. In *Rents, rent-seeking and economic development: Theory and evidence in Asia*, ed. M.H. Khan and J.K. Sundaram, 21–69. Cambridge: Cambridge University Press.

Khan, M.H. 2006. *Governance, economic growth and development since the 1960s: Background Paper for World Economic and Social Survey*. New York: UNDESA.

Khan, M.H. 2009. Governance capabilities and the property rights transition in developing countries: Draft Paper in Research Paper Series on "Growth-Enhancing Governance". http://mercury.soas.ac.uk/users/mk17/Docs/Others.htm (accessed 1 January 2010).

Khan, M.H. 2010. Political settlements and the governance of growth-enhancing institutions: Draft Paper in Research Paper Series on "Growth-Enhancing Governance". Mimeo. University of London, School of Oriental and African Studies.

Levy, B. 2010. *Development trajectories: An evolutionary approach to integrating governance and growth*. Economic Premise 15. Washington, DC: World Bank.

Makamure, J., J. Jowa, and H. Muzuva. 2001. *Liberalisation of agricultural markets. Structural adjustment participatory review initiative*. Harare: SAPRI.

Moore, M., and H. Schmitz. 2008. Idealism, realism and the investment climate in developing countries. Working Paper 307. *Centre for the Future State*, Brighton: Institute of Development Studies.

Nest, M. 2001. Ambitions, profits and loss: Zimbabwean economic involvement in the Democratic Republic of the Congo. *African Affairs* 100: 469–90.

Nkomo, J. 1984. *The story of my life*. London: Methuen.

North, D.C., J.J. Wallis, and B.R. Weingast. 2009. *Violence and social orders: A conceptual framework for interpreting recorded human history*. Cambridge: Cambridge University Press.

Nyarota, G. 2006. *Against the grain*. Cape Town: Zebra Press.

Otieno, G. 2009. *Baseline study of anti-corruption at an institutional level in Zimbabwe*. Harare: Multi-donor Trust Fund.

Partnership Africa Canada. 2010. *Diamonds and clubs the militarized control of diamonds and power in Zimbabwe*. Ottawa: Partnership Africa Canada.

Raftopoulos, B. 2005. The Zimbabwean crisis and the challenges for the left. Public Lecture, June 23, 2005. University of Kwa-Zulu Natal.

Robertson, J. 2010. Interview 12 August 2010.

Rodrik, D. 2007. *One economics, many recipes: Globalization, institutions, and economic growth*. Princeton, NJ: Princeton University Press.

Selby, A. 2006. Commercial farmers and the state: Interest group politics and land reform in Zimbabwe. PhD thesis, Oxford, University of Oxford.

Stoneman, C., ed. 1981. *Zimbabwe's inheritance*. London: Macmillan.

Tambudzai, Z. 2003. Privatisation: A review of the Zimbabwean experience 1991-2002. *Africana Bulletin* 51: 165–203.

UNDP. 2008. *Comprehensive economic recovery in Zimbabwe: A discussion document*. Harare: UNDP.

United Nations 2001. *Report of the panel of experts on the illegal exploitation of natural resources and other forms of wealth of the Democratic Republic of the Congo*. New York: United Nations.

Utete, C. 2003. *Report of the Presidential Land Review Committee on the implementation of The Fast Track Land Reform Programme 2000-2002*. Harare: Government of Zimbabwe.

Velamuri, S. 2003. *Resisting political corruption: Econet wireless Zimbabwe*. Shanghai: China Europe International Business School.

Zimbabwe Institute. 2008. *The security-military business complex and the transition in Zimbabwe*. Discussion Paper. Harare: Zimbabwe Institute.

Foreign investment, black economic empowerment and militarised patronage politics in Zimbabwe

Booker Magure

Department of Political and International Studies, Rhodes University, South Africa

> This paper seeks to analyse Zimbabwe's economic empowerment policy. It argues that while there is a felt need for Zimbabwe to redress colonially induced injustices and racial imbalances in the ownership of the means of production, a 'one-size-fits-all' approach to the indigenisation of the economy is fundamentally flawed as it deters investors and may further damage the country's already extremely fragile economy. The implementation of the land reform programme contributed to the decline of Zimbabwe's economy: lessons learnt from the programme and related economic policies of the past 15 years highlight the problems of empowerment policies that are intertwined with patronage politics. The government's negation of basic economic principles and failure to open spaces for critical engagement with all relevant stakeholders epitomises an ill-advised indigenisation and economic empowerment strategy. The policy will not promote and retain foreign investment;nor are there sustainable prospects of internally oriented accumulation strategies on the horizon.

Introduction

The creation of a Zimbabwean government of national unity after the signing of the SADC-facilitated Global Political Agreement in late 2008 raised expectations about rebuilding the economically and politically ravaged country. By late 2011, however, the optimism regarding these developments was fast waning. The implementation of Zimbabwe's 2007 indigenisation policy, meant to foster a 'deliberate involvement of indigenous Zimbabweans in the economic activities of the country, to which hitherto they had no access, so as to ensure the equitable ownership of the nation's resources' (Government of Zimbabwe 2007, 33), contributed to this pessimism. This article does not dispute the idea of taking measures meant to redress colonially induced injustices and racial imbalances in the ownership of the means of production, but suggests that the way in which the process of seeking to compensate for these historical injustices and racial imbalances is being carried out is not contributing to these aspirations: the 'sticky point' is not the principle of empowering the previously disadvantaged, but the implementation process. On this point important questions with profound policy ramifications must be asked: What lessons can be learnt from previous economic empowerment initiatives carried out in Zimbabwe? To what extent does the indigenisation policy act as an instrument of investment promotion and retention? This study contributes to the debate by seeking to answer these questions, particularly the economic implications of implementing the empowerment laws in their present form. This article's first section analyses business-state relations in a neo-patrimonial context, while the second section examines the development of the African business class in Zimbabwe. The causal relationship between Zimbabwe's economic decline and the country's land reform programme is addressed in the third section of this paper. The final section makes special reference to the banking, manufacturing and mining sectors, and the implications therein of indigenisation policies.

Business-state relations in a neo-patrimonial context

In Zimbabwe, a complex network of patrons and clients mediates the allocation of scarce resources. This 'neo-patrimonial' process means that the reciprocal needs and expectations of individuals, corporate entities, and the state are negotiated asymmetrically, with business entities needing to be close to powerful politicians who can create and protect investment opportunities.

Notwithstanding the unequal status and power often characterising patron-client relations, Sen and Te Velde (2009, 1278; and see Dawson and Kelsall in this issue) maintain that benign business-state collaboration can contribute significantly towards economic growth and prosperity. However, Seekings and Nattrass (2011, 339) argue that business-state relations in neo-patrimonial states are often unconstructive as a result of the political elite's commandist instincts. Notwithstanding the damaging and costly nature of patron-client relations to any economy, such ties remain a common method by which African rulers gain and maintain power. In Africa it is generally easy for a clique of state-based elites to promulgate policies furthering their own interests (Handley 2008, 5). As Handley puts it, given the fusion of political and economic elites in neo-patrimonial states, compounded by a weak civil society and weak political opposition, the formation of an indigenous business class is often a result of political corruption: the self-interested behaviour and incestuous relationships between the state and business elites are the order of the day due to the influence of the state on African business-class formation. The neo-patrimonial character of the state's intervention in the economy is closely related to the state's monopolisation of policy making (Handley, 9). It is against this background that some business entities strive to be aligned to the state and ruling party in order to get protection and opportunities such as government tenders. Indeed, government's policy biases reflect the power and privilege of a few societal actors whose political actions are often strongly influenced by 'expediency and necessity' (Jackson and Rosberg 1984, 423–25). Policies can be promulgated with a view to give business to certain companies aligned with influential political figures in return for kickbacks.

The state and African business-class development in Zimbabwe

According to Munslow (1980, 64) settler colonialism explains why wealth in Zimbabwe is concentrated in the hands of a few racial categories. Settler power restricted the emergence of an indigenous capitalist class across almost all sectors of the Rhodesian economy. Policies of separate development explain why many black people were excluded from participating in the mainstay of the settler economy. However, this is not to say the settler colonialists discouraged the emergence of an indigenous bourgeoisie *in toto*, rather it is the ambivalence and half-hearted nature of the white community's efforts towards uplifting black businessmen that is of concern to this conversation. The equivocal stance towards black business people can be noted when one looks at the emergence of the vibrant Native Purchase Area farmers in 1930: these farmers were budding capitalists despite the challenges wrought by colonialism (Cheater 1984, 7, 176). Thus the existence of an embryonic, indigenous bourgeoisie in Zimbabwe shortly after independence in 1980 is a legacy of settler colonialism.

Ostergaard (1994, 115) argues that this untenable situation was exacerbated by a post-colonial development strategy that continued to promote and favour settler capital at the expense of both indigenous (black) and foreign capital. The relative strength or weakness of African domestic capitalist classes is determined mainly by the economic policies of both the colonial and post-colonial states (Nicholas 1994, 95). However, this is not to suggest that the ZANU PF government gave settler capital-free reign. Rather, an economically interventionist state emerged out of the government's ambivalent attitude towards indigenous (black) and foreign capital. It should however be noted that interventionism is a legacy of the settler colonial state that equally sought to manage the economy through state ownership (Stoneman and Cliffe 1989, 16). The proliferation of state-owned enterprises after 1980 reflected the government's policy of seeking to gain firm control of the economy as opposed to indigenising and promoting African capitalism or maintaining the economic status quo.

Raftopoulos (1996) suggests that the ruling elite was opposed to the emergence of an autonomous domestic bourgeoisie primarily because ZANU PF feared it would not need to rely on ruling party patronage and thus would be less easy to control. Similarly, Nicholas (1994, 95) observes that the post independence government resisted policies promoting the emergence of an African bourgeoisie, partly because the new political elites were reluctant to share political power with them. Yet over time it became clear to ZANU PF that it was of paramount importance to nurture and promote 'a strong political relationship with the indigenous capitalist classes' (Nicholas, 110). Evidence suggests that Raftopoulos and Nicholas's observations are correct because a number of beneficiaries of the recent land reform programme are easy to control: they support ZANU PF because they fear losing their farms.

ZANU PF's indigenisation discourse in the past tended to marginalise and vilify embryonic domestic business people hoping to establish and operate businesses independent of the state and ruling party. In Mandaza's opinion, the state has done more to contain than to promote the emergence and growth of a national bourgeoisie (Tekere 2007, 11). In cases where the state allowed a national bourgeoisie to emerge, the lobby groups representing them are basically subordinate to ZANU PF and 'pursue their objectives as an integral part of ruling [patronage] party politics' (Raftopoulos 2000, 33). ZANU PF is also well known for dealing ruthlessly with business people who jump ship after having benefited from patronage party politics. For example, Mutumwa Mawere of African Resources Limited is widely believed to have used ZANU PF to acquire his wealth, but his vast business empire collapsed in 2004 after falling out with his political patrons in ZANU PF.

The 'indigenisation debate' started to gather momentum as a major theme of political discourse in Zimbabwe in 1990, shortly after the government adopted economic reforms. The Economic Structural Adjustment Programme created an enabling environment for the embryonic black middle class – as Maphosa put it, 'veteran business-people and high salaried bureaucrats in the private and public sectors' – to lobby the government to remove settler induced obstacles to their meaningful participation in the economy (1998, 185). It could be argued that this class – Wild's 'post-colonial "protobourgeoisie", consisting of veteran nationalists and middle-class professionals using the 'politics of connections' to advance their economic interests' (1997, 278) – was still pressing for more black participation and control of the Zimbabwean economy in 2011, albeit in a more forceful and combative manner, sparking debate and speculation once again. It is against this background that many Zimbabweans are deeply suspicious that the empowerment laws are not for public good but for private gain.[1]

The original indigenisation and empowerment vision espoused by the Indigenous Business Development Centre (IBDC) was not premised on the racially motivated asset stripping currently defining Zimbabwe's indigenisation culture. Raftopoulos and Compagnon note that IBDC sought to fight unemployment by increasing the size of the country's economy through the creation of new black businesses as opposed to 'taking over existing companies owned by whites' (2003, 22). However, over time the IBDC changed its course as a result of factionalism engineered by ZANU PF-aligned politicians-cum-businessmen: it was taken over by ZANU PF political businessmen more concerned with getting rich overnight. This fits Sandbrook's characterisation of the African political elite's aspiration to become a bourgeoisie as 'an opportunistic exploitation of "insider" privileges...not the development of the classic risk-taking entrepreneurial behaviour' (1985, 72): in other words many black businessmen are too risk averse to start hard-core capitalist projects that will lead to sustainable development. Ironically, Jonathan Moyo, now a key member of the government implementing the indigenisation regulations supporting this class, in 1992 implored the emergent African petit-bourgeoisie to strive to become 'hard-core capitalists' creating wealth for the benefit of future generations instead of being phony capitalists satisfied by retailing goods produced by others (1992, 323). Upon close scrutiny one cannot help but agree with an observation made by the official daily newspaper, the *Herald* about the African petit-bourgeoisie when the IBDC was launched in December 1990:

> The one thing that the vast majority of black businessmen are guilty of is that business for them means flashy cars and big houses. They want their profits tomorrow, and seem to lack the concept of business for posterity. What they need to appreciate is that making money means building up their business enterprises. More importantly, they must be reminded that business empires are not built to be enjoyed immediately. (quoted in Moyo 1992, 323)

A number of other economic lobby groups have emerged in Zimbabwe to carry on the unfinished business of indigenisation. For example, the Affirmative Action Group (AAG) was formed in 1994, partly as a result of the crisis bedevilling the IBDC. The organisation was not dissimilar to the IBDC but its lobbying strategy was more strident and laced with typical ZANU PF nationalist rhetoric (Raftpolous

1996). The continuous economic indigenisation debate reflects the lack of a clear-cut economic policy from Zimbabwe's earliest days. ZANU PF pursued capitalist economic policies while enunciating socialist rhetoric. Thirty years later, public spats still pit ZANU PF technocrats and political figures over similar policy-related issues (*The Zimbabwe Independent*, 26 March 2010; *The Herald*, 20 August 2011). In the meantime, President Mugabe's assurance to investors that their investments are safe does nothing to alleviate the concerns of foreign – or non-ZANU PF domestic – capital. Nor does the example of 'fast-track land reform', which constitutes the next section of this article.

Zimbabwe's land reform programme and economic collapse

The Zimbabwe Chamber of Mines suggests that Zimbabwe's total GDP is presently around US$4 billion, a figure that represents half the GDP of about US$8.7 billion in 1996/97 (Zimbabwe Chamber of Mines 2010, 16). This means that the economy lost about 54% of its productive potential between 2000 and 2010 (Zimbabwe Chamber of Mines 2010, 16). While the magnitude of sectoral economic recovery may be subject to varying estimates, official figures presented in this paper suggests that the Zimbabwean economy is reviving after a decade of decline. In other words, the different sectors of the economy are recovering but figures given in this paper as their present contribution to GDP are still low compared to the pre 2000 levels.

According to Zimbabwe's Ministry of Finance, the agricultural sector recorded a sustained cumulative decline of 85.7% between 2002 and 2009 (Government of Zimbabwe, *National Budget Statement*, December 2010) while it contributes around 17.6% of GDP presently (Government of Zimbabwe, *Monetary Policy Supplement*, July 2011). The debate on the successes and failures of Zimbabwe's land reform programme (Scoones et al. 2010; *Zimbabwe Independent* 3 March 2011; and Rutherford in this issue) is relevant to the current phase of economic empowerment targeting the financial, mining and manufacturing sectors. Scoones et al. (2010, 241) argue that the land reform programme was a success despite visible shortcomings indicating the importance of a land audit, which would reveal the ownership pattern of acquired farms and expose multiple farm owners, particularly among ZANU PF political elites. However for Mandaza:

> the land reform exercise... appears to have provided yet another opportunity for the parasitic bourgeoisie and comprador classes to engage in voracious primitive accumulation, with little or no real improvement in production nor the requisite contribution to industrialisation and the related increase in employment and economic growth. Indeed, today Zimbabwe is no nearer to establishing a national economy nor national bourgeoisie. (in Tekere 2007, 11)

Similarly, the Reserve Bank of Zimbabwe Governor, Gideon Gono, is on record as having warned the political leadership to guard against implementing the empowerment policy in a manner that would hurt the economy and threaten investors. According to Gono threats to investors cause panic given that 'CAPITAL [sic] is a timid commodity, which always stands ready to jump ship at the slight inclination of attack whether factual or perceived' (Government of Zimbabwe, *Reserve Bank of Zimbabwe Monetary Policy Statement*, October 2007). In a supplement to the July 2011 monetary policy statement, the Governor revealed that some people in ZANU PF were accusing him of seeking to derail the implementation of the indigenisation and economic empowerment legislation simply because he was advocating a well thought-out empowerment policy. It is worth noting that Gono's monetary policy statements issued since 2007 suggest that he is acutely aware of the predatory inclinations of some politically connected individuals who want to hijack the empowerment policy for private gain. For example between 2007 and 2011, the Governor made the following telling comments about indigenisation and economic empowerment:

> as Monetary Authorities, we also call upon Government to ensure that the empowerment drive is not derailed by a few well connected cliques, some who are already making the most noise in ostensible support of this initiative, who would want to amass wealth to themselves in a starkly greedy but irresponsible manner, whilst the intended majority remain with nothing as happened in the past with respect to other Government empowerment schemes. (Government of Zimbabwe, *Reserve Bank of Zimbabwe Monetary Policy Statement,* October 2007)

> ...any attempt to hide behind the indigenisation law... in order to commit or justify acts of economic banditry, expropriation and or unfair practices that suggest that we are not a law abiding citizenry or any attempts to parcel out pieces of the economic cake and opportunities created by this noble piece of legislation to a few connected cliques of people whilst the majority of intended beneficiaries remain with nothing, as happened in the past with respect to other Government empowerment schemes, is totally unacceptable. (Government of Zimbabwe, *Reserve Bank of Zimbabwe Supplement to the Monetary Policy Statement,* July 2011)

These quotes indicate that some well-connected party supporters want to use the indigenisation and economic empowerment policy for self-aggrandisement. The politicisation of the debate on Zimbabwe's empowerment laws also led to the ZANU PF-aligned Affirmative Action Group to allege that those opposed to the implementation of the law in its present form are simply scaremongering (*Short Wave Radio Africa*, 12 February 2010). In order to counter this view emanating from those seeking to unfairly benefit from indigenisation laws, it is important to draw important lessons from Zimbabwe's controversial land reform programme. The land reform programme destabilised the supply of agricultural inputs to a number of downstream processing industries as well as reducing demand for agricultural equipment and other farming inputs such as fertilizer and pesticides. In other words, the land reform programme ruined the agriculture sector that was the backbone of Zimbabwe's once fairly diversified economy.

The expropriation of farms saw the evictions of many farm owners on 24-hour notice. The beneficiaries also claimed ownership of standing crops, plantations, livestock and other valuable assets worth billions of dollars (Cross 2009). This occurred despite the fact that in terms of the 1992 Land Acquisition Act affected farmers were supposed to be given fair compensation by the government of Zimbabwe. These lessons are relevant to the current indigenisation debate. Many scholars note the positive link between property rights and long-term economic growth, thus any government's failure to respect property rights may lead to economic collapse (Richardson 2005, 542). While no proper costing has been done to ascertain the exact price of Zimbabwe's land reform programme, conservative figures from both Commercial Farmers' Union of Zimbabwe (CFU) and independent economists indicate severe economic damage. The CFU has estimated that the destabilisation of the agricultural sector between 2000 and 2011 has cost the Zimbabwean economy US$33 billion (*President's Address to the Commercial Farmers' Union Congress*, 2011), while Eddie Cross of the MDC argues that the land reform programme cost Zimbabwe an estimated US$20 billion (Cross 2009, 2). The pressure group Justice for Agriculture claims that more than half of the expropriated farms are derelict and abandoned (Cross 2009, 2). A Reserve Bank of Zimbabwe monetary policy supplement noted with grave concern that the 'economy is littered with cases of productive farms lying idle, farms which have been turned into grasslands instead of maize lands, soya lands...' (*Supplement to the Monetary Policy Statement,* July 2011). For example, citrus trees at Chigwell Farm in Chegutu, previously owned by Thomas Beattie but taken over by ZANU PF's Bright Matonga, are diseased owing to years of neglect. Beattie's farm used to generate between US$3 million to US$4 million annually and also employed hundreds of workers (*The Standard*, 1 August 2010).

Another case study of failed agrarian reform is the Kondozi estate, in Manicaland. Kondozi once turned over about US $15 million per annum in exports to Europe and South Africa and employed around 5000 people, but was looted by ZANU PF politicians in 2004 (*The Standard*, 17 July 2010). The courts ruled that its main financier, Barclays Bank, should have regained the stolen farm equipment it had funded, but the decision was never enforced.

Without title deeds it is difficult for 'new farmers' to borrow money from Zimbabwean banks, both foreign and locally owned, so this new form of 'property' creates very little new value. It is instructive to note that the compulsory acquisition of land also saw Zimbabwe in breach of a number of Bilateral Investment Treaties. In 2009 and 2010 the Zimbabwe government appeared before the Paris-based International Centre for Settlement of Investment Disputes in cases involving the invasion of farms owned by Dutch and German nationals. However, the Zimbabwe government refused to entertain any settlement claims brought by these farmers despite the Paris court ruling in their favour. ZANU PF's failure to offer compensation for expropriated farming-related investments supposedly protected by international investment agreements can be attributed to its predatory inclinations. Thus opponents of the current phase of empowerment through indigenisation argue that this initiative too will be hijacked by a privileged few, without creating or adding value to existing wealth.

In his address to the 2011 Commercial Farmer's Union congress, the outgoing president of the organisation, Deon Theron, said that the almost total collapse of public services in Zimbabwe can be attributed to the decline in government revenue in the form of taxes (Theron, 2011). He further noted that the continued growth of the informal economy erodes the government's tax base. Consequently the adequate provision of social services such as refuse collection, education, health, transport and energy by both the central and local government authorities remain difficult to achieve. For example between August 2008 and April 2009, Zimbabwe witnessed an unprecedented cholera outbreak as a result of failure by local authorities to upgrade and replace ageing and dilapidated water and sewerage infrastructure (Mason 2009). Increased poverty levels also explain why local authorities fail to collect rates and taxes from an impoverished population. A vicious cycle ensues because under the prevailing circumstance of uncertainty, it is very difficult to promote economic growth in Zimbabwe. Having discussed how the implementation the land reform programme contributed to the decline of Zimbabwe's economy, the next section of this paper analyses the potential costs of the empowerment policy in relation to the banking, manufacturing and mining sectors.

Sectoral analysis of the likely costs of Zimbabwe's empowerment policy
The banking sector
Despite the fact that Zimbabwe has too many banks relative to the size of its economy, the sector is also being targeted for indigenisation. This is happening although the banking sector is very sensitive to policy discord and a majority are owned by Zimbabweans. According to the Reserve Bank of Zimbabwe, the country has a total of 25 banking institutions comprised 1 savings bank, 15 commercial banks, 5 merchant banks and 4 building societies (Government of Zimbabwe, *Monetary Policy Statement,* January 2011). It is worth noting that the finance and insurance sectors presently contribute a combined average of about 8.8% to the GDP (Government of Zimbabwe, *Supplement to the Monetary Policy Statement, July 2011*). In a commentary, the privately owned *Zimbabwe Independent* on 21 October 2010 observed that:

> The empowerment recommendations were made despite stiff resistance from the Bankers Association of Zimbabwe, which in its submissions to the committee had argued that the banking sector 'was already indigenised' because 85% of banks were owned by locals. Out of the targeted foreign-controlled banking institutions, which make up nearly 45, 06% of the banking sector's total assets, Stanchart (100% foreign), Barclays (68%), Stanbic (100%), MBCA (76%) and CABS (100%) have historically been foreign-owned. However, Premier (54%) and Metropolitan (60%) banks - both formed by local shareholders - have become predominantly foreign-owned following the disposal of 70% and 60% shareholding, respectively to foreign shareholders in recapitalisation initiatives....

Developments in the banking sector are instructive. It is very difficult to implement the indigenisation and empowerment policy in the absence of a proper funding mechanism. Previously locally owned banks became foreign-owned because local shareholders failed to inject additional capital following the adoption of the multi-currency system in Zimbabwe. In 2010, the Reserve Bank of Zimbabwe revised the prescribed minimum paid-up capital requirements for banks. The central bank first extended the deadline for banks to comply with the new requirement to 31 December 2010 and further to 30 June 2011. The extension was necessitated by the central bank's realisation that many banking institutions were experiencing recapitalisation challenges. The need to recapitalise saw some locally owned banks resorting to foreign capital injections, a move that left them technically foreign-owned.

In a monetary policy statement, Governor Gono revealed that multinational banks were not keen to play an active role in supporting the domestic economy (Government of Zimbabwe, *Monetary Policy Statement,* January 2011). The banks were accused of *inter alia* paralysing the money and capital market by refusing to lend money to the productive sectors of the economy. A huge amount of locally generated deposits were simply not being made available to local business by the following multinational banks – Standard Charted, Barclays and Stanbic. The Reserve Bank of Zimbabwe reported that loans-to-deposits ratios for the said banks were as follows as at 31 December 2010: Barclays, 25, 23%, Stanbic, 33, 90% Standard Chartered, 50, 72% (Government of Zimbabwe, *Monetary Policy Statement*, January 2011). These statistics demonstrate that Barclays is reluctant to loan money to business entities, possibly as a result of lessons learnt when Kondozi, a farming concern it had financed, was expropriated in 2004.

Banks demand collateral security in order to safeguard the interests of their investors; therefore suggestions that foreign-owned banks and their locally owned counterparts are being unfair and discriminatory are simplistic. While the Reserve Bank Governor opposed the banks' 'retrogressive attitudes and practices', (Government of Zimbabwe, *Monetary Policy Statement,* January 2011) he was swift to protect the banking sector from ZANU PF Minister Kasukuwere's ultimatum to comply with the black empowerment laws or risk losing their licenses. It is instructive to note that in 2007 the governor invited domestic businessmen with an interest in the banking sector to apply for new banking licenses from the central bank rather than taking over existing foreign-owned banks (Government of Zimbabwe, *Monetary Policy Statement,* October 2007). Gono is on record saying that a cautious, as opposed to a 'one-size-fits-all', approach to empowerment is required, particularly in 'sensitive sectors such as the banking sector, where confidence should be retained at all costs' (Government of Zimbabwe, *Monetary Policy Supplement,* July 2011). While the central bank governor is articulating a position that is now fitted to the current conditions in Zimbabwe, it must be noted that he presided over the decline of the country's once vibrant economy by printing money to support ZANU PF.

Since the financial services sector is battling to mobilise local capital in order to meet the RBZ's minimum paid-up capital requirements, it follows that the situation is not different in other sectors of the economy earmarked for takeover. From this standpoint, a workable financing mechanism must be devised so as to achieve the set objectives defined in the empowerment policy. The timing of the implementation of the indigenisation policy is inappropriate given the country's efforts to emerge from decades of economic malaise. The central bank is severely undercapitalised following sustained periods of engaging in quasi-fiscal activities meant to sustain the Mugabe regime. Therefore the central bank is also in dire need of recapitalisation in order for it to be able to support the local banking sector as a lender of last resort.

In 2011 business confidence in Zimbabwe plummeted following continued threats of compulsory take-overs of foreign-owned firms in the banking and mining sectors failing to furnish 'acceptable' indigenisation plans (*Herald,* 7 September 2011). Perhaps Zimbabwe's Finance Minister Tendai Biti (of the MDC-T) should have revised Zimbabwe's growth forecasts for 2011 downward from the projected 9.3% (Government of Zimbabwe, *Mid-term Fiscal Policy Review Statement,* July 2011). The policy contradictions and inconsistencies around the controversial indigenisation programme remain detrimental to the attraction and retention of private investment. Over the years the ZANU PF government has failed to demonstrate commitment to the rule of law and protection of private property rights. To that end FDI is likely to go to countries where property rights are respected and the judiciary is independent.

The manufacturing sector

The Ministry of Finance reported that the manufacturing sector registered a cumulative decline of -91.1% between 2000 and 2008 (*2010 National Budget Statement*). Its present average contribution to GDP is around 14.5% (Government of Zimbabwe, *Monetary Policy Supplement, July 2011*), meaning that the sector used to generate more money in 2000 than now. Many Zimbabweans argue that while the economy may not be sufficiently locally owned, it is not prudent to carry out full-scale indigenisation at this stage. An analysis of on-line comments and newspaper articles on indigenisation reveals that much opinion on this issue indicates wariness about, if not total opposition to, opportunistic ZANU PF elements seeking to grab productive companies.[2] Many commentators wonder why emergent domestic business people make no effort to rescue struggling foreign-owned companies such as David Whitehead Textiles in Kadoma and Chegutu. In light of all the challenges faced by the Zimbabwean economy, one cannot help but agree with the popular view that the indigenisation policy must wait 'until the local economy recovers' (*Newsday*, 6 December 2010). What Zimbabwe needs for the time being is economic growth, which may be difficult to achieve if the country continues to alienate itself from the community of serious international investors. Towards the end of 2010, Industry and Commerce Minister, Welshman Ncube of the splinter MDC party was quoted as having said:

> Until such a time when the economy recovers and rebuilds capacity, it's not possible for every sector to achieve 51% (minimum indigenisation equity). We need foreign investors with the balance sheet and the capacity. If locals had the capacity, would we struggle to build new power stations or to rebuild our railways and roads? But the capacity is not available locally. That's why we have to engage foreign investors. (*Newsday*, 6 December 2010)

In 2010 the Confederation of Zimbabwe Industries (CZI) commissioned a manufacturing survey seeking insight into the state of the manufacturing sector with a view to develop strategies to improve its economic performance. The survey revealed the performance and challenges facing manufacturing industries in Zimbabwe, chief among them being capacity underutilisation. The average capacity utilisation for the whole economy was said to be hovering around 43.7% (CZI, *2010 Manufacturing Survey*). Captains of industry attributed this condition to the government's failure to address fundamentals required to attract and retain foreign direct investment. It is very difficult for manufacturing concerns to fully recover costs of production in the absence of adequate capacity utilisation. Without fresh capital injection (for which increased FDI would help immeasurably) capacity under-utilisation will remain a perennial problem in Zimbabwe. It is therefore not surprising that the cost of a number of locally produced goods and services remain astronomically high. In a functional economy, optimal capacity utilisation would necessarily result in economies of scale and relatively cheap and affordable goods and services. A stagnating economy affects downstream industries whose traded volumes are affected by low demand for their goods and services. A growing economy creates more jobs, increases disposable income, creates a high demand for locally manufactured goods and also contributes to the national purse through various taxes.

Antiquated machinery, breaking down constantly, results in time loss and increases in production costs in Zimbabwe's industrial sector. Finance Minister Tendai Biti has reported that a local fertilizer manufacturing company, Sable chemicals in Kwekwe, still used 'old electrolysis technology that consumes massive quantities of electricity' (*Herald*, 20 June 2011). Once again FDI appears to be the only route industry can use to access new and advanced technology. The CZI-commissioned survey also noted that the industrial sector's failure to obtain state of the art technology has compromised quality and made the country's products less competitive globally. This is aggravated by limited investment in research, product development, and high production costs. Without appropriate measures to stop this industrial decay, it is highly unlikely that the economy will be able to get back on track.

The government of Zimbabwe has failed dismally to turn around the declining economic fortunes of state-owned enterprises such Air Zimbabwe, National Railways of Zimbabwe, Noczim, Agribank, Cold Storage Company, the Grain Marketing Board, and mobile telephone networks NetOne and TelOne. These companies continue to be perennial loss-making entities. The first four reported an aggregate loss of $38.9 million in the first half of 2010 (*Newsday*, 6 December 2010). They are joined by the Zimbabwean Electricity Supply Authority (ZESA) and the Zimbabwe United Passenger Company (ZUPCO) that are making heavy losses and struggling to recapitalise. For instance, ZESA recorded a loss of over US$ 100 million between January and June 2011 (*Herald*, 30 September 2011). Regarding the issue of foreign ownership more generally, Minister Biti's advice is instructive – 'I'm one of the people who believe that it's better to own 10% of an elephant than 90% of a rat' (*Newsday*, 6 December 2010). Strategic partnerships with foreign investors may be the only way to ensure that the wheels of industry and commerce turn again. The power shortages that have damaged Zimbabwe's economy for nearly two decades could easily be resolved if foreign investors were given a role to play.

Income levels and domestic savings in Zimbabwe are generally low as a result of the longevity of its economic crisis. The problem was further compounded by the dollarisation of the economy introduced as a measure to stem hyper-inflation and restore monetary credibility (Noko 2011, 339). The introduction of the multicurrency regime also saw many people and businesses losing their deposits in banks, given that the Zimbabwean dollar was no longer a legal tender. Zimbabwe's gross domestic savings as a percentage of GDP between 1990 and 2005 were as follows: 1990 (17. 5%), 2002 (7.1%), 2003 (6. 2%), 2004 (4. 1%) and 0.60% in 2005 (*World Bank Africa Development Indicators* 2010). (The lack of data from 2006 to 2009 may be due to the paucity of reliable data given the hyper-inflationary environment during that period.) According to the Ministry of Finance, Zimbabwe's gross domestic savings remain below 10% of GDP against the desired 20–30% necessary for economic growth (2010 *National Budget Statement*). A favourable economic environment can potentially generate domestic savings that could finance productive investments (UNCTAD 2007). Domestic capital generated from local savings should complement foreign capital in order for a country to achieve sustainable growth. However, in the absence of domestic savings it becomes even more compelling for Zimbabwe to attract and retain FDI.

The ZANU PF aligned Affirmative Action Group submitted that Zimbabwe no longer has a middle class as 'more than 90% of workers earn less than US$200 per month' (*Affirmative Action Group* November, 2010). Thus it is safe to say that the majority of Zimbabweans cannot afford to pay for stakes in the companies earmarked for indigenisation. Ironically, AAG still insists that locals can afford to buy shares in companies such as Nestlé and Barclays, which the government is forcing into majority shareholding deals with Zimbabweans. It is most likely that rich people from ZANU PF will be the major beneficiaries.

As indicated above, Zimbabweans are not opposed to indigenisation *per se*, but they want the process to be carried out in a rational and fair manner to avoid a situation where the initiative is hijacked to benefit a privileged few.[3] Many Zimbabweans did not benefit from the land reform programme despite having applied for land from the responsible ministry. The uncertain economic environment ushered in by the indigenisation policy has already sparked a spate of company closures, particularly in Zimbabwe's second capital city of Bulawayo, and also in Kwekwe and Gweru. According to the AAG 'We have a situation here where some companies are deliberately closing down, stripping assets and selling machinery so that they are not included when the indigenisation drive is in full swing' (*The Standard*, 8 May 2011). This capital flight must be understood in the context of the profit seeking and risk-averse nature of both domestic and foreign investors. As Fatehi (1994, 187) notes, domestic and foreign capital may leave a country where they face an 'unacceptable business risk' tied to political instability. Under circumstances in which existing businesses are closing due to threats by hostile government policies, it becomes increasingly difficult for Zimbabwe to attract foreign investors capable of injecting fresh capital. Uncertainty brought about by the chaotic implementation of the empowerment act has already resulted in company closures and job losses in Bulawayo, Kwekwe and Gweru. The problem has been compounded by off-the-cuff remarks by politicians and their proxies in black economic empowerment groups such as AAG that 'any means necessary' will be used to indigenise the economy. The AAG is also on record stating that it will work hand in glove with the government to close foreign-owned business entities resisting the policy. Furthermore, little progress has been made in attracting another form of 'foreign' capital – the diaspora's. Exiled Zimbabweans participating in online debates about Zimbabwean politics are not keen to invest in the country as a result of policy uncertainty.[4]

What is even more disturbing for foreign business owners is the MDC's equivocal stance on the indigenisation debate. At one moment the party condemns the move as discouraging foreign direct investment (*Newsday*, 12 September 2011), but at the next it says the law is flexible and must not be seen as nationalisation or expropriation (*Businessday*, 2 September 2011). This suggests that the inclusive government is built on shaky ground and investors are worried about the lack of policy clarity. For example, Econet shares have reportedly lost more than US$169 million in value since January 2011 as 'investor perception deteriorated and foreign investors sold local shares' (*Sunday Mail*, 11 September 2011). This development is said to be closely related to the implementation of the indigenisation and empowerment legislation notwithstanding the fact that the company is owned by a Zimbabwean (Strive Masiyiwa) and therefore only distantly threatened by the ZANU PF empowerment crusade.

The indigenisation debate has even included threats to evict foreigners operating retail shops across Zimbabwe. For example the Affirmative Action Group, the

Zimbabwe Indigenous Economic Empowerment Organisation and another ZANU PF aligned group called *Upfumi Kuvadiki* ('wealth to the youth') stated that all foreigners operating retail businesses should be evicted. AAG President Supa Mandiwanzira said

> The law is clear on this issue. We cannot let foreigners to come all the way from China and come bake bread here [sic]. These are the areas which our people should take up, and as AAG we are going to push the government to apply the law'. (*The Zimbabwean*, 7 September 2010)

In February 2011 the Harare-based *Upfumi Kuvadiki* demonstrated against a tender awarded to manage the city's car parking to the South African company, EasiPark. During the same period suspected ZANU PF supporters also looted some shops owned by owned by West African and Chinese nationals at Harare's Gulf shopping complex. ZANU PF did not condemn these violent acts of xenophobia and thuggery; instead it blamed the MDC for orchestrating the clashes.

The mining sector

The mineral sector is estimated to contribute an average of about 3.2% to the country's GDP (*Monetary Policy Supplement,* July 2011) but the Zimbabwean Chamber of Mines puts the contribution at least at 15% (*Chamber of Mines* 2010). For Saunders (2008, 68) the mining sector in Zimbabwe is currently in a state of flux – characterised by what he terms 'contradictory tendencies seen in investment flows and outcomes'. To support his argument it is important to examine how the indigenisation debate evolved with respect to the mining sector since 2010. At its 11th National People's Conference held in Mutare in December 2010, labelled *Total Control of our Resources through Indigenisation and Empowerment*, ZANU PF resolved to accelerate and broaden the indigenisation and empowerment programme. The current emphasis on the implementation of the indigenisation and empowerment in Zimbabwe can be understood in the context of the resolutions passed at this conference, after which ZANU PF-aligned black empowerment lobby groups seem began behaving towards foreign-owned business entities more combatively.

The Chamber of Mines is not in favour of the indigenisation initiative primarily because it is scaring away potential investors in the mineral sector *(Chamber of Mines 2010)*. The cloud of uncertainty has led some mining houses to attempt to implement delaying tactics (until a new government is elected), but to no avail. Foreign-owned mining companies accused by ZANU PF politicians of seeking to derail the indigenisation programme include Murowa Diamonds, Pan American Mining, Zimplats, Blanket Mine, Mimosa Holdings and Duration Gold Mine. However, the reality is that mining exploration, commissioning and production expansion all demand significant capital inflows not locally available. It is therefore important for the government to strike a balance between indigenisation and attracting foreign investment in the mining sector given its importance to the Zimbabwean economy. Saunders (2008, 83) summarised the situation in the minerals sector by noting that:

Mining investment in the past decade has been over-determined by a high risk political and an economic environment compounded in more recent years by weakened state policy-making and regulatory institutions, and the heightened impact of ruling party elite factional conflict in shaping economic and particularly empowerment interventions. Structural adjustment in the 1990s and militarization in the 2000s gutted much of the professional bureaucratic capacity of the state, and made policy making and implementation more ad hoc, reactive, unpredictable and narrowly partisan. With regard to the critical question of empowerment and participation, for example, Zimbabwe saw the emergence of elite-driven approaches rather than the articulation of a policy seeking the sustainable transfer of strategic production into accountable hands. The recent changes to the mining indigenisation and empowerment policy starkly reflected government's precarious capacity and equivocal will to pursue a transparent, more widely beneficial approach to indigenisation.

Saunders' telling observations account for the disagreement between Zimbabwe Platinum Mines Limited (Zimplats) and the government of Zimbabwe over the latter's indigenisation policy. The South African-owned Zimplats – currently the biggest investor in Zimbabwe's mining industry – was singled out as 'failing to submit acceptable indigenisation and empowerment plans as directed by Government...[and] leading the band of delinquent foreign-owned mining firms' (*The Herald* 8 September 2011). ZANU PF's Youth Development, Indigenisation and Empowerment Minister, Saviour Kasukuwere, responsible for indigenisation, announced that the company's license will be cancelled, citing a deadlock with the platinum mining giant that employs about 4000 workers. At time of writing, conflicting reports circulated in the media in relation to the exact status of the Zimplats mining stake and license. While the responsible ministry revealed that processes were underway to cancel the company's license, Zimplats insisted via a press release that there was no deadlock and discussions with government were ongoing. These developments do not augur well for current and potential investors in the Zimbabwean economy.

Conclusion

This paper sought to provide a sectoral analysis of the likely costs of Zimbabwe's economic empowerment policy. Findings suggest that the most damaging aspect of the implementation of the empowerment policy is its tendency to cast a cloud of uncertainty over the country's investment outlook. ZANU PF's militarised patronage system under the guise of indigenisation provides a perfect opportunity to well-connected members of the Zimbabwean ruling party-state complex to become rich overnight. Indications so far are that the implementation of the empowerment policy is vindictive and lacks transparency. The fast track indigenisation programme across all sectors of Zimbabwe's economy is likely to have a knock-on negative effect on economic growth and poverty alleviation. In the long run it can be argued that patronage politics are both economically and financially unsustainable as they run against the very basic notions of wealth creation meant to alleviate poverty and redistribute wealth. Current indigenisation policies in Zimbabwe seem to continue that trend.

Notes

1. This perspective was gained after analysing online debates that often follow some stories carried by both domestic and international online newspapers on Zimbabwe's political economy.
2. See, for example, the online conversations that followed the *Herald*, 20 August 2011 headline- 'Gono blasts Kasukuwere ultimatum'. About 65 people aired their views on Zimbabwe's indigenisation policy. Similarly the *Herald*, 22 August 2011 headline – 'Minister Kasukuwere lays down the law', saw 96 people contributing to the online debate on the indigenisation topic.
3. As already noted, this view was popular on online newspaper debates.
4. See, for example, online debates referred to in footnote 2 of this article.

Note on contributor

Booker Magure is an Andrew Mellon post-doctoral research fellow in the Department of Political and International Studies at Rhodes University, South Africa. His current research focuses on black economic empowerment and money politics in Zimbabwe and South Africa and the role of spirit mediums in contesting the dominant structures of power and authority in emerging democracies. In his doctoral study he examined civil society's quest for democracy in Zimbabwe: its origins, impediments encountered and prospects.

References

Affirmative Action. 2010. Affirmative action group's position. Paper presented at the Kimberley Process Conference in Jerusalem, Israel 1– 4 November 2010.

Cheater, A.P. 1984. *Idioms of accumulation: Rural development and class formation among freeholders in Zimbabwe*. Gweru: Mambo Press.

Cross, E. 2009. The cost of Zimbabwe's continuing farm invasions. *Cato Institute Economic Development Bulletin* 12: 1–2.

Fatehi, E. 1994. Capital flight from Latin America as a barometer of political instability. *Journal of Business Research* 30, no. 2: 187–95.

Government of Zimbabwe. 2007. *Indigenisation and Economic Empowerment Act, [Chapter 14:33] 2007*.

Government of Zimbabwe. 2007. *Mid-Year Monetary Policy Statement issued in Terms of the Reserve Bank of Zimbabwe Act, 1 October, 2007*.

Government of Zimbabwe. 2009. *Statement on the 2009 Budget, Government of Zimbabwe, the Ministry of Finance, 17 March, 2009*.

Government of Zimbabwe. 2010. *The 2010 National Budget Statement, Government of Zimbabwe, Ministry of Finance, 2 December 2009*.

Government of Zimbabwe. 2011. *Monetary Policy Statement issued in Terms of the Reserve Bank of Zimbabwe Act. January, 2011*.

Government of Zimbabwe. 2011. *Supplement to the Monetary Policy Statement issued in Terms of the Reserve Bank of Zimbabwe Act, July 2011*.

Government of Zimbabwe. 2011. *Mid-Term Fiscal Policy Review Statement, July 2011*.

Handley, A. 2008. *Business and the state in Africa: Economic policy-making in the neo-liberal era*. Cambridge: Cambridge University Press.

Jackson, R.H., and C.G. Rosberg. 1984. Personal rule: Theory and practice in Africa. *Comparative Politics* 16, no. 4: 421–42.

Maphosa, F. 1998. Towards the sociology of Zimbabwean indigenous entrepreneurship. *Zambezia* 25, no. 2: 173–90.

Mason, P.R. 2009. Emerging problems in infectious diseases, Zimbabwe experiences the worst epidemic of cholera in Africa. *The Journal of Infection in Developing Countries* 3, no. 2: 148–51.

Moyo, J.N. 1992. State politics and social domination in Zimbabwe. *The Journal of Modern African Studies* 30, no. 2: 305–30.

Munslow, B. 1980. Zimbabwe's emerging African bourgeoisie. *Review of African Political Economy* 19: 63–9.

Nicholas, S.M. 1994. The state and the development of African capitalism in Zimbabwe. In *African capitalists in African development*, ed. B. Berman and C. Leys, 95–113. Boulder: Lynne Rienner.

Noko, J. 2011. Dollarization: The case of Zimbabwe. *Cato Journal* 31, no. 2: 339–65.

Ostergaard, T. 1994. The role of the national bourgeoisie in national development: The case of the textile and clothing industries in Zimbabwe. In *African capitalists in African development*, ed. B. Berman and C. Leys, 115–37. Boulder: Lynne Rienner.

Raftopoulos, B. 1996. Fighting for control: The indigenization debate in Zimbabwe. *Southern Africa Report* 11, no. 4: 3–7.

Raftopoulos, B.. 2000. The state, NGOs and democratisation. In *NGOs, the state and politics in Zimbabwe*, ed. S. Moyo, J. Makumbe, and B. Raftopoulos, 21–45. Harare: SAPES Books.

Raftopoulos, B., and D. Compagnon. 2003. Indigenization, the state bourgeoisie and neo-authoritarian politics. In *Twenty years of independence in Zimbabwe: From liberation to authoritarianism*, ed. S. Darnolf and L. Laakso, 15–33. New York: Palgrave.

Richardson, C.J. 2005. The poss of property rights and the collapse of Zimbabwe. *Cato Journal* 25, no. 3: 541–65.

Sandbrook, R. 1985. *The politics of Africa's economic stagnation.* Cambridge: Cambridge University Press.

Saunders, R. 2008. Crisis, capital, compromise: Mining and empowerment in Zimbabwe. *African Sociological Review* 12, no. 1: 67–89.

Scoones, I., N. Marongwe, B. Mavedzenge, J. Mahenehene, F. Murimbarimba, and C. Sukume. 2010. *Zimbabwe's land reform: Myths and realities.* London: James Currey; Johannesburg, Jacana.

Seekings, J., and N. Nattrass. 2011. State-business relations and pro-poor growth in South Africa. *Journal of International Development* 23, no. 3: 338–57.

Sen, K., and D.W. Te Velde. 2009. State business relations and economic growth in sub-Saharan Africa. *Journal of Development Studies* 45, no. 8: 1267–83.

Stoneman, C., and L. Cliffe. 1989. *Zimbabwe: Politics, economics and society.* London: Pinter Publishers.

Tekere, E. 2007. *A lifetime of struggle.* Harare: SAPES Books.

The Confederation of Zimbabwe Industries. 2010. *The Confederation of Zimbabwe Industries (CZI) 2010 Manufacturing Survey.*

Theron, D. 2011. President's Address to the Commercial Farmers Union Zimbabwe Congress, Wild Geese Lodge, Harare, 26 July 2011.

United Nations Conference on Trade and Development (UNCTAD). 2007. *Economic development in Africa: Reclaiming policy space*, Geneva: United Nations.

Wild, V. 1997. *Profit not for profit's sake: History and business culture of African entrepreneurs in Zimbabwe.* Harare: Baobab Books.

World Bank. 2010. *Africa development indicators 2010.* Washington, DC: World Bank.

Zimbabwe Chamber of Mines 2010. *Zimbabwe Chamber of Mines Journal*, May–June 2010.

Teachers' and bank workers' responses to Zimbabwe's crisis: uneven effects, different strategies

Tapiwa Chagonda

Centre for Sociological Research (CSR), University of Johannesburg, South Africa

> While other studies have examined worker experiences in the informal sector during the crisis, this study is the first to focus on the formal sector, comparing the experiences of teachers and banking sector workers. The study shows that the Zimbabwean crisis (2000–2008) had uneven effects which elicited differential responses from workers. During the peak of the crisis in 2008, the teaching sector almost collapsed as most of the primary and secondary school teachers responded to hyper-inflation that had eroded their incomes by joining the diaspora or Zimbabwe's burgeoning speculative informal economy. The establishment of the Government of National Unity (GNU) saw the dollarisation of the Zimbabwean economy and the shelving of the Zimbabwean dollar in April 2009. These changes saw the teaching sector showing signs of revival, as some of the teachers who had left the profession re-joined the sector. This was largely because the dollarisation of the Zimbabwean economy 'killed off' the speculative activities that were sustaining a large proportion of the teachers in the informal economy during the crisis. In stark contrast, the banking sector thrived during the peak of the crisis, as most banks became key players in highly speculative activities such as Zimbabwe's bullish stock exchange and real estate. The profits realised in the banking sector trickled down to its workers who became the best remunerated amongst all the sectors in Zimbabwe. In a twist of irony, the banking sector was adversely affected by the dollarisation of the economy, as the speculative activities that were reaping huge rewards for the banks were wiped out overnight by the adoption of currencies more stable than the precarious Zimbabwean dollar. This spelt disaster for the banking fraternity. Most banks in the first few months of dollarisation struggled to pay their workers in hard currency; many were forced to downsize their operations and lay-off some employees.

Introduction

The main argument in this article is that the Zimbabwean crisis in the 2000s, and the subsequent stabilisation of the economy made possible by the Government of National Unity (GNU) and the dollarisation[1] of the Zimbabwean economy in 2009, had uneven outcomes for teachers and bank workers. The teaching sector disintegrated partially in the 2000s, as large numbers of teachers left the profession due to hyper-inflation that was wiping away their incomes. The official dollarisation of the Zimbabwean economy in April 2009 (Noko 2011) however saw the teaching sector re-composing, as most teachers who had left the profession returned to work.

In contrast to the teaching sector, the banking sector boomed during the crisis–the Zimbabwe Congress of Trade Unions' (ZCTU) monthly remuneration inventory in 2008 saw the banking workers topping the lists consistently. However, the dollarisation of the Zimbabwean economy turned the tables on this once prosperous sector, as some bank workers, such as the bank tellers and other clerical workers, were laid-off while most banks struggled to remunerate their workers in hard currency.

Giddens' (1984) structuration theory is of considerable utility in highlighting the agency demonstrated by both the teachers and bank tellers in surviving adverse structural forces (an unfavourable political climate and economy). Despite ensuring the sustenance of some households, the survivalist responses to the crisis of some teachers and bank tellers had the effect of contributing to a culture of corrupt and illicit activities that fuelled a 'get rich quick' mentality among some sections of Zimbabwean society.

The paper is based on a larger study conducted in Harare to ascertain the different individual responses at both the work place and household level employed by teachers and bank tellers in the face of hyper-inflation and a political crisis (Chagonda 2011). Between August 2008 and May 2009 semi-structured interviews were carried out with 16 primary school teachers and the same number of bank tellers, with an equal number of interviews of men and women.[2] Key informants, mostly trade union leaders in the teaching and banking trade unions, were also interviewed to obtain their views of their respective sectors during Zimbabwe's period of crisis and the immediate period following the dollarisation of the economy.

Urban studies on the Zimbabwean crisis

Urban studies on the formal working class during Zimbabwe's decade of decay are scant. Literature on the labour movement and the working class in Zimbabwe by scholars such as Sachikonye (1995), Phimister and Raftopoulos (1997) and Raftopoulos and Sachikonye (2001) has traced the movement's history from the colonial era into the post-colonial period. Alexander (2000), Dansereau (2001), Gwisai (2002), Raftopoulos (2006, 2008) and Matombo and Sachikonye (2010) have also looked at the links between workers and the Movement for Democratic Change (MDC). These studies either predate the time of the greatest impact of the crisis or they have not focused on the day-to-day survival and other strategies of workers.

The few urban studies conducted during Zimbabwe's crisis decade focus mostly on the survival strategies employed by informal sector workers to stem the effects of the crisis. This article, however, focuses on formal sector workers, namely primary school teachers and bank workers, thus filling a gap in the Zimbabwean literature on the responses of workers in formal employment to the crisis. During the early stages of gathering data for this article in 2008, Jeremy Jones and Philani Moyo were undertaking doctoral research on how informal traders in the country were coping with Zimbabwe's hyper-inflationary environment. Jones (2008, Jones (2010)) seeks to understand the effects of hyper-inflation and economic decline on young men in Chitungwiza, a working class township just outside Harare. Jones examines the development of a new logic of everyday economic action and argues that the *kukiya-kiya* economy–in local parlance, *kukiya-kiya* refers to multiple forms of 'making do' that are sometimes illegal[3]–replaced the 'real' economy after 2000. For Jones, people participated in the *kukiya-kiya* economy as an individual survival strategy. Jones contends that the *kukiya-kiya* activities in Zimbabwe's informal sector during the peak of the crisis had far reaching repercussions on the ethics and morality of the Zimbabwean people in general, as the culture of surviving through means that were not straight appeared to have taken root in the country.

Moyo (2009) investigates and analyses livelihood strategies employed by the urban poor in an endeavour to bridge household food gaps under conditions of food insecurity and macro-economic meltdown. He investigates the effectiveness, viability, and sustainability of livelihood strategies, the role and capacity of the state in addressing the food crisis, as well as state policies, laws and the 'politics of the stomach', and whether or not they have been a constraint to people's livelihood strategies. Moyo focuses on the urban poor in Bulawayo and the majority of his subjects are unemployed people. In contrast, this article focuses on the working class people of Harare. A shortcoming of Moyo and Jones' studies is that they make *a priori* judgments that survival strategies are the only responses that Zimbabweans came up with in the face of the hyper-inflation and political crisis that Zimbabwe faced in the 2000s. Thus, they adopted a methodological bias towards the household, obscuring what happens at work and at the level of politics.

Zimbabwe's economic crisis, 1997–2008

Before presenting details of the case studies, it is necessary to present a synopsis of the economic crisis between 1997 and 2008. The UNDP (2008) traces the onset of the economic crisis in Zimbabwe to the so-called 'Black Friday' crash of the Zimbabwean dollar by 75% on 14 November 1997. This was precipitated by the government's unbudgeted payments of a Z$50,000 gratuity and Z$2000 monthly pension to the country's war veterans. To make these payments, the government was forced to print Z$4.5 billion (US$450 million; Moore 2002). The designation of 1471 white-owned farms for compulsory acquisition in November 1997, and Mugabe's statement (not for the first time) that he would only pay compensation for land improvements and not for the land itself, also caused uncertainty, as did his subsequent warning that he would not be derailed by the courts, which ruled in favour of farmers who challenged the designations (Selby 2006, 239, 246)

In 1998, the Zimbabwean government decided to participate in the conflict in the DRC, which further contributed to the ballooning fiscal deficit. Nest (2001, 470) contends that Zimbabwe went into the DRC war for three reasons. First, Mugabe wanted to assert himself as the premier leader of SADC, upstaging then President Nelson Mandela, who was in his last years in office, as the region's key statesman. Secondly, the SADC charter includes a collective security provision stating that in the event of a member country being invaded, other members will come to its assistance. SADC would be viewed as an ineffectual organisation if it could not protect its new members such as the DRC, which had joined in 1997. Mugabe wished both to preserve the integrity of SADC, and to demonstrate the importance of the organisation. Thirdly, Mugabe had lent Laurent Kabila several million dollars for his war effort against Mobutu. If Kabila lost power, there would be no possibility of this debt being re-paid. The DRC war was rumoured to cost the government of Zimbabwe over US$1 million a day (Moore 2002).

The chaotic and violent land reform programme, beginning in 2000 and christened the *'third Chimurenga'* by ZANU (PF), resulted in a steep decline of commercial agriculture, and also caused economic sanctions to be placed on leading ZANU (PF) officials by western countries. These sanctions included travel bans and foreign asset freezing.

Rampant inflation, ballooning to hyper-inflation, proved to be a severe problem for Zimbabwe in the 2000s. Inflationary pressures built up from 1997, when the inflation rate rose from 19% to 56% by 2000, to over 1000% by 2006 and to an astronomical 231 million percent by July 2008. Leading economists in Zimbabwe such as Hawkins and Kanyenze claim that the July 2008 rate was higher still. In early 2007, hyper-inflation set in. In February the month-on-month inflation rate reached 50%, translating to a 12,875% year-on-year rate, the benchmark for hyper-inflation according to Hanke (2008, see also UNDP 2008). Hanke (2008) posits that Zimbabwe's year-on-year inflation peaked at a stupendous 89.7 sextillion (sextillion has 21 zeroes) percent by November 2008: the second highest rate of hyper-inflation in recorded history.

Robinson (2007, 8) notes that 'hyper-inflation is...notorious for concentrating incomes in the hands of the rich while impoverishing the poor, often making already highly unequal societies even more divided'. In the Zimbabwean situation, this undesirable process was magnified by high levels of patronage. Key resources in a highly distorted environment, such as cheap credit and foreign currency at the official rate, were allocated to selected individuals and groups, enabling them to amass enormous levels of wealth in a very short space of time. Those with political leverage borrowed heavily from the banks and then declined to re-pay loans, waiting for inflation to remove the burden of the original debt (Robinson 2007). But, as this article will show, the banks and even bank workers managed to reap benefits from hyper-inflation.

Table 1 shows Zimbabwe's other economic indicators reveal the severity of the crisis. Average annual GDP growth, employment growth and formal employment figures continued to plummet, most notably during the period of extreme crisis.

Real wages of the working class fell continually during Zimbabwe's crisis period. Real average earnings peaked in 1982, when wages were adjusted in line with the Poverty Datum Line, as recommended by the Riddell Commission.[4] However, following the adoption of a wage-restraint policy in 1983, real wages fell, a trend that was repeated during the period of ESAP (1991–1995), when wage setting was deregulated and prices rose (UNDP 2008). A period of worker militancy resulted in real wage increases between 1995 and 2000.[5] However, by 2004–when the Central Statistical Office (CSO) data on real wages ends–real average earnings were far lower

Table 1. Zimbabwe's Macroeconomic Indicators, 1980–2006.

Economic indicators	1980–1990	1991–2000	2001–2006
Average annual GDP growth (%)	4.30	0.90	−5.7
Employment growth (%)	1.90	0.40	−7.5
Average population (millions)	9.74	11.34	11.95
Formal employment (% of population)	12.20	10.90	7.00

Source: Zimbabwe Central Statistical Office, 2008.

than during the final years of UDI (1975–1979) (UNDP 2008, 18). The trend of real wage decline for the working class continued until 2008. This is why large numbers of workers left their jobs, either to join the informal sector or look for work in other countries.

The Reserve Bank of Zimbabwe (RBZ) was forced to revalue the Zimbabwean dollar thrice in as many years (2006–2009) because of rampant hyper-inflation. In August 2006, in an operation called 'Sunrise 1', the RBZ removed three zeroes from Zimbabwe's currency and promised to introduce a new currency in the near future. In August 2008, exactly two years after the first revaluation, the RBZ's 'Sunrise II' slashed a further ten zeroes from Zimbabwe's currency, and another 12 zeroes were erased in early February 2009 in 'Sunrise III'. Thus, a staggering 25 zeroes had been slashed from the Zimbabwean currency within a space of only three years. When the Zimbabwean dollar was officially shelved in April 2009, the highest single denomination was a 100 trillion dollar note. When this was introduced on 16 January 2009, it was worth US$30 on the parallel market.

Zimbabwe's economy contracted by 14.1% in 2008, while public spending collapsed, pushing unemployment and poverty to 'catastrophic' levels (IMF 2009, 19). The IMF Report claimed an estimated 14% fall in real GDP in the Zimbabwean economy in 2008, on top of the 40% cumulative decline during 2000–2007. The economic implosion in Zimbabwe was, however, halted by the formation of the GNU and the dollarisation of the Zimbabwean economy in early 2009.

The teaching sector before and during the crisis

During the first decade of Zimbabwe's independence, the government claimed to follow a socialist path. The main principle was 'Growth with Equity' (Government of Zimbabwe 2001). This principle was adopted so that the government could redress the inherited inequities and imbalances in access to basic needs such as education, health facilities and other public services. Thus, the Government of Zimbabwe invested heavily in the education sector, such that it could claim that primary and secondary education enrolments expanded by 79% and 841%, respectively, in the period 1980–1989 (Government of Zimbabwe 2001). Primary school education was made free. This resulted in gross admission rates rising by well over 100%, and by the end of the first decade of independence, Zimbabwe had achieved universal primary education (Government of Zimbabwe 2001). As primary and secondary education expanded at a rapid pace, the number of teachers also increased, and by 1997, when the Zimbabwean crisis began, the Zimbabwe Teachers Association (ZIMTA) estimated that there were about 100,000 primary and secondary school teachers in Zimbabwe's public schools.

The strides made in the education sector in the first two decades of independence were undone during the Zimbabwean crisis (2000–2008), as teachers left the profession because of poor remuneration. ZIMTA and the Progressive Teachers Union of Zimbabwe (PTUZ) claimed in 2009 that during the past decade 45,000 teachers out of about 100,000 in the civil service's records quit the profession and most sought jobs in the diaspora (Interview with Tendai Chikowore, the President of ZIMTA on 30 April 2009 and Raymond Majongwe, Secretary-General of PTUZ on 2 May 2009). The teaching sector suffered immensely during the period of hyper-inflation between 2007 and 2008. The ZCTU monthly lists of salaries consistently showed the teachers to be amongst the lowest paid workers. From October to December 2008, the teachers' average salaries were Z$729,000, Z$3 million and Z$12 million, respectively (*The Worker*, October 2008, November 2008, December 2008). When converted to the prevailing exchange rates *vis-a-vis* the US dollar during that time, teachers were earning less than US$10 for each of the three months. The October 2008 income was the worst: when the teachers earned Z$729,000, it was equivalent to US$0.72 on the widely used parallel money market. This is why in the last half of 2008 most remaining teachers in the public schools left the chalk and the classrooms to embark on an indefinite protest against their miserly salaries. Thus, the teaching sector experienced a form of partial disintegration in terms of numbers of teachers who were actively teaching in schools. By the end of 2008, most public sector teachers had stopped teaching and there were only a few teachers in the private schools still teaching.[6]

The concept of the disintegration or decomposition of certain classes or particular sectors in a country's economy has been theorised in the sociology of work. Eley and Nield (2000) assert that the working class in the West showed signs of disintegration in the early 1980s at the ideological and organisational levels, as trade unions became weaker in comparison to previous decades. They argue that this class ceased to be united in the classical Marxist sense of being a class for itself, as a consequence of the onslaught from the right-wing politics and economics of Reagan and Thatcher in the 1980s (Eley and Nield 2000). The decline in the numbers of particular sections of a class, as occurred in sectors such as manufacturing, catering and teaching in Zimbabwe during the peak of the Zimbabwean crisis, can also be conceived of as the disintegration of a class in numerical terms.

Migrating to other countries as a response to the implosion of the economy

Many teachers chose to migrate to other countries in response to Zimbabwe's economic implosion. A wave of emigration including teachers began soon after the disputed general elections in 2000 and commencement of the fast track land reform programme (Zinyama 2002). The destinations varied from neighbouring Southern African countries to New Zealand, Australia, the United Kingdom and the United States.

Interviews conducted with teachers confirmed that many of the profession left Zimbabwe as the economic situation worsened. Ben Chatuka, a teacher who stopped working from September 2008 because of the poor salaries explained the extent of teacher migration from his school:

> When I joined the primary school that I was teaching at in 2004, the staff complement was 21 teachers, including temporary teachers, but by September (2008) when I stopped teaching, 12 teachers had left for South Africa, Botswana and Swaziland in order to look for better teaching posts in these countries. When the PTUZ called for an industrial action just before the start of the third term in September, there were only seven permanent teachers in the whole school, including the headmaster, who were still coming to school to teach.[7]

Memory Chipunza stopped teaching in May 2008. She recalled the exodus of teachers from her primary school in Glen View:

> When I joined Glen View 1 Primary School in 2006, there were 16 teachers, but when I decided to quit in May this year (2008) none of the teachers that had been at the school when I joined, were still teaching at the school. Most did not say where they were going. You would just hear from the grape-vine that so and so is now in Botswana or South Africa.[8]

Thus, migrating to other countries by teachers due to their collapsing salaries meant that this component of the working class had partially disintegrated by the time dollarisation was officially introduced in April 2009.

The informal sector as a means of survival for teachers

As Zimbabwe's economic crisis deepened and the formal sector shrank, the informal sector burgeoned and sustained many livelihoods. The significance of the informal economy is in stark contrast to what the informal economy was like at the advent of independence in 1980. Then, the informal economy in Zimbabwe was relatively small, accounting for less than 10% of the labour force (Mhone 1992). All 16 teachers interviewed were engaged in some informal sector activity that ranged from petty commodity trading to cross-border trading and foreign currency dealing.

The largely speculative nature of Zimbabwe's informal economy during the period of hyper-inflation was a dominant feature. The informal economy, also known as the 'black market', was very lucrative because of the shortages of foreign currency and most basic commodities in Zimbabwe. As a result, there was a thriving 'black market' in foreign currency dealing, fuel, and basic goods like mealie-meal, sugar, cooking oil, and soap, brought by cross-border traders into Zimbabwe from neighbouring countries such as South Africa and Botswana. A speculative informal economy will in most cases thrive in hyper-inflationary situations, because it provides an opportunity for people to hoard goods and re-sell them later at inflated prices rather than keeping money which loses value. In this case, speculative activities assist people to hedge against the devastating effects of hyper-inflation (Hanke 2008). The 'black market' also thrived in countries that faced hyper-inflation in the past such as Germany during the Weimar Republic (1920–1923), Argentina (1988–1989) and Yugoslavia (1992–1994), as most goods became available in the informal economy (Dornbusch, Sturzeneggar, and Wolf 1990; Carmen 2002; Petrovic, Bogetic, and Vugosevic 1998).

Nine of the 16 teachers interviewed were involved in cross-border trading in the informal economy. The teachers were well placed to engage in cross-border activities because from 2005 to 2009 Zimbabwean civil servants could visit South Africa without the need to obtain a visa: without this privilege visas cost about US$200, although in early 2009 the fee was waived. The school holidays and the almost year-long industrial action by teachers in 2008 also meant that some teachers had 'free time' to engage in cross-border trading. Primary school teacher Tracey Chamboko narrated how cross-border trading became pivotal for the survival of her family:

> I started engaging in cross-border trading in 2006 and it has helped my family a lot because the salary that I earn as a teacher is not enough to do anything with. The teaching that we have been doing for the past few years now, has just been a community service, because teachers have been working for nothing. So, because of the meagre salary, I decided to become a cross-border trader, while I continued to teach by the side.

I have been going to South Africa, mostly to Musina, to buy goods like sugar, cooking-oil, soap, rice and hair extensions, which I have been re-selling here in Zimbabwe.[9]

Edith Madombwe, another primary school teacher, explained how cross-border trading was helping her cope with the crisis:

From about 2002, our economic situation as teachers has worsened, and we have become the laughing stock of society because of our meagre salaries. As I am talking to you now, my salary last month (September 2008) was Z$812, 000 which was equivalent to US$2 on the parallel market which is widely used. Tell me, what do I do with US$2 as a salary for the whole month? So I am engaged in cross- border trading, and I go to South Africa twice a month to buy groceries like sugar, cooking-oil, mealie-meal, flour and rice which I re-sell here.[10]

Tracey and Edith's accounts reveal the important role of cross-border trading as a survival strategy and how teachers took advantage of school holidays and the crippling teachers' strike of 2008 to engage in cross-border trading.

Foreign currency dealing (combined with remittances of stable foreign currency) was also a way of weathering Zimbabwe's hyper-inflationary environment. Sam Dhana, who was a primary school teacher in Highfields, claimed that he was able to sustain his family through foreign currency dealing:

Every month, I receive between £50 to £100 from my brother who is in England. I use some of the money to buy food for my family but mostly, I use this foreign currency to buy Zim dollars. I will then use the Zim dollars to buy more forex from other people who want to dispose their forex at favourable rates, that ensure that I buy more US dollars than I would have had previously. I repeat the cycle continuously, and at the end of the day, I make a lot of profit in forex terms.[11]

Revival of the teaching sector in the wake of dollarisation of the economy

When the GNU was formed in Zimbabwe in February 2009, one of the first measures the GNU implemented was to dollarise the Zimbabwean economy, in order to bring some semblance of macro-economic stability, and to stem the scourge of hyper-inflation.

In line with dollarisation, the GNU decided to pay every civil servant an allowance of US$100, regardless of one's post or educational qualifications. This move by the government resulted in the resuscitation of sectors that were 'dead' such as the teaching and nursing professions because teachers and nurses who had not been working for the greater part of 2008 went back to their jobs. The PTUZ reported in April 2009 that out of about 100,000 teachers in public schools before the crisis, 60,000 had gone back to work after the GNU started paying civil servants in foreign currency (*The Worker*, May 2009). The PTUZ went on to say that the outstanding 40,000 were mostly those teachers who went to other countries and got better paying teaching posts or other opportunities. The Union added that, by April 2009, 6000 teachers had returned to Zimbabwe from South Africa, and that about 3000 of them were teaching again in government schools. The other 3000 had deserted their teaching posts, so the Ministry was mulling over whether or not these teachers should be re-engaged without punitive measures being taken against them (*The Worker*, May 2009).

Most of the teachers interviewed said that they had gone back to the classrooms because the US$100 that they were getting in 2009 was much better than the worthless trillions of Zimbabwean dollars they had been getting from the government before the dollarisation of the economy. Elizabeth Mpariwa summed up the feelings of most teachers about the US$100 they were receiving:

> The US$100 that we are getting from the government may not be enough to sustain an individual for a month, let alone a family, but, I believe that this is a good starting point, given the economic crisis we are coming from as a country. I had stopped teaching in April 2008, but I have decided to go back to work because I believe that if the GNU works properly, our salaries will improve with time, to be in line with the Poverty Datum Line. But for now, at least I can buy a few groceries and afford my transport costs so that I can report for work, unlike in the past.[12]

The accounts of most teachers interviewed reveals that most strove to come up with survivalist strategies in the face of a crisis that had almost totally eroded their salaries.

The banking sector during the crisis

In 2008, the banking sector had 15 commercial banks. Three had some degree of state ownership while the others were wholly privately owned. There were also six merchant banks, three discount houses and four building societies (UNDP 2008). Four of the private commercial banks, the South African-owned Stanbic Bank, Merchant Bank of Central Africa, and British-owned Standard Chartered Bank and Barclays Bank were multi-national corporations commanding 55% of the commercial banks market share (UNDP 2008). The three banks with a degree of state ownership, the Commercial Bank of Zimbabwe, ZB Bank and the Zimbabwe Allied Banking Group, were gaining market share through preferential treatment from the state.

The banking sector was generally doing very well during the peak of the Zimbabwean crisis because of the speculative activities in which most banks were engaged, attempting to cushion themselves from the hyper-inflation. Thus, most banks were trading in the best performing stocks on the Zimbabwe Stock Exchange (ZSE), also doing very well during the period of the crisis, as individuals and companies chose to trade on the bourse's best performing shares as opposed to saving rapidly eroding money. The exceptional performance of the ZSE defied stock market analysts' widely held belief that events that stimulate GDP growth inevitably drive up stock prices while events that hurt GDP growth push stock prices down, and led Koning (2008) to challenge this purported linkage as simplistic. Koning (2008) argues that the Zimbabwe Stock Exchange (ZSE) was the best performing stock exchange in Africa, with the key Zimbabwe industrials index going up by 595% over a period of 12 months in 2007. Koning (2008) and Hanke (2008) are of the opinion that one of the ways for people to hedge against hyper-inflation was to buy stocks of the best performing counters on the ZSE. Another way of hedging against the hyper-inflation was to buy property. Thus, real estate and the ZSE boomed during the crisis as individuals and companies scrambled to maintain and even add to the value of the Zimbabwean dollars that they had. Banks were no exception and profited greatly from the booming ZSE and the property market.

The above activities in the banking sector led the Reserve Bank of Zimbabwe (RBZ) Governor, Gideon Gono to accuse most banks of engaging in activities that were not their core activities (Gono 2008). Such criticism was paradoxical, coming from the RBZ Governor, whose central bank was engaged in quasi-fiscal and speculative activities as well as printing the money fuelling hyper-inflation (IMF 2009).

Workers in the bank sector during the crisis

The profits being made by the banks trickled down to the working class sections of the sector, such as the bank tellers and other junior bank clerks. Commercial bank teller Paula Porusingazi narrated the good working conditions she and her colleagues enjoyed:

> Even though working conditions in Zimbabwe are generally tough because of inflation, but my bank has been trying to give us remuneration that is better than what most workers get in other companies. We earn salaries twice a month and last month, my two salaries amounted to Z$120 million. [In October 2008 this was equivalent to between US$100 and US$120 on the forex black market]. Each person also gets a fuel coupon of up to 50 litres, which one can sell to other motorists, if one does not have a car.[13]

Miriam Sithole, a 26-year-old Stanbic Bank teller of three years, echoed Paula's statement when she described the relatively better working conditions and remuneration in the banking sector:

> I have been a bank teller with Stanbic Bank for three years now and although the salary that I receive is not enough to buy all my needs, especially household furniture, but I think I am better off than my friends who work as secretaries in private companies in town because my salary is always higher than theirs, even though our academic qualifications are almost the same. Last month (October 2008) I got a salary of Z$73 million (US$146 on the parallel market in Zimbabwe at the end of October 2008). We also get paid twice a month and this is quite helpful in ensuring that we always have some money to buy basics and to be able to report for work.[14]

The bank workers also benefitted from foreign currency transactions. One popular foreign currency transaction scheme labelled 'burning money' made people instant quadrillionaires and trillionaires in Zimbabwean dollars. This 'burning of money' was a form of bank transfers done through a banking system known as Real Time Gross Settlement (RTGS). If a person gave US dollars to the bank and requested that the money be transferred into their accounts as Zimbabwean dollars, that individual would get Zimbabwean dollars that were many times higher than the prevailing exchange rates. The advantage for bank workers was that they could withdraw much more money every single day than the withdrawal limits that had been placed on everyone else. With the large amount of Zimbabwean dollars withdrawn, most bank workers were able to buy foreign currency on the streets and repeat the 'burning of money' process *ad infinitum,* thus making a lot of money in the process. A number of the bank tellers interviewed said they hoped the Zimbabwean crisis would continue indefinitely, because it was benefitting them a lot.

Other bank tellers interviewed were going to countries such as Dubai and China to buy electronic goods to resell in Zimbabwe. The 'burning of money' helped people to fly with Air Zimbabwe for almost nothing as they would 'burn' a few US dollar and then pay for their airfares with the quadrillions or quintillions of Zimbabwean dollars obtained in the RTGS transactions. In reality the national airline was making huge losses.

Even though the working class in other sectors of the economy was showing signs of disappearing, in sectors like banking the working class remained intact and appeared to be able to cope relatively better with the economic crisis because of engagement in accumulation strategies, as compared to the teachers for instance, who had to leave formal employment and engage in largely petty commodity trading. However, the introduction of dollarisation spelt the death of such speculative activities and changed the situation dramatically for the banks and their workers. Most banks became unable to remunerate their employees in hard currency because of depressed deposits.

Reversal of fortunes: the banking sector in the era of dollarisation

The Worker of April 2009 reported that a massive retrenchment exercise was looming in the banking sector as most institutions were struggling to adjust to the dictates of a dollarised economy. Godfrey Kanyenze, the director of the Labour and Economic Development Research Institute of Zimbabwe, contends that most banks struggled during the early stages of dollarisation because Zimbabwe's central bank required banks to be strictly capitalised in hard currency (Interview 14 May 2009). Most banks were also not getting many deposits from clients, because of their low hard currency incomes. Several banks such as Zimbank, CABS and Stanbic had already closed some of their branches in reaction to the slump in business (*The Worker*, April 2009). The Zimbabwe Banking and Allied Workers' Union (ZIBAWU) reported that contract workers and those in the lending and advances departments had been the most adversely affected, as banks were no longer issuing loans. In general, few people visited banks, thus forcing them to streamline their operations. Consequently, the working class in the banking sector faced serious threats of disintegration because of the dollarisation of the economy.

Teachers and bank workers' agency in the face of crisis

Giddens' (1984) structuration theory is helpful in explaining the agency of the teachers and the bank tellers (survival and accumulation strategies) in the face of a hostile structure (political and economic context). According to Giddens, as agents/actors, the teachers and bank tellers in Zimbabwe are able to monitor their own thoughts and activities as well as their physical and social contexts. This implies that actors (the teachers and bank tellers living under an unfavourable structure such as hyper-inflation and a political crisis) were capable of rationalisation, which in Giddens' work means the development of routines enabling them to deal with their social lives efficiently. Consequently, Giddens' agents–and certainly those in the Zimbabwean context–have the ability to make a difference in the social world and improve their situation. Giddens certainly recognises that there are structural constraints on actors, but this does not mean they have no choices (in the Zimbabwean case, the different responses to the hyper-inflation by workers in Zimbabwe).

Giddens' structures are not fixed 'girders', in the Durkheimian or Parsonian sense. Thus, the agency displayed by the teachers and bank tellers had the effect of reshaping the economic and social structure. Illicit activities in the highly speculative informal economy were abetting a 'get-rich quick' and 'dealer' culture among some working class sections of the society and institutions and this in turn promoted corruption and illicit activities in institutions like banks. The influential economist Henry Hazlitt (1992, 8) was not wrong when he argued: 'the consequences of inflation are malinvestment, waste, a wanton redistribution of wealth and income, the growth of speculation and gambling, immorality, corruption, disillusionment and social resentment... and eventual collapse'. Hazlitt's characterisation of high levels of inflation corroborates Jones' (2010) depiction of Zimbabwe's *kukiya-kiya* economy during the crisis.

Workers' agency at the political level (partyism) which entailed support and voting for the MDC was however partially successful, as the MDC won the March 2008 parliamentary elections that led to the formation of the GNU and the dollarisation of the economy. The MDC victory however was not outright, meaning that the political agency of the majority of the workers voting for the MDC was not able to totally reshape the repressive political structure or system that was responsible in part for the Zimbabwean crisis. The Zimbabwe case also suggests the limits on the primacy that is placed by Giddens on the power of agency to reshape structures. The fact that many of the teachers also barely stayed afloat in the face of the Zimbabwean crisis also cautions us against romanticising the agency that was displayed by some sections of the working class.

Conclusion

The article has argued that the crisis in Zimbabwe in the 2000s and the period in the immediate wake of dollarisation from April 2009 had uneven effects on primary school teachers and bank tellers. The responses to the crisis by the teachers and the bank workers were also different as the former strove to merely survive, while the latter were well placed to engage in accumulation strategies that were being fuelled by a highly speculative economy. During the period of crisis, the teaching sector partially disintegrated as most teachers either left the country or decided to join Zimbabwe's informal economy on a full-time basis. Militant responses at the workplace level, such as embarking on industrial action, did not help the plight of the teachers as their salaries continued to be eroded by hyper-inflation. Consequently, petty commodity trading, cross-border trading and foreign currency dealing became the best option for the survival of the teachers. However, the dollarisation of the Zimbabwean economy changed the situation for the teachers, as that development 'killed-off' most of the speculative activities in the informal economy and, together with improved salaries paid in US dollars, encouraged teachers still in the country to go back to formal employment, thus resulting in a gradual re-integration of the teaching sector.

In contrast, the banking sector thrived during the crisis, remaining intact because of the profits banks made from speculative activities. The situation however changed dramatically for this sector when dollarisation was effected. Most banks suddenly struggled to pay their workers in hard currency, with some even forced to downsize their operations, retrench their workers and close some of their branches. The banking sector faced a decline because of a slump in business as deposits dwindled and speculative activities disappeared due to the dollarised economy. Thus, dollarisation proved to be a double-edged sword as it was able to wipe-off hyper-inflation in no time and lead to the gradual revival of sectors such as public sector teaching. On the other hand, dollarisation of the economy brought with it difficulties for sectors such as banking, as liquidity levels in the country were generally low in the immediate period after dollarisation.

The responses of the teachers and some of the bank tellers displayed a sense of agency in the face of the Zimbabwean crisis, albeit that it also contributed to compromising Zimbabwean society's principles.

Notes

1. Bloch (2009) defines dollarisation as the substitution of a domestic currency by a more stable foreign currency. Bloch further adds that it does not necessarily imply that only one foreign currency is introduced or adopted: currencies such as the US dollar, the South African Rand, the British Pound Sterling and the Botswana Pula are all accepted as legal tender in Zimbabwe.
2. Please note that all names used in this paper are pseudonyms in order to protect the informants' identities.
3. *Kukiya-kiya* has also been referred to colloquially as *kujingirisa* by people taking part in informal sector activities.
4. The Riddell Commission was a Presidential Commission that was set up in 1981 in Zimbabwe to make enquiries and recommendations on incomes, prices and conditions of work of employees.
5. There was a wave of strikes between 1995 and 2000 in Zimbabwe, in both the private and public sectors. The biggest strikes were by the civil servants in 1996 and 1997.
6. Teachers in private schools were being paid more money by the affluent parents who could afford to send their children to private schools. In some cases, these teachers were being paid in hard currency while teachers in the public schools were being given worthless Zimbabwean dollars.
7. Interview with Ben Chatuka on 4 October 2008.
8. Interview with Memory Chipunza on 6 August 2008.
9. Interview with Tracey Chamboko on 6 August 2008.
10. Interview with Edith Madombwe on 3 October 2008.
11. Interview with Sam Dhana on 10 August 2008.
12. Interview with Elizabeth Mpariwa on 26 April 2009.
13. Interview with Paula Porusingazi on 8 December 2008.
14. Interview with Miriam Sithole on 11 November 2008.

Note on contributor

Tapiwa Chagonda is a Post-Doctoral Fellow at the Centre for Sociological Research (CSR) at the University of Johannesburg. His current research focuses on the responses of Zimbabwean workers in both formal and informal employment to the dollarisation of the Zimbabwean economy. In his doctoral thesis he investigated the response of Harare's working class in Zimbabwe to hyper-inflation and the political crisis in the 2000s.

References

Alexander, P. 2000. Zimbabwean workers, the MDC and the 2000 election. *Review of African Political Economy* 85: 385–406.
Bloch, E. 2009. The Zimbabwe dollar farce. *The Zimbabwe Independent*, 13 March.

Carmen, M. 2002. *Some lessons from modern hyperinflation.* Chicago: University of Chicago Press.
Central Statistical Office, 2008. *August report on July inflation statistics.* Harare: CSO.
Chagonda, T. 2011. The response of the working class in Harare, Zimbabwe to hyper-inflation and the political crisis, 1997-2008. PhD thesis, University of Johannesburg.
Chamboko, T. 2008. Teacher, Interview on 6 August 2008. Harare.
Chatuka, B. 2008. Teacher, Interview on 4 October 2008. Harare.
Chikowore, T. 2009. President, Zimbabwe Teachers' Association. Interviewed 30 April 2009. Harare.
Chipunza, M. 2008. Teacher, Interview on 6 August 2008. Harare.
Dansereau, S. 2001. Zimbabwe: Labour options within the MDC. *Review of African Political Economy* 89: 403–14.
Dhana, S. 2008. Teacher, Interview on 10 August 2008. Harare.
Dornbusch, R., F. Sturzeneggar, and M. Wolf. 1990. Extreme inflation: Dynamics and stabilisation. *Brookings Papers on Economic Activity* 0, no. 2: 1–64.
Eley, G., and K. Nield. 2000. Farewell to the working class? *International Labour and Working Class History* 57: 1–30. Cambridge University Press.
Giddens, A. 1984. *The constitution of society: Outline of the theory of structuration.* Berkeley: University of California Press.
Gono, G. 2008. *Zimbabwe's casino economy: Extraordinary measures for extraordinary challenges.* Harare: Zimbabwe Publishing House.
Government of zimbabwe, 2001. *The developments in education: The education system at the end of the 20th century, 1980-2000.* Harare: Government Printer.
Gwisai, M. 2002. *Revolutionaries, resistance and crisis in Zimbabwe: Anti-neoliberal struggles in periphery capitalism.* London: New Clarion Press.
Hanke, S. 2008. Hyperinflation: Mugabe versus milosevic, Globe Asia.
Hazlitt, H. 1992. *From Bretton Woods to world inflation. A study of causes and consequences.* Chicago: Regnery Gateway.
International Monetary Fund, 2009. IMF Country Report No.09/139.
Jones, J. 2008. Everybody's doing it. Young Township Men and Zimbabwe's Kukiya-kiya Economy 2006-8. Paper presented at international conference on Political Economies of Displacement in Post-2000 Zimbabwe, Nordic Africa Institute and Forced Migration Studies Programme, Wits University, 9–11 June 2008.
Jones, J. 2010. Nothing is straight in Zimbabwe': The rise of the kukiya-kiya economy 2000-2008. *Journal of Southern African Studies* 32, no. 2: 285–99.
Kanyenze, G. 2009. Director, Labour and Economic Development Research Institute of Zimbabwe. Interviewed on 14 May 2009. Harare.
Koning, P. 2008. *Zimbabwe: Best performing stock market in 2007?* New York: Ludwig Von Mises Institute.
Madombwe, E. 2008. Teacher, Interview on 3 October 2008. Harare.
Majongwe, R. 2009. Secretary-General, Progressive Teachers' Union of Zimbabwe. Interviewed on 2 May 2009. Harare.
Matombo, L., and L. Sachikonye. 2010. The labour movement and democratisation in Zimbabwe. In *Trade Unions and Party Politics: Labour movements in Africa,* ed. B. Beckman, S. Buhlungu, and L. Sachikonye, 109–30. Pretoria: HSRC.
Mhone, G. 1992. *The informal sector in Southern Africa: Structural status and constraints.* Harare: SAPES Trust.
Moore, D. 2002. Zimbabwe's triple crisis: Primitive accumulatiom, nation-state formation and democratisation in the age of neo-liberal globalisation. *African Studies Quarterly* 7, no. 2 and 3: 1–18.
Moyo, P. 2009. Urban food insecurity, coping strategies and resistance in Bulawayo, Zimbabwe. PhD thesis, Leeds University.
Mpariwa, E. 2009. Teacher, Interview on 26 April 2009. Harare.
Nest, M. 2001. Ambitions, profits and loss: Zimbabwean economic involvement in the Democratic Republic of Congo. *African Affairs* 100: 469–90.
Noko, T. 2011. Dollarization: The case of Zimbabwe. *Cato Journal,* no. 2: 339–65 (Spring and Summer 2011).

Petrovic, P., Z. Bogetic, and Z. Vugosevic. 1998. The Yugoslav hyperinflation of 1992-1994: Causes, dynamics, and money supply process. *Journal of Comparative Economics* 27: 335–53.
Phimister, I., and B. Raftopolous. 1997. *Keep on knocking: A history of Zimbabwe's labour movement, 1900–1997*. Harare: Baobab.
Porusingazi, P. 2008. Commercial Bank Teller, Interview on 8 December 2008. Harare.
Raftopoulos, B. 2006. The Zimbabwe crisis and the challenges for the left. *Journal of Southern African Studies* 32, no. 2: 203–19.
Raftopoulos, B. 2008. *Elections, mediation and deadlock in Zimbabwe?*. Cape Town: SPT.
Raftopoulos, B., and L. Sachikonye, ed. 2001. *Striking back: The Labour Movement and the post-colonial state in Zimbabwe 1980-2000*. Harare: Weaver Press.
Robinson, P. 2007. Macro-economic paper produced for the Zimbabwe Institute, Cape Town.
Sachikonye, L., ed. 1995. *State and social movements in Zimbabwe*. Harare: SAPES Books.
Selby, A. 2006. Commercial farmers and the state: Interest group politics and land reform in Zimbabwe. PhD thesis, Oxford University.
Sithole, M. 2008. Commercial Bank Teller, Interview on 11 November 2008. Harare.
The Worker, October 2008. Harare: Zimbabwe Congress of Trade Unions.
The Worker, November 2008. Harare: Zimbabwe Congress of Trade Unions.
The Worker, December 2008. Harare: Zimbabwe Congress of Trade Unions.
The Worker, April 2009. Harare: Zimbabwe Congress of Trade Unions.
The Worker, May 2009. Harare: Zimbabwe Congress of Trade Unions.
UNDP, 2008. *Comprehensive economic recovery in Zimbabwe. A discussion document*. Harare: UNDP.
Zinyama, L. 2002. International migration and Zimbabwe: An overview. In D.S Tevera and L. Zinyama, eds. *Zimbabweans Who Move: Perspectives on International Migration in Zimbabwe. Migration Policy Series 25*, 7–41. Kingston: SAMP.

'New realities' and tenure reforms: land-use in worker-peasant communities of south-western Zimbabwe (1940s–2006)[1]

Vusilizwe Thebe

Department of Development Studies, National University of Lesotho, Roma, Lesotho

> This article is about rural people, what they value and consider as important in their lives, and state policy to ameliorate rural conditions. It is an analysis of the tenure system and landholding patterns in operation among a community of Zimbabwean worker-peasants vis-à-vis the post-colonial state's attempts to reform former Native Reserves (communal areas) after the country's independence in 1980. Based on ethnographic research on the semi-proletarian Gwayi Valley, in Lupane District, the article equates the communal tenure system in practice to Scott's hidden transcripts. The tenure system was a result of constant negotiations and manipulation by households, in response to environmental challenges, and over the years, became central to the very survival of households. The post-colonial state's attempts to reorganise communal areas to make them legible and productive, were opposed to the new culture. The deployment of land-use planning tools to redefine communal area agrarian systems represented a social engineering process which was geared at remoulding households' livelihoods.

In 2004, I became interested in Zimbabwe's land reform process – hoping to add my voice to the unremitting debate on what is termed by the Zimbabwe African National Union- Patriotic Front (Zanu-PF), the Third *Chimurenga*. I received active support from a PhD supervisor who at one time in her academic career had done work on the country's agrarian formation. The field was highly congested, with all kinds of interests – partisan, critical, and neutral. If this mix was no place for an academic still trying to cut his teeth, it changed after a chance meeting with a war veteran during a bus trip to one of the resettled farms. 'I was one of the first people into this farm. I had land here, which I abandoned for land in the communal areas where landholding is more secure', he told me as we drove past a resettled farm in uMguza District. Yet, if we follow the general narrative justifying communal area reforms, landholding in communal areas is insecure, and the resource inalienable. What then did he mean by 'secure landholdings' in communal areas? To put it differently, how communal was communal land, and communal to whom? Some of these questions have long-term implications to the future of rural areas in Zimbabwe. Tenure relations in communal areas are not that communal anymore. Through a process of negotiation and adaptation, a new tenure system, different from the ideological model, has emerged. I equate this process to Scott (1990)'s 'hidden transcripts', which exist alongside the 'public transcripts'.

Scholarship on tenure relations in Zimbabwe has focused on agrarian communities in eastern Zimbabwe, leaving a dearth in the analysis of such processes in worker-peasant Ndebele communities, where landholding provide a different livelihood option from crop production. Using four administrative kraal units in the Gwayi Valley in Lupane District as a case study, I argue that the tenure in practice is not communal, if by communal, we mean not transferable and inflexible. The tenure system that emerged reflects households' culture, shaped overtime by local interests in the fragmentation of labour (Bernstein 2004) or the 'co-existence of subsistence farming and migrant labour' (O'Flaherty 1998, 538). I contend that post-colonial attempts at internal resettlement were a stark departure from the culture that had emerged, and were part of the state's attempt at a social engineering of rural livelihoods.

I draw on material from an extended case study carried out between 2004 and 2006 and a close reading of related work. I focus on governance and landholding practices during different phases in the country's political transition (1940s–2006), and examine how landholding practices depart from the ideal, as well as the processes that have informed the tenure system in practice. I base my evidence on processes and governance issues in four administrative kraal dynasties and life histories from 107 households in the Gwayi Valley, Lupane District.

Rural development interventions in Zimbabwe

Rural Development interventions in Zimbabwe can be understood only in the context of the protracted history of social engineering, made prominent by the Todd administration in the mid-twentieth century, and given intellectual backing by Emory Alvord (Bush and Cliffe 1984; Wolmer and Scoones 2000). The re-enactment of history by post-colonial Zimbabwe was not surprising, given Zanu (PF)'s policy of moderation and reconciliation (Alexander 1994; Drinkwater 1989). Thus, the post-colonial state did not only adopt Rhodesian policies, centrally formulated and coercively implemented, it also inherited Rhodesian institutions – the bureaucracy, the legal apparatus, etc (Alexander 1994; Chaumba, Scoones, and Wolmer 2003). Land-use planning had become institutionalised in technical and bureaucratic thinking of the inherited structures, it had become very difficult to question, and hence its persistence as a rural development tool after independence (Chaumba, Scoones, and Wolmer 2003). While this is certainly part of the story, rural transformation was also geared at improving productivity in communal areas (O'Flaherty 1998). As expressed by various scholars (Weinrich 1975; Yudelman 1964) and commissions (Riddell 1981; Chavunduka Commission, GoZ 1982), communal tenure has always been dismissed as economically unviable (O'Flaherty 1998, 537). Thus, post-colonial policies attempted to re-mould rural communities by reconfiguring rural livelihoods in ways that served Zanu (PF)'s pseudo-socialist transformation agenda.

Worby (2001, 490) has observed:

> Rural development in Zimbabwe, ... has been about moral judgment, 'the civilizing project' masquerading as disinterested social engineering. In theory, what is engineered, optimized or rationally managed, is the relation between the nation's citizens and the nation's natural body (what the economists call its 'human' and 'natural' resources). This impulse ranks among the most notable continuities in practices of state power that survived the end of white minority rule ....

As Adams (1999) noted, while social engineering is geared at improving human conditions, it also attempts to impose structure upon diverse social elements, thus replacing 'socially and ecologically diverse polycultures with highly simplified, commercially-oriented monocultures'. Usually, intervention is the state's attempt at administrative ordering of nature, what Scott (1998) terms state simplifications. Even so, state simplifications interfere with man/nature interaction. While man is robbed of an intimate natural environment, which is usually transformed and stripped of its relevance to the local population, it remains highly 'visible, and legible, to the synoptic view of the state' (Adams 1999, 262). Social engineering is about visions, and visions do not depict reality. James Scott looks at visions as abridged maps, which do not successfully represent the actual activity of society they depict. Such maps represent only that slice of it that interest the visionary. Nonetheless, when these maps are allied with state power, they 'would enable much of the reality they depicted to be re-made' (Scott 1998, 3). Social engineering is therefore about legibility not reality.

Background to rural social engineering in Zimbabwe

Areas reserved for African settlements were created through military conquest and legislative statutes. The precursor was the Gwayi and Shangani reserves, created under the Matabeleland-Order-In Council (1894), and legitimised by the Land Apportionment Act of 1930 (Moyana 1984; Okoth 2006). The creation of African areas was significant in the development of a capitalist mode of production in the new territory (Arrighi 1970; Johnson 1992). Thus, state policy to banish Africans to agro-ecological hostile environments deprived indigenous Africans of their means of subsistence in order to incorporate African labour into the capitalist mode of production. The policy proceeded simultaneously with the denigration of African traditional production systems, while protecting white-settlers from African competition in the product markets (Bush and Cliffe 1984; Duggan 1990). However, although unintended, the policy created a worker-peasantry (Bernstein 2004; Bush and Cliffe 1984; Yeros 2002), reinforced later by influx control measures, which left many families 'forcibly' divided (Potts and Mutambirwa 1990, 678). Rural agricultural production remained in the hands of farmer-housewives (Potts 2000) and livelihoods became increasingly dependent on both hoe and wage (Cordell, Gregory, and Piché 1996) or wage and hoe (Bernstein 2004).

While the *status quo* in the reserves served the settler economy well, there was a policy shift in favour of active interventions in the rural economy, of which the linchpin was the Native Land Husbandry Act of 1951 (Phimister 1993). Boosted by substantial financial backing from the World Bank and supported by scientific justifications, state plans on issues of land, agriculture production, and environment conservation were put into implementation (Duggan 1990; Phimister 1993; Wolmer and Scoones 2000). State policy was geared at redefining African agrarian systems by first, reorganising landholding and use patterns (Thompson 2004), and secondly, to conserve the environment and promote good husbandry (Duggan 1990). As Wolmer and Scoones (2000, 596–7), reminds us, 'the ordering of space and rationalisation of "messy destructive practices" was a mechanism through which power could be exerted'. The act empowered colonial administrators to intervene extensively in rural agricultural processes, directing peasant production and determining who could have access to land (Thompson 2004). Through the policy of indirect rule, traditional leaders were afforded a central role in rural governance, controlling land and enforcing colonial conservation policies (Ranger 1982). On a different level, the act represented state attempts to eliminate the worker-peasantry, by fixing the number of people dependent upon the land (Duggan 1990) and creating a permanent urban proletariat (Bush and Cliffe 1984). The interventions typified a process of social engineering of the highest order, where state attempts to remould the relations of productions departed from the culture that had emerged in the African reserves (O'Flaherty 1998). While this was certainly the case, state social engineering came in a neutral cloak of 'modernisation and civilisation' of African agriculture (Berry 2002; Wolmer and Scoones 2000). According to Berry:

> Rural development and rural governance entailed a dual strategy of modernization and control. Technical demonstrations and improved economic incentives for "progressive farmers" went hand-in-hand with increased state regulation of rural economic life. From compulsory terracing as a guard against soil erosion, to forced de-stocking as a cure for overgrazing, colonial regimes placed onerous new demands on African labor and capital in the name of conservation and development (2002, 647–8).

Nevertheless, the agricultural betterment package was not intended for all rural dwellers but a selected agriculture elite (Duggan 1990), leaving many Africans impoverished, without land and any means of subsistence (Bush and Cliffe 1984; Thompson 2004, 2007). In general, however, the science of civilised agriculture was not only guided by the assumption that traditional agriculture was backward and inefficient, it was mutually compatible with state designs to transform the communal tenure system (Phimister 1993), providing instead, individual security of tenure (Wolmer and Scoones 2000). As Thompson (2004) noted, the colonial state's civilising mission met with a lot of rural resistance because the project interfered with core African productive systems.

The post-colonial state's policies

The post-colonial state was born on the background of the colonial legacy of land alienation; neglect and coercive state interference in African agriculture and settlement patterns; and rural resistance to state plans. In addition, the customary powers conferred by the Tribal Trust Land Act of 1967 had largely disappeared by independence (Cheater 1990; Ranger 1982). The highly skewed pattern of land distribution, resulting from various colonial legislations provided the post-independence administration with a rationale for reform, particularly land redistribution (Cheater 1990). Even so, the reform path was charted by Britain, in the Lancaster House Constitution, following the Kenyan experience. As Bush and Cliffe (1984, 86) observed, ' ... land had to be largely individually owned, and kept as far as possible, in "economic" sized holdings, which, if it has any meaning, means capable of generating a marketable surplus'. It is interesting to realise that the reform path and the objectives were in line with colonial reforms, widely resisted by rural people (Alexander 1994; Drinkwater 1989; O'Flaherty 1998). As Alexander (1994) noted, policy continuities after independence were dictated by Zanu (PF)'s policy of moderation and reconciliation towards the white population. Indeed, through moderation, the Rhodesian bureaucratic structures remained intact and former officials maintained influential positions within government policy circles.

On the other hand, government sought to redress the legacies of colonial policies, reforming the education and health sectors, land and agriculture, and communal area governance (Alexander 1994; O'Flaherty 1998). While reform had the ostensible purpose of substituting traditional institutions with elected decentralised structures for effective development, economically the programme was geared at increasing the production of commercial crops (O'Flaherty 1998). Hence, the Communal Land Act of 1981 did not only fail to return the land to chiefs, it also took away their authority over rural areas, giving these rights to District Councils under the Communal Land Act of 1982 (Mohamed-Katerere 2003; O'Flaherty 1998). Government interest in sidelining traditional institutions may be three-fold: first, the realisation that traditional institutions could not be representative in a changing society; secondly and more sinister, punishment for the role it played during the colonial era (Mohamed-Katerere 2003); and finally, chiefs and headmen were seen as a conservative guard of an unproductive system and thus, an impediment to government efforts to improve communal area productivity (O'Flaherty 1998). Again, there were threads of continuity with colonial thinking on communal areas – the myth of African farmers as subsistence-oriented and inefficient; the inefficiency of traditional tenure systems; and state obsession with eradication of the worker-peasant (Alexander 1994; O'Flaherty 1998).

While reform centred on new institutions, the traditional political system continued to enjoy widespread support among households, and traditional leaders continued to assert their right to allocate land (O'Flaherty 1998). It would seem that despite the quest for reform, traditional institutions remained important in Zanu (PF)'s political project (Alexander 1994). Unsurprisingly, the government sought to preserve and conserve traditional institutions in the guise of reconciliation: chiefs sat as ex-officio members in the new councils; chiefs and headmen remained on government payroll while vidcos and wadcos received no remuneration; and to protect 'tradition and dignity', chiefly appointments remained a central government prerogative (Kriger 1992, 225, cf. Alexander 1994). In 1998, the traditional system was given legitimacy through the Traditional Leaders Act, creating a dual structure of rural governance (Mohamed-Katerere 2003). Nonetheless, even before enactment of the act, Zanu (PF)'s pseudo recognition of traditional institutions was in itself a proclamation of their indispensability in communal areas, and more importantly, their centrality in constituency building and policy implementation (Alexander 1994).

Communal area reforms

In the context of the above, improved communal area productivity could not be achieved within the communal tenure system, and efforts were directed at internal resettlement in communal areas as part of the land reform exercise (O'Flaherty 1998). Internal resettlement involved realigning land resources and settlement patterns optimally to achieve agriculture productivity and facilitate infrastructural provision to improve economic viability of the rural sector (Gasper 1988; cf. Alexander 1994). The policy of internal land-use reform had its origins in the general slow-down in land distribution after 1983 (Alexander 1994), and was given intellectual and empirical backing by two post-independence commissions (Riddell and Chavunduka commissions). Both commission reports were damning of communal area practices and recommended change of the tenure system (Chavanduka Commission, GoZ 1982; Riddell, GoZ 1981). In fact, debates towards communal area reforms gained momentum following three years of droughts and subsequent drops in grain output (Drinkwater 1989). The cost of drought relief, which in the three financial years (1982/83–1984/85) cost the government Z$111.1 million, resulted in the launch of a 'green revolution' package of inputs and credits to boost communal area production (Drinkwater 1988, 121–22).

The policy was launched in 1986 with a pilot villagisation programme in each of the country's 55 district council areas (Drinkwater 1989). Programme objectives were articulated in the Ministry of Lands, Resettlement and Rural Development's *Communal Lands Development Plan* of 1984/85. It needs to be stressed here that programme implementation followed Alexander (1994)'s observations that agrarian reforms during the 1980s were managed by government ministries with little reference to people for whom plans were developed. The programme was centrally planned: the District Administrators was to select the vidco area for the project; the Department of Agricultural Technical and Extension Services (Agritex) was to be responsible for land-use planning (demarcating arable and grazing areas, and for assessing water requirements for human, stock, and irrigation purposes); and the Department of Physical Planning had the mandate to plan consolidated village settlements (Drinkwater 1989). Also, the programme took a lot from Rhodesian agrarian policies. Jocelyn Alexander observed:

> in June 1985 the Ministry of Land revealed its *Communal Lands Development Plan*. Strangely, the later report relied on 1970s research and reports, ... The plan criticised communal tenure and its allegedly ill effects .... Like the NLHA, it saw a solution in the creation of surveyed, planned and demarcated 'economic units', consolidated villages, and increased state control over tenure through a leasehold system which would exclude those who were not farmers (1994, 332).

Indeed, following colonial thinking, land-use planning was seen by key actors as an indispensable tool for rural development. Thus, villagisation as an aspect of the programme gained prominence after 1986, and was given budgetary support through the country's First Five Year Plan (Alexander 1994). While villagisation was about legibility and orderly settlements, it was by all intents and purposes, an agrarian reform strategy geared at rationalising land-use, and improving productivity (GoZ 1986). There was no room for traditional institutions in state designs, thus, ignoring the crucial role played by the traditional political system in ensuring household survival in communal areas (O'Flaherty 1998). In large measure, in line with Rhodesian agrarian policies, coercion was deployed to enforce compliance (Gasper

1990, cf. Alexander 1994). Unsurprisingly, like Rhodesian policies, the programme was met with hostility by communities and their representatives (Alexander 1994).

Creating a worker-peasantry in the Gwayi Valley

The Gwayi Valley in Lupane District is a small strip of territory, sandwiched between the Gwayi River to the south-west and the A8 Highway north-easterly, and these two landmarks dissect two dense forests. The Gwayi River separates the communal area from the commercial Sotane Safari Ranch, and meanders north towards the Zambezi River (see Figure 1). Large parts of the area constitute Menyezwa Ward 14 – a collection of five villages – defined more by primary schools serving the communities than any recognisable physical boundaries or a defined number of households. Whereas each village divides into administrative divisions or kraals, the composition is arbitrary, with some villages having more kraals than others, and the kraals being randomly constituted. The administrative kraal units are not associated with clearly defined boundaries and physical tracts of land, but households allied to a particular headman (*sabhuku*). Until the enactment of the 1998 Traditional Leaders Act, they conformed to O'Flaherty (1998, 548)'s description of a *musha* – 'bounded resource-holding units associated with and named after an influential lineage in the area, which controlled the hereditary title of *samusha*'.[2]

Whereas, the majority of soils at the Sotane Ranch are richer, with good grazing grass and vegetation cover, the majority of soils in the communal area are the poor *gusu* type (Worby 2001). Using Penman's (1948) formula of classifying physical regions in Matabeleland, the Gwayi Valley would fall in Prescott (1961)'s region II – with a growing season of between 75 and 95 days and 9–14 inches of effective rainfall. While the territory experiences semi-arid climatic conditions, characterised by moderate dry spells and occasional droughts, drought-resistant crops are

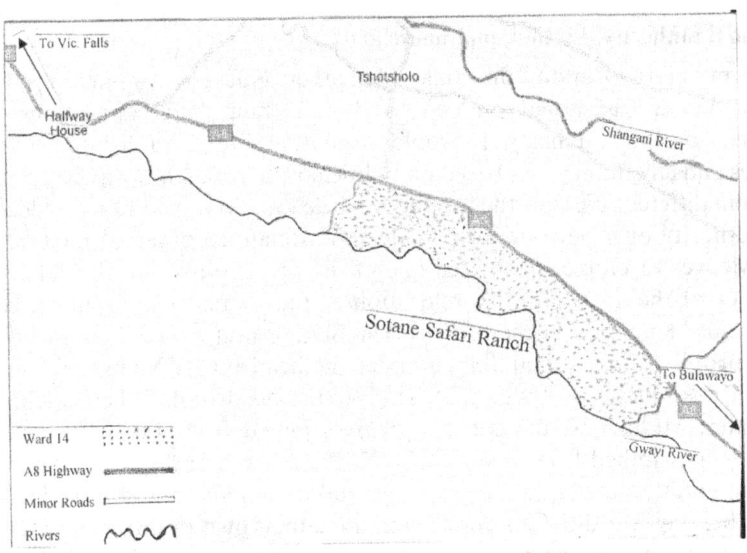

Figure 1. Map of Gwayi Valley, Menyezwa Ward 14 and surrounding area.[3]
Source: Adapted from Collins Maps (2011).

produced with moderate success. However, due to erratic rainfall and persistent droughts, crop failure is common. This territory, currently under Chief Mabhikwa Khumalo, experiences contrasting land fortunes, with some kraals experiencing severe land constraints and others being sparsely populated, with households laying claims to extensive tracts of both arable and abandoned land. The territory is an epitome of semi-proletarianism, characterised by high rates of labour migracy and dual households (Thebe 2009). It is rural but not remote – connected to centres of administration and employment by the A8 Highway. Given the climatic conditions, livelihoods are diversified but highly dependent on the formal and informal sectors, locally, in the cities and across the country's borders in Botswana and South Africa.

Now home to Ndebele-speaking households, the area was initially home to hunter-gathering San lineages, some of which remained and were absorbed into Ndebele culture. As noted in Thebe (2009), the area is a colonial legacy and a living example of displacement of Africans by the conquering white-settlers from their ancestral land. The Gwayi Valley was part of the Shangani Reserves, created for Ndebele groups, evicted from land expropriated for white settlement by the settler administration (Alexander, McGregor, and Ranger 2000; Moyana 1984). The households which relocated to the area after WW II had developed a semi-proletarian culture at their places of origin. Hence, Alexander, McGregor, and Ranger (2000) defined the people as the men of the store and the 'factories'. Land expropriation and the constraint exerted by the tenant system, had driven both males and females to the formal sector in Bulawayo. Given the above, at arrival in the reserves, the majority of males held formal jobs. Nevertheless, semi-proletarianisation was also exacerbated by a harsh new environment, and households' attempts to make sense of the environment and to adopt strategies for survival. More importantly, households also had the social networks, which became central in the movement and absorption of labour into the formal sector.

Traditional authority, kinship, and households

Despite proletarianisation, the area, like other Ndebele communities in former reserves, had a traditional outlook, and everything had connections to either chieftaincy or kraal dynasty. It would seem that the relationship between kraal dynasties and chieftaincy was based on political rather than kinship ties, since groups came from different parts of the former Ndebele kingdom, and resettled leaders were given authority over new areas or made subordinate to others (Lan 1985; Ranger 1982). Menyezwa Gumede, who led one of the first groups into the valley, held the chieftaincy of the area, until his relocation to the Zambezi escarpment, ceding the area to Chief Khumalo in the process. The Sivuwe households had joined Gumede and his people from Nyamandhlovu under the headship of Mahlwayi Ncube (after his death, his oldest son Sikhonzi took over the headship). Other Ndebele groups joined later: Mkhuzi Ncube and his relatives joined from Tshayile, while another Ncube dynasty joined from Insuza. The Ndebele invasion displaced the indigenous hunter-gathering San, but some San households remained and were incorporated into Ndebele culture, although they maintained their own traditional structure. Over time, the territory grew as headmen (*osabhuku*) enrolled more households.

What is interesting here is the development of a complex system of kraal building by different headmen in spite of the authority of the chief, who ideally controlled

Table 1. Kraal dynasties and kraal building.

Kraal	Composition	Origin	Gwayi Valley
Sivuwe	Households related to Ncube lineage	Nyamandlovu	-took in more householdson recommendations. -took over land left by households that relocated with Gumede -low population density
Tshayile	Households related to Ncube lineage	Tshayile	more relatives joined & more household members established own homes. -took in more households. -high population density.
Ngabetsha.	San households	San	-authority over Ngabesha lineage in Gumede -took in more households. -low population density.
Mathetshane		Inyathi	-arrived as a small group. -took in more people into his book -low population density

Source: Field data (2006).

land on behalf of the state (see Table 1). There is evidence that some kraals experienced rapid growth due to in-migration and disintegration of extended households, as land for both settlements and pastures became increasingly scarce. Other kraals grew rather slowly due to stricter regulations on in-migration. Among the four headmen, Sikhonzi appear to have adopted a stricter land allocation regime, with outsiders only offered land on references by other community members. It is therefore significant that the few households that joined the kraal were worker-peasants, mainly recommended by community members working in the city.

Emerging tenure relations

The current tenure relations in the area are communal, only because the statutes define them as such, but in practice landholding depicts Cheater's (1990, 189) observations that 'there are vast discrepancies between the ideologised models and the very different realities of both holding and use'. Basing my observations on the four kraals, I realised that, not all land was common property, and what appeared common to an outside was not common to households, both in definition and in use. The headman remained the custodian of the land and exercised the right to initial allocation, but once land was allocated, he relinquished all responsibility and claims over it. The households would exercise freedom of utilisation and disposal thereof.

Individualised ownership?

The first point of departure from the ideological model was that certain arrangements allowed communal land occupants to sell or rent-out their land, a process that Chimhowu and Woodhouse (2006, 1), term 'vernacular rural land sales and rental markets'. Such land sales were often disguised as compensation for the residential buildings, yet the package included all other land claims that the seller held. What is interesting here is that buyers came from the kraal in question – usually people from extended households, whose land needs could not be satisfied by the intra-household land redistribution system. The second point of departure was that once land was allocated to or purchased by a household, it became the property of the household, and the landholder had freedom to allocate it to other people, who included outsiders. Evidence suggests that households used their land allotment to create a network of relationships – they would allocate land to their members, relatives and acquaintances from outside the community. Thus, it was common practice for heads of households working in the cities to cede land within their land claims to working colleagues.

Of even greater interest in land transactions was the system of land leases between households, independent of the headman or any other authority. Land leases were made by households whose land exceeded their needs, either to locals or new households. However, land leases were not made to any person. Households would lease land to people they perceived to be of higher status – rich or influential in their own circles, particularly at places of work. In the event that an outsider was allocated land by a household, the role of the office of the headman was limited. Once the newcomer was presented to the kraal and approved by the kraal court, the headman would register the new household in the kraal register. Even then, land allocation remained the sole responsibility of the former and not the headman. Thus, through fission of land, the landholder would extend his social networks. In certain cases the newcomer was also leased a piece of cropping land by another household in the community. However, the leased land remained the property of the household that leased it out. Leases did not attract rent of any kind, and the leaser reserved the right to reclaim the land at a later stage. Nonetheless, through such land leases the leaser would build social contacts, which were key livelihoods decisions.

The third point of departure was that in the event that a household relocated from the kraal, the land did not revert to the kraal, but was often taken over by close relatives remaining in the community. Thus, households that held large land claims were households, which took-over land from relatives, and through the additional land, these households increased their chances of extending their social networks, and therefore, livelihood options. However, they would still release the land to descendants of relatives who relocated if they returned to reclaim the land. The final point of departure was that households' claims to land were not defined by clear boundaries, and they were not limited to the residential plot and fields, but extended to cover any arable land in the vicinity of the fields and residential plot. A household's landholding therefore depended on the distance between the household and its neighbours and the distance between their fields and neighbouring fields. Land claims differed from household to household. Households that originated from Nyamandlovu, Insuza and those of San origin, held extensive land claims (arable and fields), while the Tshayile households faced severe land stress (Thebe 2009).

Some households have held their land claims since they were established, while others acquired additional land after relatives left the community, and others still have divided their land between themselves and other household members. In this community and in Ndebele culture in general, household land is important for future expansion (Thebe 2009). Sons and other household members move on after marriage and are ceded land from the main household's landholding. It is interesting to note that intra-household land allocations did not require the approval of the headman, who was often informed of the allocation by the landholder. In this unprecedented situation, the new households were included in the kraal register. In a very real sense, these households were important in the livelihoods of the main household. These households were sources of remittances and support in the form of labour input, and in situations where the assets of the main household were obsolete; they provided the assets, which were critically important for agricultural production. Households often equated new households to an alternative investment:

> Children are our investment. We look after them when they are growing and they look after us when we are old. But in such a situation, proximity is important, and available land for their use keeps them closer to us. What will happen to us if we fail to provide them with land and they relocate? Here, where the harvest is poor, children provide the means for survival and to purchase agricultural inputs for the next planting season. More importantly, these children also own assets that are important in agricultural production. They also have the resources to rebuild livestock after a drought (interview, 13 July 2006).

Through collaborative and share-cropping arrangements, these assets were often pooled-together to the benefit of the whole kin network. However, the importance of labour-migrants as contacts in the cities, for kin in their search for jobs cannot be ignored (Thebe 2009).

Households' behaviour towards their land claims

Despite the fact that under the Communal Land Act (1982), the underlying principle of tenure was usufructuary rights rather than private possession (O'Flaherty 1998, 540), the behaviour of households towards their land claims depicted some form of ownership. In fact, a household would often refer to these claims as 'my place' (*indawo yami*). Thus, all households would hold onto land they abandoned (*amafusi*), and protect such land against any form of encroachment by other community members. Evidence suggests that the land was reserved for people, some working in the cities and even outside the country. Interestingly, some of these people working outside the community were educated, had no need for rural land and had their own city homes (interview, 27 July 2006). Unsurprisingly, reservation of land for people working outside the community was guided by the support – financially and materially – that the household received. Such a situation was also exacerbated by the old Ndebele tradition where only sons inherited land. From this perspective, widows would often refer to the home (and the land) as belonging to an absent son or sons.

It is therefore not surprising that well-off households fenced-off their land to prevent encroachment by their neighbours. A community elder confessed that fencing was an old practice in the community: ' ... households would also guard against any form of exploitation of resources in their arable land, and preserved flora and fauna' (interview, 27 July 2006). As a strategy of conservation, households would collect firewood from the commons rather than cut down trees in their land. They would also graze their cattle in the commons, reserving their land for emergency grazing. It is important to emphasise here that, although there were no physical demarcations separating one household's land claims from another, households knew where each claim ended. Without any physical boundaries, encroachments by some households into other households' land and land conflicts were common, usually resolved at kraal level.

What is of interest here is that these processes were not confined to a particular era, but did cut-across different phases in the administration of rural areas. Evidence points to an informal land ownership regime without official titles, justified through initial allocation and subsequent payment of taxes. It was ownership modified by households, yet unrecognised by policy-makers obsessed with the social engineering of rural lives. On average, over half the households owned *amafusi* at the time of research, and other households recognised such ownership. There were similarities in behaviour towards land between land-rich and land-poor households, with every formal land allocation enjoying endorsement from the traditional leadership. Household had rights to formal complaint in the event of encroachment, and cases of encroachment were often treated with disdain by the kraal.

Headmen and land administration

Land in the Gwayi area is held under the communal tenure system and this has been the system of landholding in the history of the area. The land-use patterns reflect the mixed agriculture model, with households being allocated residential stands and fields and also being allowed to keep livestock, where pastures are communally utilised. Despite administrative and political transformation since the 1950s, present tenure relations depart from the legal model embodied in the post-independence Communal Land Act (1982), and it would seem that traditional authority has stood the test of time. From the perspective of households, traditional leadership is and has always been the custodian of land, and no other authority enjoys an unquestioned right over land issues. The headman/households relationship is revealing for understanding the continued influence of traditional leaders in Zimbabwe's rural areas. Since the Ndebele occupation, kraals have never been associated with well-demarcated boundaries but were resource-owning units, representing households that were allied to a kraal dynasty. These households paid allegiance to a particular headman due to kinship ties or through his relatives through whom they acquired land.

It is significant that people in the area remembered the application of technical land-use management and modern agricultural practices because they have remained a visible reminder in their fields even today, but not the authority over land by the colonial District Commissioner. Through the system of indirect rule, headmen through kraal messengers were visible *de facto* colonial policemen in their communities, and monitored adherence to colonial land-use practices. For their part, households conformed to traditional authority and grudgingly accepted any form of sanctions, which were often passed by the kraal court (*inkundla*). It is important to emphasise here that courts were attended by all households and decisions were made after extensive deliberations. Thus, decisions were kraal decisions rather than headmen decisions. I identified three key periods in the administration of land in the area.

Table 2. Legislation and practice in land governance.

Time	Framework	Practice
Before	1969 Native Land Husbandry Act (NLHA 1951)	Custodian by headmen
1970–77	Tribal Trust Land Act (TTL 1969)	-Official administration by headmen
1977–80	Land Tenure Act	-Madiro (Zipra guerrillas introduce declare protected zones, & freedom of settlements -Households continued to consult their headmen on land matters.
1981–99	Communal Lands Act (1981)	-Parallel authority by traditional leaders -allocated land -endorsed intra-household land redistribution by households
	District Councils Act (1982)(Land admin by elected councils)	
		-VDCOs had no land to allocate
1999-	Traditional Leaders Act (1999)	-Legitimate land administration by chiefs & headmen.

Source: Field data (2006), legislations.

Ambiguity in land management

Colonial land administration in the Gwayi Valley portrayed the ambiguity inherent in the colonial administration's policy on the reserves as revealed in Ranger (1982) – the desire to implement the Native Land Husbandry Act and the regime's reliance on traditional leadership to bring about compliance in the reserves. There is evidence that some provisions of the NLHA were extensively implemented in the territory, characterised by contour ridging, storm drains and compulsory dipping of cattle. However, the most prominent were colonial land-use planning measures, particularly the separation of land according to areas of utilisation (the zoning system).

In the area, the authority of headmen over land and implementation of conservation measures remained visible, even before the enactment of the Tribal Trust Land Act of 1967. People approached their headmen for land and trusted their courts for the resolution of land disputes. The envisaged role of traditional authority in the management of communities emerges clearly in any discussions with senior citizens in the community:

> Headmen played central roles in managing their people and the land they occupied .... and their roles extended beyond land management and allocation. Through their messengers, they played a monitoring role in the implementation of conservation measures and the management of the commons. Households were expected to adhere to strict grazing patterns and time-tables. Headmen assumed the role of gate-keepers, declaring a particular zone open for utilisation or closed, and enforcing compliance through fines (interview, 17 August 2006).

With growing nationalism, their role became a major concern for nationalist leaders and guerrillas, and as the liberation war filtered into Lupane District, their position within the colonial system threatened to alienate them from their people. Their monitoring role had reduced them to Johnson (1992, 121)'s *de facto* government policemen in the countryside'. Sikhonzi Ncube was particularly singled out for being heavy handed in land administration – both allocation and management of pastures. A war veteran who operated in the area told me:

> He behaved like a little lord, treating land as his personal possession. He chose what land to allocate, what land to keep, and to whom land was allocated. He was too close to the colonial office and his people, and derived allegiance, through the kinship system, relationships built through inter-marriages and gratitude for land received (interview, 3 September 2006).

The war of liberation and the promotion of *madiro*

It was precisely their tag as '*de facto* policemen' that compromised their authority during the mid-1970s. As Cheater (1990) noted, by the turn of the decade, they had completely lost legitimacy, as the Zipra fighters operating in the area gave households rights to utilise land as they saw fit – a process called *madiro* in Shona terminology. According to guerrillas, land belonged to all citizens, and due to their history in land management, traditional leaders were seen as 'sell-outs' and enemies of the people and the struggle. In 1977 Headman Hlabangani in Menyezwa Village was thrown into a dip tank for his role in the colonial administration. In 1977 and 1978, Chief Mabhikwa Khumalo was subjected to armed attacks by guerrillas while for the duration of the war, Sikhonzi Ncube and his household were treated with suspicion, even though two members of his household had joined the liberation forces.

In the absence of a local monitoring agency, households abandoned all colonial land-use practices: they abandoned the zoning system; stopped contour-farming, and ploughed on existing storm drains (Thebe 2009). Zipra fighters also stopped people from taking their cattle to dip and instructed local youths to destroy the local dip tank, arguing that dip sessions were the basis for cattle culling. Even then, Zipra guerrillas did not interfere with existing patterns of landholding, leaving Sikhonzi and his household with large tracts of land, inherited from relatives who relocated with Chief Gumede. He thus, continued to allocate land to outsiders, especially kin and household friends. Households also maintained consultative relationships with him and other heads, although the courts could not sit. Despite the granting of *madiro*, random settlements remained unpopular in the areas occupied by the Sivuwe, Insuza and households of San origin, mainly because of the informal ownership arrangements. Due to these land ownership patterns, even unoccupied land had a community-recognised claimant. What became popular, however, was what officials would call the indiscriminate clearing of land for fields and gardens, without official land surveys and pegging. By independence in 1980, every household had extended its fields into arable land, abandoned parts of the officially pegged fields, and had a garden plot. It seems clear that land clearances were not clandestine but a response to environmental constraints. In a community like the Gwayi Valley, where soils are poor and climatic conditions uncertain, the quest for fertile land was part to a perpetual struggle.

Post-independence administrative reforms

After independence, the government passed the District Councils Act (1980) and the Communal Land Act (1982), the provisions of which transferred legal authority over communal areas to local government (Alexander 1994; O'Flaherty 1998). In the study area, authority lay with the Kusile District Council, thus officially relegated Chief Mabhikwa and his headmen to ceremonial figures. In addition, a 1984 Prime Ministerial directive established local development committees – the village and ward development committees (vidcos and wadcos) – as decentralised structures at the level of communities. Theoretically, the Communal Land Act transferred land administration to District Councils, which held the land in trust for communal area people (O'Flaherty 1998), with vidcos and wadcos providing the participation channels at local levels. In practice, the new framework remained ambiguous, and was difficult to implement in the absence of holistic changes in landholding. In the context of the study area, where previous allocations were treated as personal possessions, there was little land available for allocation by vidcos and wadcos. It is ironic that people in the new structures had a stake in the *status quo* – they held land in the community, and like others, they also had fenced-off their land allotments, which they continued to utilise alternately as a strategy to avoid the allocation being revoked under the new regulations. Unsurprisingly, they did not challenge the *status quo*, and were content with the role of organising occasional 'Food for Work' programmes, while the real power remained with a distant authority, which households struggled to associate with, thereby leaving a power gap at local level. It is interesting to note that headmen and households continued to exercise their pre-war rights over land. This is illustrated by the number of households that Sikhonzi took-up between 1982 and 1990, and those brought to the community by other households during the same period.[4] Households also continued to consult their headmen on land-related issues, ignoring the elected councillors, vidcos and wadcos.

It would seem that the local authority ignored the continued encroachment by traditional leaders into what was legally council domain or it did not have the capacity to intervene. The first point to note is that due to conflict over borders and resources, the amalgamated Rural District Council Act of 1988 only saw implementation in June 1993 (Alexander 1994). The second relates to conflict between policy and central government actions with regards to the traditional system. As Alexander (1994, 328) noted: 'the central government instituted or perpetuated a number of measures which retained chiefs' status if not, initially, their late colonial powers'. But in the area, vidco structures were superimposed on structures that for long, had defined community relations. For example, the first vidco chairperson was the wife to the heir-apparent to the Ngabetsha kraal dynasty, and given the complex web of relationships, other people in the new structures had links with the other three dynasties. Clearly, the difficulties in implementing the new regime were inherent in the very structure of communal areas, and the semi-proletarian culture that had emerged. Thus, the answer to the administrative difficulties rested on radical reforms of communal areas, which came in the form of an internal resettlement package (villagisation) between 1985 and 1989 (Alexander 1994; O'Flaherty 1998).

It needs to be stressed that while the traditional system was seen as impeding on this new thinking on communal areas (Alexander 1994, 333), the government made a complete policy u-turn and re-instated the power of traditional leaders through the Traditional Leaders Act in 1998. Thus, land allocation was to be exercised in consultation with the relevant traditional structures (Mohamed-Katerere 2003). Again, in the area, at least the statute merely gave legal backing to functions that headmen and the kraals were already performing. Although all the substantive headmen had died, the kraal courts still functioned through acting appointments (Thebe 2009). It is important to emphasise here that land requests or allotments, whether by households or the headmen, were subject to endorsement by the kraal.

However, if the act signified government intentions to return the governance of communal areas to traditional leaders, it was also an attempt to institutionalise rural governance along the new thinking on communal areas. At local level, section 8 of the act authorised the chief to nominate headmen, who were duly appointed by the Minister of Local Government and Public Works. Instead, largely on the basis of these nominations and appointments, an inflated traditional structure of seven kraals of 25 households each, replaced the four traditional dynasties in the study area. Even some of these heads, particularly those outside the traditional dynasties, were left with no land to administer and less than 25 households under their jurisdiction. In the absence of guidelines to allocate households to cell settlements, and boundaries between administrative units, households had the freedom to choose where to belong and to leave when it suited them. In theory, by virtue of his/her appointment, each headmen administered households in his/her kraal register on behalf of the chief, but in practice the authority of the three headmen outside the traditional dynasties, remains hollow. They convened meetings, collected levies and purchased grain on behalf of households, but households still managed their land allotments as private property. Thus, they continued to allocate land for both residence and fields to their members and relatives from outside the community, and headmen continued to register these new households and to collect levies. Nonetheless, land transactions remained social rather than economical, with landholders deriving no direct financial returns from the transactions.

Conclusion

How do we fit the post-colonial state's communal area reorganisation project into this process of negotiation and manipulation? Did the project reflect the new culture that emerged in rural communities like the Gwayi Valley or did it accommodate some aspects? The answer to these questions is no, because it was not meant to. Rural development policies are generally formulated based on assumptions about how processes take place in rural communities, and in most cases, policies are designed to reshape these processes to reflect the interests and views of policy formulators. However, these rural processes, especially models of land-use that emerge after years of constant negotiation are complex and unique to each context. They represent Scott (1990, 4)'s 'hidden transcripts', are guided by certain constraints and experiences, and stand apart from the 'public transcripts' or what policy-makers consider to be the ideal. There was no room for the consideration of the hidden transcripts in the post-colonial state's internal resettlement project. The policy process more generally, revealed a complex rural development agenda, supported by a range of ideological positions that did not necessarily reflect the situation on the ground for the majority of rural Zimbabwe. The policy was mainly dictated by the hand of the 'invisible ghost' of the country's history of technical development and the accompanying assumptions about traditional agricultural systems. The historical process of land disenfranchisement and neglect gave the political leaders legitimacy to impose their visions and ideologies on the rural populace. Following Scott (1998, 3), the post-colonial state's rural vision could be equated to 'abridged maps', which failed to successfully represent the actual activity of society they depicted, but represented only that slice of it that interested the visionary policy formulators.

Notes

1. In an attempt to understand new environments and to construct strategies of survival, new realities emerge in rural communities and replace what is generally considered as ideal by officials. The story of the Zimbabwean worker-peasantry is one of resilience. The worker-peasantry has refused to die in communal areas of Zimbabwe, even in the face of adversity and appears to be on the rise. This is a class with distinct land needs and distinct livelihoods, and my story focuses on their strategies of survival and resilience.
2. The act provided for the nomination and appointment of headmen by the chief and Minister of Local Government & Public Works, respectively. In line with other reforms in communal areas, kraals were streamlined into units of 25 households each. Thus, traditional kraal dynasties had to shed some households to appointed headmen.
3. Ward boundaries are arbitrary, based on the number of households rather than whole communities. Even then these have shifted markedly since the launch of the post-colonial local government project. This has implications on the boundary used here. Also, the boundary represents communal land as of 2006, after the land north of the A8 was taken over by the Shangani River Valley Pilot Grazing Scheme.
4. In total there were 12 new households during the period, all categorised as internal allocations. No allocation was made to outsiders by the council through the local representatives, the vidcos and wadcos.

Note on contributor

Vusilizwe Thebe is associated with the Department of Development Studies, National University of Lesotho, Roma 180, Lesotho.

References

Adams, J. 1999. Review of James Scott, seeing like a state: How certain schemes to improve human conditions have failed (Michigan: Thomson Shore). *Rural History* 10, no. 2: 261–3

Alexander, J. 1994. State, peasantry and resettlement in Zimbabwe. *Review of African Political Economy* 61: 325–45.

Alexander, J., J. McGregor, and T. Ranger. 2000. *Violence and memory: One hundred years in the dark years in the 'Dark Forests' of Matabeleland*. Oxford: James Currey.

Arrighi, G. 1970. Labour supplies in historical perspective: A study of the proletarianization of the African peasantry in Rhodesia, *Journal of Development Studies* VI: 198–233.

Bernstein, H. 2004. 'Changing before our very eyes': Agrarian question and the politics of land in capitalism today. *Journal of Agrarian Change* 4, nos: 1 & 2: 190–225.

Berry, S. 2002. Debating the land question in Africa. *Comparative Studies in Society and History* 44: 638–68.

Bush, R., and L. Cliffe. 1984. Agrarian policy in migrant labour societies: Reform or transformation in Zimbabwe? *Review of African Political Economy* 29: 77–94.

Chaumba, J., I. Scoones, and W. Wolmer. 2003. From Jambanja to planning: The reassertion of technocracy in South-Eastern Zimbabwe? *Journal of Modern African Studies* 41, no. 4533–4.

Chavunduka Commission, Government of Zimbabwe. 1982. *Report of the commission of inquiry into the agricultural industry*. Harare: Government Printers.

Cheater, A. 1990. The ideology of communal land tenure in Zimbabwe: Mythogenesis enacted? *Africa* 60, no. 2: 188–206.

Chimhowu, A., and P. Woodhouse. 2006. Customary vs private property rights? Dynamics and trajectories of vernacular land markets in Sub-Saharan Africa. *Journal of Agrarian Change* 6, no. 3: 346–71.

Cordell, D.D., J.W. Gregory, and V. Piché. 1996. *Hoe and wage: A social history of a circular migration system in West Africa*. Boulder, CO: Westview Press.

Drinkwater, M. 1988. The state and agrarian change in Zimbabwe's communal areas: An application of critical theory. PhD diss., Norwich: University of East Anglia.

Drinkwater, M. 1989. Technical development and peasant impoverishment: Land use policy in Zimbabwe's Midlands province. *Journal of Southern African Studies* 15, no. 2: 287–305.

Duggan, W.R. 1990. The Native Land Husbandry Act of 1951 and the rural African middle class of southern Rhodesia. African Affairs 79, no. 315: 227–340.

Gasper, D. 1988. Rural growth points and rural industries in Zimbabwe: Ideologies and policies. *Development and Change* 19: 425–66.

Government of Zimbabwe. 1986. *First Five Year National Development Plan, 1986–90, 1*. Harare: Government Printers.

Johnson, D. 1992. Settler farmers and coerced African labour in southern Rhodesia, 1936–46. *The Journal of African History* 33, no. 1: 111–28.

Lan, D. 1985. *Guns and rain: Guerrillas and spirit mediums in Zimbabwe*. London: James Currey.

Mohamed-Katerere, J. 2003. Participatory natural resources management in the communal lands of Zimbabwe: What role for customary law?*African Studies Quarterly* 5, no. 3. http://web.africa.ufl.edu/asq/v5/v5i3a7.htm.

Moyana, H.V. 1984. *The political economy of land in Zimbabwe*. Gweru: Mambo Press.

O'Flaherty, M. 1998. Communal tenure in Zimbabwe: Divergent models of collective land holding in the communal areas. *Africa* 68, no. 4: 537–57.

Okoth, A. 2006. *African nationalism and the decolonisation process*. Nairobi. East African Educational Publishers Press.

Penman, H.L. 1948. Natural evaporation from open water, bare soil, and grass. *Proceedings of the Royal Society of London A* 193: 120–45.

Phimister, I. 1993. Rethinking the reserves: Southern Rhodesia's Land Husbandry Act Review. *Journal of Southern African Studies* 19, no. 2: 225–39.

Potts, D. 2000. Worker-peasants and farmer-housewives in Africa: The debate about 'committed farmers', access to land and agricultural production. *Journal of Southern African Studies* 26, no. 4: 807–32.

Potts, D., and C. Mutambirwa. 1990. Rural-urban linkages in contemporary Harare: Why migrants need their land. *Journal of Southern African Studies* 16, no. 4: 677–98.

Prescott, J.R.V. 1961. Overpopulation and overstocking in native areas of Matabeleland. *The Geographical Journal* 127, no. 2: 212–25.

Ranger, T.O. 1982. Tradition and travesty: Chiefs and the administration in Makoni District, Zimbabwe, 1960–80. *Africa* 52, no. 3: 20–41.

Riddell Commission, Government of Zimbabwe. 1981. *Report of the commission of inquiry into incomes, prices and conditions of service*. Harare: Government Printers.

Scott, J.C. 1990/98. *Domination and the arts of resistance Hidden transcripts*. London: Yale University Press.

Scott, J.C. 1998. *Seeing like a state: How certain schemes to improve human conditions have failed*. Michigan: Thomson Shore.

Thebe, V. 2009. *Searching for a new rural development narrative: Rural reality and the state's peasant models in Zimbabwe's land reform policy (1980–2003)*. Koln: LAP.

Thompson, G. 2004/2007. Cultivating conflict: Agricultural 'betterment', the Native Land Husbandry Act (NLHA) and ungovernability in colonial Zimbabwe, 1951–1962. *African Development* XXIX, no. 3: 1–39.

Thompson, G. 2007. Is it lawful for people to have their things taken away by force? High modernism and ungovernability in colonial Zimbabwe. *African Studies* 66, no. 1: 39–77.

Weinrich, A.K.H. 1975. *African farmers in Rhodesia: Old and new peasant communities in Karangaland.* London: Oxford University Press.

Wolmer, W., and I. Scoones. 2000. The science of 'civilized' agriculture: The mixed farming discourse in Zimbabwe. *African Affairs* 99: 575–600.

Worby, L.E. 2001. A redivided land? New agrarian conflicts and questions in Zimbabwe. *Journal of Agrarian Change* 1, no. 4: 475–509.

Yeros, P. 2002. Zimbabwe and the dilemmas of the left. Historical Materialism 10, no. 2: 3–15.

Yudelman, M. 1964. *Africans on land: Economic problems of African agricultural development in Southern Africa, with special reference to southern Rhodesia.* London: Oxford University Press.

Two perspectives on Zimbabwe's National Democratic Revolution: Thabo Mbeki and Wilfred Mhanda

David Moore

Department of Anthropology and Development Studies, University of Johannesburg, South Africa

> The concept of the 'National Democratic Revolution' (NDR) is often used by left-leaning scholars and political actors in attempts to explain or justify the lack of socialism in third-world societies governed by rulers who consider themselves 'scientific socialists'. It has been invoked in analyses of Zimbabwe by both the former president of South Africa, Thabo Mbeki, in 2001 as he was embarking on his 'quiet diplomacy', and Wilfred Mhanda, a Zimbabwean guerrilla leader imprisoned by the Mozambican government in the late-1970s for posing problems to the leadership aspirations of Robert Mugabe, who later became president of the country posing problems for Thabo Mbeki among others. Analysis of both these political intellectuals' writing sheds light on the concept of the NDR (evoked often in contemporary South African politics and Zimbabwean discourse about the current crisis) as well as the theoretical and practical aspects of the authors' careers.

In early 2000, shortly before his death the next year, Govan Mbeki – once National Chairman of the African National Congress, executive member of the South African Communist Party, Secretary of *Umkhonto we Sizwe*, author of the classic *Peasant Revolt in South Africa* (1964), and father of the man who was then President of the Republic of South Africa – presented an evening lecture to students of a part-time MA in Politics programme at the then University of Port Elizabeth,[1] in the city where 'OomGov' resided. One of the students asked the 90-year-old struggle veteran, who had held the class spellbound with his tales of espionage and analysis of modern South African history for nearly an hour, what he felt about the progress of South Africa's 'National Democratic Revolution' (NDR). He replied with 'the National Democratic Revolution takes a long time'. Another asked the well-practised raconteur to reflect upon the disagreements he and Nelson Mandela had encountered during the days approaching South Africa's democratic denouement, when according to folklore the two icons had stopped speaking to each other because Govan Mbeki espoused a longer struggle in order to bring socialism somewhat closer to fruition whilst Mandela was happy to see a quicker end to violence and warfare. Mbeki – criticised by some as a 'Stalinist' – replied that he and the purportedly more liberal Mandela 'debated' the fate of their movement with mutual respect and decorum: they never stopped talking about strategy and tactics, and out of robust arguments a better movement would evolve. Yet one more student wondered what 'OomGov' would do if he were in his elder son's shoes: he answered that they were probably too big for the father, but that Thabo Mbeki seemed to fit into his footwear quite well.

The concept of the NDR is invoked often by African nationalists with a Marxist orientation. It appears to be born out of Marx and Engels' recognition that socialism needed capitalism's productive forces (including 'modern' rationality superseding the superstitious super-structures of pre-capitalist modes of production) to be exhausted by their own contradictions before the promised land could appear on the horizon. But given the apparent success of Marxist-Leninism in societies where capitalism was only partially started (such as in Russia and, later, China), something for the revolutionary project inspired by its intellectual fountainheads had to be rescued for the colonies and other underdeveloped social formations. These nascent leaders were struggling for 'national' independence or for their capitalist energies to be unbound from those of the 'imperialist' economies, be they colonial or neo-colonial in form – and/or for socialism (even though it may have been prefaced by a particularity called 'African' in some cases). Stalin's proposition that there could be 'socialism in one country' made the aspiration of many revolutionaries seem achievable: they would not have to wait until the whole world reached the pinnacles of capitalist development (starting in the 'west' and finishing in a mimicked form somewhere other than that) but they could direct their societies in a socialist direction with a combination of concerted state action and the nurturing of their proletariat, which remained the true reservoir of socialism. The NDR was but another stage on the way to socialism and then the communist utopia. This would require a form of what might now be called 'the developmental state', which would dispense with notions of the 'free market' – and thus imperialist intervention – in varying degrees, creating the conditions and/or substituting for the national and patriotic bourgeoisie. To nurture the proletariat would require the right (or rather, left) thinking intellectual, political and cultural vanguard running the development state to contrive a judicious combination of rigorous socialist leadership with the requisite amount of democracy allowing the proletariat to develop the capacity to lead the state and society one day in the (not too distant) future, and simultaneously to build up the forces of production. Even without a fully developed working class (part and parcel of the contradictions of capitalism, of course), the intelligentsia in control of the state could at least become 'socialist-oriented'. During the Cold War this could be facilitated by the correct foreign-policy choices: third world social formations would be well on the way if they chose the Soviet Union to assist them along the path towards 'socialist oriented states' (Chirkin and Yudin 1978) or, less excitedly, the 'non-capitalist path' (Solodovnikov and Bogoslovsky 1975), as advised by the 'scientific socialist' analysis on Africa coming out of Moscow's Progress Press. If after the mid-1960s they happened to favour the Maoist brand of the NDR (or vice versa: if Beijing favoured them) they could make the necessary noises against the 'social imperialism' emanating from Moscow, but still maintain adherence to the NDR.

The difficulties of managing this project even in the best of times are apparent: for example, when do restrictions on freedom for capital turn into the repression of the working class? It is not hard to see why Govan Mbeki answered that the NDR will take a long time to reach fulfilment, nor is it difficult to foresee many twists, turns and potholes on that road.

Yet during the Cold War, when many people of Govan Mbeki's generation and those succeeding it – his son Thabo Mbeki, for example (Gevisser 2007) – learned their politics, the NDR's problems were not foremost in their minds: its prospects were. Most colonialists – especially those of a 'special type' in South Africa and other settler-colonies (Slovo 1976) – were hardly democrats, so liberalism always held hypocritical hues of privilege, and the travesties of Stalinism and Maoism were barely known: the USSR and China were sources of ideological and material sustenance. Perhaps, too, the legacy of American New Deals and Labour's British form of socialism suggested that developmental statism, welfarism, and democracy could be combined anywhere. Today, however, the socialist USSR is but a figment of history and so too might be the social democratic project in capitalist societies (Judt 2008), so the NDR problematic would appear to be more vexed than ever.

However, there are many leaders and intellectuals in the 'third world' – much younger than the late Govan Mbeki – still steeped in the hopes that their societies can escape the ravages of capitalism as it moves into its frontiers, and bound intellectually to the NDR's precepts. In South Africa, for example, the NDR holds considerable purchase within the South African Communist Party, as well as – but with more trepidation – for many in the third member of the 'triple alliance', the Congress of South African Trade Unions. Many on the left outside of the tense troika (or inside, but not fully convinced that it is the way forward) also hinge their debates on the NDR, whether in praise or condemnation. As Pillay (2011) has put it, left critics worry about the NDR legitimating 'conservative class interests – a coalition of white and emerging comprador black capital... and a professional black middle class' while deceiving the 'organised working class... into supporting the ANC against their own class interests'. Its defenders, however, say that triple alliance's use of NDR ideology helps keep it glued together: otherwise the interests of the working class and the poor would be lost in a fragmented and 'dangerously fractious contest over resources' only benefiting 'predatory right-wing forces' (Pillay 2011, 31–2).[2] It is safe to say that in a context of decreasing democracy and increasing inequality, holding on to the NDR may entail many contortions. Nonetheless, it offered much theoretical sustenance to those waging liberation wars against colonialism yet wanting more substance at the end of the battle than a mere changing of the governing guard.

Thus Govan Mbeki's words are still relevant to anyone equating the concept of 'progress' in Africa with something approaching social justice and even socialist democracy. The road to these ends will not be travelled overnight, the route should be debated democratically – and rigorously – and it is not too wise to try to put on the shoes of those with the task of pursuing the NDR. They might be too small and cramped to apply the necessary pressure on the brake pedals, or too big and clumsy to negotiate clutch and accelerator as many downward and upward gear shifts are executed. The trials and tribulations of the NDR are many: too much democracy and/or socialism can lead to 'ultra-leftism' and too much statism can lead to authoritarianism and the construction of a 'state bourgeoisie' known for its consumerist excesses and bureaucratic sloth – not to mention corruption – instead of applying a Protestant work ethic to the grindstone of industrialised productivity.[3] Too much 'realism' can lead to making the necessity of capitalist policies – even neo-liberalism – a virtue, while exalting 'democracy' on its own can result in idealism cloaked in liberalism.[4] When all fails to rally, one is left with the fig-leaf of patriotism and sovereignty, the last refuges of scoundrels and scholars,[5] more often than not wrapping up a retreat (especially in the once-colonies of a special type) into the discourse of racial redress (Southall 2004, 2008).

This article will attempt to discuss two conceptions of the 'NDR' applied to Zimbabwe. One is an essay by Thabo Mbeki, written while he was embarking on his 'quiet diplomacy' vis-a-vis Zimbabwe as South Africa's president and 'facilitator' for the Southern African Development Community's (SADC) efforts to bring peace and good government to its region (Mbeki 2001).[6] The second is from the maelstrom of Zimbabwe's war of liberation, in the form of a 'prison notebook' by a young cadre sent to Mozambique's prisons for daring to challenge Robert Mugabe's conception of the war's way forward (Mhanda 1978, 2011; Moore 1995a, 1995b, forthcoming). The two perspectives will be compared: they share much, although Mhanda's emphasises 'democracy' more than Mbeki's, while 'sovereignty' and 'race' are given less import than the former president's. The proof is in the pudding, too. Mhanda pursued the notion of democracy consistently throughout Zimbabwe's post-2000 era while Mbeki arguably did not. Whether this has more to do with the theory than other factors is open to questions that are not within the purview of this article.

The NDR in Zimbabwe: Mbeki's view

Not long after Zimbabwe re-entered the rest of the world's consciousness with its land invasions in early 2000 and June elections nearly putting the first effective Zimbabwean opposition party into power (Moore 2001), the relatively new president of South Africa turned his mind to the increasingly repressive and economically nose-diving country on his northern borders. His first – and as yet only, aside from short letters to some of his critics in Zimbabwe's Movement for Democratic Change (MDC)[7] – sustained intellectual intervention on the nature of the Zimbabwean crisis is a mid-2001 'discussion document' of 29 pages entitled 'How Will Zimbabwe Defeat Its Enemies!', circulated as part of a much longer policy compendium to members of the African National Congress. Stephen Chan describes the essay as a 'long letter' to Mugabe that is almost 'pastoral', but very critical (2011, 97–8). Most important for the purposes of this article, however, is the way in which it applies the nostrums of the NDR to Zimbabwe.[8]

According to Mbeki the first stage of the NDR in Zimbabwe is complete. 'The struggle for liberation from foreign and white minority rule and the establishment of a national democratic state' have been accomplished, 'with ZANU-PF at the helm' (2001, 370).[9] The second phase must bring 'poverty and underdevelopment among the formerly colonised masses' to an end, bridging the gaps 'between the formerly colonised and the former colonisers in terms of wealth, income and opportunity'. The 'political' part of this phase must further entrench democracy by increasing the involvement of the 'masses of the people in the system of governance, while ensuring the continued allegiance of the masses of the people to the party of revolution' (Mbeki 2001, 371). Zimbabwe had failed, said Mbeki, on both of these counts – over half the population had lost faith in the ruling party, and the party had come very close to destroying the economy through a form of public profligacy born of trying to 'bribe' the masses. ZANU-PF had become prey to the wishes of the only source of support it had left: the 'lumpen-proletariat' war veterans (Mbeki 2001, 385). It had better wake up, hasten the democratic process (even to the extent of having free and fair elections!), listen to the advice of the International Monetary Fund, and make its peace with white capital. The further stages of the revolution were still a long way off, and would not start until these basic steps had been taken.

Aside from the fact that Mbeki failed to do much to implement his advice, the document has provisos that make these claims less than genuine. His warnings about how anti-revolutionary forces were in prime position to take advantage of ZANU-PF's setbacks seem to caution against going too far down the democratic road. These forces, Mbeki indicates, are not just opposed to the way in which ZANU-PF has ruled Zimbabwe, but are against the ideas of the NDR in and of themselves. They do so because they elevate 'property rights over the very right to life', but also because the people who lost their property in Zimbabwe were their 'kith and kin' there and in the 'rest of southern Africa' – that is, in South Africa too. These people 'have decided, internationally, that they are opposed to Zimbabwe's party of revolution', basing 'this determination on the assessment that the party is anti-democratic and therefore does not respect the rule of law...equally, it does not respect human rights'. According to Mbeki these forces 'control the means of communication', so will influence and 'entrench' global views of Zimbabwe. They 'interpret...both the leader of the party of revolution and the party itself [as] a force for dictatorship and the corrupt abuse of power' and 'neither the party of revolution or the national democratic [sic] has the capacity to defeat this offensive' (2001, 391).

Yet, seemingly to reverse this pessimistic forecast, Mbeki claims that ZANU-PF could be resurrected if it worked really hard to mobilise all the social forces in Zimbabwe who would benefit objectively from the NDR. This includes every social group – 'all the people of Zimbabwe' is repeated, including white commercial farmers – with the 'support of the Cupertino [sic: old Micrsoft spell-checks turned unhyphenated "co-operation" into Cupertino, the centre of Silicon Valley!] of the international community' (2001, 393).[10] However, the subjective element could be the determining one: Mbeki warned of 'committed forces of racism in Zimbabwean society' which must be 'isolated' to 'ensure their final historic defeat'. Not all whites are included in these remnants, but the committed racists do have a 'natural historical base' in 'the minority that benefited from colonialism and racism' and continue to be privileged today – including (again) white commercial farmers. Mbeki emphasises that the 'material interests' of the 'major sections' (2001, 393-4, my emphasis) of the whites are on the side of the NDR (although he does not elucidate why), and therefore can be won over to ZANU-PF's side, but 'the erstwhile colonial forces' opposing the 'party of revolution' will be encouraged by the results of the 2000 constitutional referendum (in which ZANU-PF lost its wager) and election results which gave the MDC the ability 'to position itself internationally, as the credible successor' to the ruling party (2001, 393-4).

There is much blurring when the 'subjective' and 'objective' meet – or do not. Mbeki's advice was for ZANU-PF to implement a social contract around the Pollyannish Zimbabwe Millennium Economic Recovery Programme, and above all it must 'avoid driving away anyone both domestically and externally...it will have to accept that resort to anti-imperialist rhetoric will not solve the problems Zimbabwe is facing' (2001, 396, 398). However – aside from the fact that Mbeki did very little to advance his embracing ideas in Zimbabwe – his theoretical slippages made his interpretation of the NDR very weak. By linking the unclearly identified last redoubts of racism with an equally shadowy international group opposed to ZANU-PF – and saying that this group controls the 'means of communication' – Mbeki verged on the sort of thinking that had HIV-AIDS invented by the international pharmaceutical industry. There is more than just the title 'How will Zimbabwe Defeat its Enemies!' to indicate a sense of conspiracy that would allow Robert Mugabe to go his own way. Mbeki's theory of the 'NDR' slips between 'race' and 'nation', and verges on the same 'kith and kin' discourse as Mugabe's. Mbeki's NDR did not have to travel far until the Movement for Democratic Change was a puppet manipulated by 'the west', key elements of which valued property rights more than human rights. In spite of an intellectual edifice of neo-liberal platitudes there was very little, ideologically speaking, that separated Mbeki's NDR from Mugabe's Third Chimurenga.

Zimbabwe's NDR: 'Dzino's' View

In 1978 a young Zimbabwean expelled from ZANU's camps in Mozambique for appearing to challenge Robert Mugabe's nascent hegemony, wrote 'A Treatise on Zimbabwe's National Liberation Struggle: Some Theoretical Problems' (Mhanda 1978). Although framed in quite abstract and historical terms, the 35,000 word treatise is at its heart an attempt to explain to himself and his comrades in the short-lived Zimbabwe People's Army why they had been imprisoned by the new Mozambican government on behalf of the leaders of the Zimbabwean liberation movement (especially Robert Mugabe) who had arisen, Phoenix-like, from the ashes of détente[11] (Moore 1995a, 1995b, forthcoming). Wilfred Mhanda – named during the war as Dzinishe 'Dzino' Machingura – has published his memories of these and other events (2011) with light ideological varnish,[12] but the treatise is an effort to explain the history and politics of the Zimbabwean struggle for national liberation in terms of the Marxist frameworks on offer to intellectually curious guerrilla cadres: in Mhanda's case, at the time these consisted of many leftist works gathered at Dar es Salaam's bookstores, in the camps, and some 'formal' instructions in basic Maoism of the 'red book' sort, added to by a trip to China in the early years of his induction into the higher realms of ZANU's military hierarchy.

'A Treatise' does not begin with a celebration of Zimbabwe's 'party of revolution' passing Stage 1 successfully: rather, it starts with a very negative prognosis:

> The Zimbabwean national liberation struggle has been beset by monolithic problems ever since the advent of African nationalism.... These problems have hitherto arrested the full development of the liberation struggle. Little or insignificant development has been made in terms of concrete realisation of the basic goals of African nationalism; political power has not been transferred to the nationalists nor have any significant compromises been made to increase their representation and participation in organs of power and the decision-making process.... The Zimbabwe African nationalist movement has, since its inception, been characterised by intense political inertia punctuated by a series of setbacks manifest in the frustrated hopes of the nationalists and periodic dislocation of action programmes. The gains that have so far materialised have been incommensurate with the costly human and material sacrifices. The movement has also been rocked by factional recriminations that have only served to misdirect and dissipate efforts. Consequent on these setbacks, the nationalist movement has shown great pliability to manipulation by imperialists, falling victim to one imperialist manoeuvre

after another, with costly and unpalatable consequences for the development of the nationalist struggle (Mhanda 1978, 1).

There is no effort here to paste over difficulties with bromides, even in the opening paragraphs. Here the language of 'scientific socialism' bears some resemblance to Mbeki's essay: Mhanda promises an 'objective' historical analysis of Zimbabwe and its nationalist movements 'discussed against the background of a brief analysis of the social character of Zimbabwe; the principal determinant of the nature of the struggle to be waged to achieve victory'. Indeed, 'a broad conception of the problems of the nationalist struggle in their proper historical perspective' is needed to realise 'the direction in which the subjective efforts of the national liberation struggle have to be channeled to achieve victory'. In fact, Mhanda writes that such 'awareness creates an objective platform from which a critical, sober and scientific analysis of the current course of the liberation struggle can be made', and the 'subjective efforts of the national liberation struggle' can be guided to the strategy and tactics that will lead to victory (1978, 1). Without this, the nationalist movement will 'inevitably' stagger 'from blunder to blunder in search of an elusive victory' (1978, 2). In other words, theoretical and historical reflection has material consequences. The intellectuals – perhaps 'organic' ones; perhaps hubristically – may contribute to the power that can change the world; scientific knowledge has objective force. Although Mhanda's treatise is chock full of recognition of the power of 'international monopoly capital', with the 'white minority settlers' in a form of 'double economic domination' (1978, 4–6), there is enough subjectivity in his analysis to suggest that even peripheral capitalist countries do not have to bow to the will of the IMF, etc., contrary to the 'science' Mbeki offered in his analysis.

After analysing the early history of Rhodesia and African resistance (the first resistance to Rhodes was 'waged on a national plane and within the framework of traditional society'), Mhanda's class analysis follows the 'phases in the development of capitalism and the relative development of the urban areas': '... workers, intellectuals and petty-bourgeoisie' were 'awakened ... to the consciousness of social injustices brought about by the racist white minority rule'. As early as 1911, 'this awareness generated popular discontent among the African elite and organizations championing the cause of the African elite and workers were formed' (1978, 14–5), albeit without a broad base and a national character. By the end of World War II, however, in the context of an altered global configuration and more radicalism in neighbouring colonies, what Mhanda calls 'passive African nationalism' (1978, 15) emerged in Rhodesia between 1945 and 1956. Trade unions 'mushroomed', as did urban residents' associations such as the African Youth League. It was not until 1957 however, that with the formation of the African National Congress 'active reformist nationalism' (1978, 16) took hold.[13] Its reformism was predicated on its hopes that their political objectives could be fulfilled 'on the basis of harmonious cooperation between Africans and the Europeans': this 'continued to cast a dark shadow on the revolutionary commitment of the African Nationalists' – even until, it is written between the lines, Mhanda put pen to paper (1978, 17). Even when the nationalist movements took the tactic of sabotage on board, this 'did not represent a shift to the strategy of confrontation with the settler authorities but only served to accentuate the pressure in search of a constitutional settlement', as did the 'increase in the number of industrial strikes, protest marches, political demonstrations and more civil disobedience in both the urban and rural areas' (1978, 18). This was enough, however, for the Rhodesian state to clamp down, forcing the by then widely known Zimbabwe African People's Union (essentially the same party as the African National Congress: the regime's banning of parties simply encouraged the birth of new ones) to go underground.

With subterranean activity, however, came the split in the nationalist movement that has dogged Zimbabwe's modern history. Mhanda pours ice-cold water over the assertion that the people who formed the party that went on to rule Zimbabwe were in any way more 'radical' than ZAPU.[14]

> There is no evidence to suggest that the split was a consequence of any major differences in political strategy other than personality differences and minor difference in emphasis in tactics within the general framework of pressure and leverage strategy against the racist settler minority rule. Any claim to the contrary, suggestive of deep seated ideological contradictions or any fundamental difference in strategy are completely without foundation and not borne by subsequent developments. Up to this moment in the national liberation struggle, the two organisations have an identical ideological outlook and the development of their strategic concepts has closely followed the same pattern corresponding in both time and content (1978, 19).

Rather than 'new or radical political developments on the political scene' the split served only to produce 'mutual hostilities and bloody vendettas' threatening 'to paralyse the nationalist movement and engulfed it in bitter political recriminations' (1978, 19). This diverted the 'political energy and attention of the African masses to...partisan political squabbles' that 'played into the hands of the racist settler authorities who watched with glee and folded arms as the two sides slugged each other in the African townships' (1978, 19). Combined with this, Ian Smith's Unilateral Declaration of Independence in 1965 brought the first phase of 'active nationalism' to an end. Mhanda's judgement up to then was damning: compared to 'the achievements of other nationalist movements elsewhere in Africa, the Zimbabwean nationalist movement had been a remarkable failure', calling for a 'review of strategy in political struggle given the peculiarity of the Rhodesian situation' (1978, 19).

After UDI, the nationalist leaders considered the armed struggle more seriously, but still with the hopes of it adding to the pressure for a constitutionally altered settlement led by the British, by 'fomenting internal disorder through widespread sabotage activities and isolated military action' thereby encouraging British intervention. From 1966 to 1970 sporadic military actions took place in Zimbabwe's north, but this was 'designed to play only a supplementary role to the constitutional struggle' and 'was waged by nationalist organizations that lacked a background in military affairs' (1978, 20). The guerrilla soldiers were trained poorly, lacked sufficient equipment, and were not disciplined: combat security 'left a lot to be desired'. Furthermore, 'political work among the local population in the rural communities' was noticeable by its absence: 'little pains were taken to mobilize and organize the masses of rural peasants' so they 'became vulnerable to attacks by the better trained and equipped Rhodesian army' (1978, 20). Claims made by the nationalists that these efforts were aimed at removing the Rhodesians militarily were 'misleading, unjustified and completely without foundation and devoid of any factual basis'. They were 'unscrupulous attempt[s] to disguise and mask the political naïvety of the nationalists that drove these adventurist operations at a high cost of lives' (1978, 20). However, the move to armed struggle introduced a new element – indeed, perhaps a new team – to the playing field. 'The guerrilla fighters, the unwilling victims of political opportunism and military adventurism of the nationalist leadership...laid a firm base for subsequent better planned and organised military operations' (1978, 21–2) based on the principles of classic guerrilla warfare, and were soon to constitute a political challenge to the nationalist's reformism, which was based in the misled belief that their struggles would be achieved with the help of the British, rather than setting their sights on the much more important settler element.

The next stage of 'militant nationalism' came about when even the nationalist leaders recognised that the British were not coming to their aid: they would have to confront Ian Smith's regime directly with arms. This entailed a move to guerrilla war, launched in 1972 by ZANLA in Zimbabwe's north-east, and was thus a 'leap from reformism' but, 'regrettably, the movement continued to be plagued by most of its earlier weaknesses' (1978, 23). This, combined with the gaining of independence by the Portuguese colonies in 1974, pushed South African and Zambian leaders into an attempt to stem the radicalisation of the Zimbabwean struggle by bringing the old school of nationalists, imprisoned in Rhodesia for approximately a decade, into negotiations with the Smith regime. According to Mhanda détente succeeded in destabilising the Zimbabwean liberation movement and practically brought the liberation war to an end, to the satisfaction of Ian Smith and John Vorster and their imperialist masters. Not a single shot was fired at the Rhodesian forces by the nationalist guerrillas for close to a year (1978, 24).

The day was only saved by the Zimbabwe People's Army (ZIPA), an 'initiative by ZANLA and ZIPRA combatants on their own to form...a united front of the two armies to resuscitate the armed liberation struggle.... ZIPA confined the détente exercise to the dustbin of history' (1978, 24). By the end of November 1975 the war was restarted.[15] Within 10 months, half of Rhodesia was subjected to guerrilla operations, forcing the Smith regime to respond with increased call ups for the war, prolongation of the period of national service, instituting convoy system for transportation, introducing the curfew system and mobile martial courts to deal with guerrilla supporters. The Rhodesian forces changed their counter insurgency strategy from that of clear and hold to a general offensive (1978, 24).

Five thousand ZIPA troops were in the 'semi-liberated' eastern half of Zimbabwe, while 20,000 more were waiting in Mozambique. 'Plans to set up liberated zones that it could defend from enemy attacks were at an advanced stage and scheduled to come into effect in early 1977' (1978, 25). The USSR had pledged to assist ZIPA by October. American Secretary of State Henry Kissinger was moved to action, persuading Smith to swallow his 'no majority rule in 1000 years' promise and getting British Secretary of State Anthony Crosland to call another conference of the nationalists and their nemesis in Geneva, in October.[16] Furthermore, ZIPA had persuaded the key nationalists and the Frontline state presidents that the military alliance they represented should be taken on at the political level: thus was the Patriotic Front conceived. At Geneva, moreover, ZIPA 'exposed and foiled...the imperialist machinations and dirty intrigues'. All of this contributed to the fact that a few weeks after the Geneva conference, which had dragged on to December, came to an inconclusive end, 'most regrettably, at this critical juncture, ZIPA's revolutionary thrust was emasculated through the arrest of its core leadership in Mozambique' (1978, 25), and Robert Mugabe consolidated his hold on the nationalist movement.[17] 'The age old nationalist rivalry between ZANU and ZAPU' was revived, '[transporting] the national liberation struggle to the pre-ZIPA days characterized by confusion within the ranks of the nationalist movement' (1978, 26). This is the time from which the ZIPA leaders were imprisoned. Eighteen months later – while Smith was forging an 'internal settlement' with Bishop Abel Muzorewa and others such as Ndabaningi Sithole, the first leader of ZANU – the treatise was composed and typed.[18] It does not stop there, however: it continues for another forty pages to analyse the characteristics of the Zimbabwean struggle that led to ZIPA's spending the rest of the period of the war in the custody of the Mozambican state.

Form and content in the National Liberation struggle

Mhanda cautions the readers of his treatise against confusing form and content. In 1978, 'militant nationalism' took the 'outward form of advanced nationalism or as it were revolutionary nationalism', but was 'conservative, narrow and bourgeois in essence' (1978, 27). The Zimbabwean liberation movements' outward projections – including the assertion they were 'under the influence of proletarian ideology [with] the basic interests of the workers at heart' – were actually 'propaganda couched in progressive and revolutionary ideas that conform to an anti-imperialist stance' seeking to 'identify with the world struggle against imperialism'. This is, writes Mhanda, 'posturing' at 'waging a genuine national liberation struggle to overthrow national oppression and restore the democratic rights of the people of Zimbabwe'. If this is so, Thabo Mbeki's assertion that Mugabe's 'party of revolution' had surpassed the first stage of the NDR by 1980 disagrees with Mhanda. The rest of the treatise would reveal the essence and content of Zimbabwe's liberation struggle counterpoised with its form, along with the theory and strategy to realise the liberation struggle's principles.

The root of the NDR's dilemma is the proletariat's lack of development: in the 'Third World' at large and in Zimbabwe ca. 1978 in particular, the carrier of Marx's revolution is simply not up to the task.[19] Mhanda's treatise is clear on that matter. Although workers and the semi-proletariat were key to the emergence of nationalism's early phases (1978, 15; Phimister and Raftopoulos 1997; Scarnecchia 2008) and 'like its sister proletariat elsewhere is endowed with immense leadership potential and has an historic duty to deliver humanity from oppression' (1978, 55) it is – contrary to a school of thought that was quite influential within ZIPA – unable to 'stand as a viable independent political force at this point in time (1978, 56). This was due to Zimbabwean capitalism's 'low level of development as yet' (1978, 56): it had been in existence for only 75 years and had 'not had much time to produce a sizeable force of workers', well below a million. Moreover, the Zimbabwean workers had not organised themselves as a 'class for itself', thus there was no well-formed workers' movement in Zimbabwe, let alone a 'movement for socialism' (1978, 56). As well, its rates of literacy, and cultural and technical levels were low in comparison with the petty and national bourgeois leadership elements in the nationalist movement. The working class had not been 'steeled in struggle' and there was 'no other school than to actively participate in the national liberation struggle to acquire the requisite experience in struggle' (1978, 56).

Although the petty and national bourgeoisie were the 'leading force' and 'the backbone' of the struggle (whilst the workers and peasants were the 'motive force'), these classes were 'not enthusiastic for socialism', instead hoping 'to inherit, albeit in modified form, the present socio-economic base in Zimbabwe', it would be unwise to ignore their power: 'proceeding to organise a proletarian party regardless of the strength of their aversion to it, will not only split the liberation movement but could also result in an ill-fated liberation project' (1978, 57). Thus:

> At the current stage of our struggle, the national democratic revolution, and the specific circumstances and nature of our struggle, national unity is indispensable and should be tirelessly striven for by all revolutionary and patriotic forces rather than be thrown into jeopardy through reckless and shortsighted ultra-leftist tactics. Such an approach would not only bring about the danger of defeat for the liberation struggle but would also be counter-productive to the cause for socialism (1978, 57).

Yet although the task of the day was to 'overthrow national oppression by the white settler minority as a guise of British colonialism and restore the peoples' democratic rights in the realm of politics, the economy and culture' – not 'to overthrow capitalist relations of production and capitalist private property' (1978, 57) – in order to keep both items firmly on the agenda it was necessary to construct 'a heterogeneous... revolutionary mass movement... that transcends the limits of moribund nationalism' (1978, 55). This movement is 'an alliance of the working class with other progressive and patriotic forces... in favour of fighting for genuine national liberation that restores the people's inalienable rights... [and] that will consummate the national democratic revolution' (1978, 58). Although, strictly speaking, its class composition is not very different from those who would stop at something less than even 'reformist' nationalism,[20] its 'ideological content' (1978, 59) differentiates it from conservative forces. The revolutionary mass movement's ideology aims at 'the attainment of thoroughgoing and complete national liberation', focusing on 'colonialism and imperialism, monopoly capitalism and not national capital': thus it will not be satisfied with the attainment of power for power's sake. It is different from orthodox nationalism because it 'falls within the revolutionary orbit of consistent anti-imperialism and wages a resolute struggle against imperialism' – it is not 'confined to narrow nationalism'. Thus the revolutionary mass movement 'spearheads a struggle that is genuinely an integral part of the progressive world's struggle against imperialism' and maintains the 'ideal of transforming the Rhodesian state complete with its institutions and attendant structures into a new Zimbabwe reflecting the will and serving the interests of the majority of its formerly oppressed people'.

'Narrow [African] nationalism' is merely a mirror image of white nationalism. African nationalist leaders are as racist as the white settlers, 'bourgeois in essence' and incapable of setting up anything but a neo-colonial state. 'Propped up by imperialism', this state would 'leave the existing socio-economic order with its attendant structures and institutions; the bedrock of our oppression, intact' (1978, 29–31). The nationalists' political programme stops 'short of a deep social analysis'[21]; thus it cannot grasp 'the social character of the society undergoing revolution' and subsequently 'cannot facilitate the articulation of the basic political demands... corresponding to the prevailing socio-economic situation... in clear and concise terms' (1978, 30). Yet their programmes 'state in general terms about overthrowing settler minority rule and replacing it with a socialist oriented Zimbabwe where the political rights of all Zimbabweans will be guaranteed'. They are 'replete with glowing Marxist-Leninist terms mechanically transplanted from Marxist literature completely out of touch with the social realities in Zimbabwe'. Marxist literature is 'plagiarised' as the nationalists 'feign themselves Marxist revolutionaries whereas in reality they are pseudo-revolutionaries. This is a fashionable trend among the petty bourgeoisie', who do not even understand the 'decorative Marxist terms... What they actually aspire and strive for is to step into the shoes of the white settler minority and continue to exploit the broad masses in pursuit of their selfish ends and insatiable avarice' (1978, 30–1).

Given the lack of social analysis and a realistically defined political programme, the Zimbabwean nationalist leaders have been:

> characterised by incessant splits, power struggles, antagonisms and hostilities between various political factions, rivalry and competition in diplomatic activity aimed at the total exclusion and paralysis of sister organisations, misdirection of efforts to political infighting within the movement, superficial and divisive organisational and propaganda work among the masses, degeneration into the parochial pursuit of tribal interests, etc. etc. (1978, 32).

The list of problems with the leadership of the Zimbabwean nationalist movement goes on for the next few pages of Mhanda's treatise, leading him to conclude his analysis of the leaders who threw him into prison that but were it not for the fact that in spite of them the flame of nationalism was still 'burning in the hearts and minds of the people of Zimbabwe' their 'political blunders... thus far border on being politically reactionary'. Aside from that flame, they would be 'worthy of total condemnation as they are now more of a liability than an asset to the liberation struggle'. The whole liberation struggle was being held to 'ransom on account of the pursuit of personal and clique power' (1978, 33).

Perhaps today one could add that the leaders about whom Mhanda was speaking nearly 35 years ago have learned the art of the accumulation of huge sums of wealth for themselves since then, but the flame of nationalism has died along with the rest of Zimbabwe's economy.[22] The problem remains, however: without a strong working class to counter these reactionaries, who could carry the revolution forward? Mhanda's answer is a variation on what he says is Lenin's call for an emphasis on organisational capacity (1978, 33). Again, the reader is regaled with the problems of organisation replete throughout the nationalist movement. However, the fact that the struggle for liberation took an armed form meant that guerrilla cadres had the opportunity to develop firm relationships with the 'people' and simultaneously with a 'Marxist-Leninist world outlook at variance with that of the Nationalists' (1978, 36), to a point where it influences 'the organisational and political views of the guerrilla forces'.

> This inevitably sets the guerrilla forces on a collision course with the nationalist petty bourgeois political leadership. With the latter lacking a correct general political line and the requisite military know how this contradiction will eventually develop to hamper the qualitative development of the national liberation struggle itself (1978, 36).

Of course, this is what happened to Mhanda and his comrades: their collision with the 'narrow nationalists' resulted in incarceration for more than three years.[23] However, the saving grace within the analysis of this phase of Zimbabwe's struggle rests in the following phrase. Mhanda suggests that the real source of his removal from the scene rested in *'the restriction of internal democracy within the ranks of the nationalist armies'* (emphasis mine). This intolerance of 'alternative approaches' became the 'hotbed of tension' resulting in the jailing of some of the best military (as well as ideological) minds in the liberation army, thus 'limiting the combat effectiveness of the army and arresting the initiative of the masses' (1978, 36). Later, he emphasises that contrary to the workings of the Zimbabwean liberation movement to date,

> it is a *democratic* style of work that gives full play to the initiative, resourcefulness and creative capabilities of the broad masses of the people and the fighters. A *democratic* style of work enhances the revolutionary character of the liberation movement and serves to motivate both the masses and the fighters to participate in the liberation struggle with heightened enthusiasm (1978, 62, my emphasis).

It is this emphasis on democracy that differentiates the 'revolutionary mass movement' from the narrow nationalists.[24] Without 'bestowing...hitherto suppressed and stifled...democratic rights...the attainment of full democracy' alongside 'overthrowing national oppression' (1978, 59–60), only one side of the NDR's coin is accomplished. To be sure, the class basis of the revolutionary mass movement is unclear, especially compared to the certainties of the proletarian movement. Mhanda's treatise attempts to make up for this class uncertainty. The workers, the peasants, and the other 'progressive and patriotic forces that are in favour of fighting for genuine national liberation...including revolutionary intellectuals...[and] sections of the national and petty bourgeoisie...although they cannot be firmly relied on to persevere and prosecute the struggle to complete victory...with a revolutionary core as its vanguard' (1978, 59, 63) will perform the task – with ideological, political and organisational transformation. This includes blending local party-political structures with increased guerilla democratisation, which can only be combined effectively with the transformation of semi-liberated zones into liberated ones, free of domination by Rhodesian troops (1978, 43–5, 64), combined with 'support from the world forces of socialism' (1978, 58).[25]

The tension within this formula lies not only with its lack of clarity on the class basis of the movement (which is inevitable, given the uneven development of class and capital in social formations such as Zimbabwe), but also in the amount of weight placed on the 'vanguard', which sometimes seems to take the place of the 'proletariat' in more classical evaluations of revolutionary situations. In a case where the 'petty bourgeois' is both the class in charge of 'narrow nationalism' and is also the base of the 'revolutionary intellectuals', one wonders how long 'an effective critical mass of revolutionary cadres within the ranks of the liberation movement' can 'guarantee...the revolutionary character of the movement' (1978, 62). Perhaps the notion of democracy could fill the gaps in this revolutionary theory, although it remains to be seen how it could have been institutionalised in the throes of guerrilla war, especially before the advent of liberated zones (Mhanda notes that over-reliance on foreign assistance – i.e. the benevolence of the Mozambican state in the absence of the ability to be self-reliant in substantial areas of Zimbabwe – left the liberation forces very vulnerable to the whims of others). It certainly adds a new dimension to rather deterministic perspectives on the NDR that suggest advances in the concept have to await the completion of a 'bourgeois democratic phase' or something more amorphous – and probably much more authoritarian – in Stalinist, populist, or 'developmental statist' forms.

Conclusion: comparing NDR perspectives and praxis

As indicated in the introduction, Mhanda's and Mbeki's interpretations of the NDR as applied to Zimbabwe share a Marxist perspective and indicate that 'democracy' is a way out of the cul de sacs of this theory when it is applied to the 'third world'. However, when push comes to shove – i.e. with the test of praxis, the actions inspired by theory taken at the moments of historical necessity – Wilfred Mhanda seems to have pushed the boundaries of the NDR much further than his much more powerful contemporary. Mhanda and his Zimbabwe Liberators' Forum, by continuing to push for 'bourgeois democracy' (the rule of law, even for 'property', civil liberties, and free and fair electoral contests to test and measure the desires of a country's populace for new rulers) and far beyond[26] against the combined forces of the Zimbabwean party-state and the 'war veterans' enrolled to its assistance, have contributed much to the struggles for the enlargement of choice started by the nationalists (including, of course, the 'revolutionary mass movement' they started in the midst of the liberation war) and by the newer generation who formed the National Constitutional Assembly and then the Movement for Democratic Change. In this sense, Mhanda may be seen as following the tradition of most of the rest of Zimbabwe's civil society groups (or 'civics' in local parlance) based more on liberal notions of human rights than social democratic ones; although his analysis of what to do with the economy is far from liberal.[27]

Thabo Mbeki, in contrast, although writing in *his* treatise on Zimbabwe that fully free and fair elections would be a *sine qua non* for ZANU-PF taking the second phase of the NDR forward in the 2002 presidential elections, backed down in the name of sovereignty and SADC solidarity when it came time to condemn them for lacking the basic pre-requisites of a fair and free contest – ignoring even the report of some High Court judges he sent as a second observer team (Lipton 2009, 337, 344). That is probably all he would have had to do to ensure a denominator for the NDR that did not stop at 'national'. As it happened, the most he could do – six years and thousands of lives later (through direct killings organised by the party he helped stay in power, and indirectly through early deaths due to easily preventable diseases such as cholera) – was help organise a 'transitional government' (Raftopoulos 2009) keeping an unelected party in power, that could most charitably be described as the result of a 'passive revolution' (Raftopoulos 2010). The reader may make his or her choice as to whether Mhanda's or Mbeki's view of the NDR is more propitious to 'progress' in Zimbabwe.

Acknowledgements

Thanks to John Hoffman and Brian Raftopoulos for helpful reflections: fortunately for them only I can be blamed for my misinterpretations of fact and theory.

Notes

1. It is now called the Nelson Mandela Metropolitan University.
2. A University of Johannesburg/South African Research Chair on Social Change seminar led by Professor John S. Saul in September 2011, for example, engendered intense debate on the utility of the NDR idea, with members of the Democratic Left Front – 'a broad coalition of left formations representing small groups of community activists and intellectuals from around the country' (Pillay 2011, 45) – both for and against. Saul closed the seminar with the comment that he would prefer the phrase 'class struggle' to 'NDR'. Aside from the unfortunate way in which the concept has been misused by leaders such as Stalin, though, there is no logical reason why the NDR precludes class struggle: it simply positions it within a post-independence phase. As John Hoffman has commented on this paper, it is 'right to stress the need for "bourgeois democratic" institutions, so often left out of the NDR which then becomes a pretext for old-fashioned authoritarianism'. One presumes trade unions and even leftist political parties are part of 'bourgeois democratic' institutions. For an analysis suggesting the worst possible fate for the NDR in South Africa – 'Zanufication' – and doubts that South Africa is heading that way, see Hamill and Hoffman (2011).
3. Compagnon (2010, 191–220) is convinced that the 'state bourgeoisie' in Zimbabwe will never become a productive one, given its patrimonial and destructive tendencies – thus to use NDR language, its 'revolution' will not succeed. In contrast, Stephen Chan (2011, 269–70) gives the 'corrupt, possibly even before their children' the chance to invest their 'wherewithal [in] joint ventures with external investors, for instance. Just as it will be those who stole the largest farms who will be in a position to help revitalize large-scale agro-industry'. This begins to sound like the NDR is on the road, until Chan indicates that the route ends at Zambia.
4. Suttner (2010) could fall into this category, although his injunction not to let the NDR remain 'fixed' is a welcome move away from the Stalinist perceptions – invoked in defence of capitalism – often repeated by the South African Communist Party.
5. As exemplified in the public letter of a number of South African scholars and 'public intellectuals' bemoaning the United Nation's support for NATO's 'invasion' of Gaddafi's Libya: the letter looks too much like special pleading for dictators to gain the respect of democrats (Daily News 2011; Kirchick 2011).
6. South Africa's foreign policy efforts regarding Zimbabwe have been much analysed and debated, with many arguing that the Zimbabwean crisis would have been worse if not for South African forms of diplomacy. Nor should it be assumed that the South African state was united: there were strong pushes after the March 2008 election to implement an inclusive government to forestall the violence of the June 'runoff' from which Morgan Tsvangirai withdrew (Sachikonye, 2010), but this notion was set aside by those who wanted to follow the constitution and see the run-off through. On South African Zimbabwe policy see Freeman (2005), Graham (2006), Habib (2009), Hamill and Hoffman (2009), Lipton (2009), McKinley (2004) and the Southern Africa Liaison Office (2009).
7. Thabo Mbeki wrote a public letter to MDC leader Morgan Tsvangirai in late 2008, responding to MDC Secretary-General TendaiBiti's criticism of his handling of the negotiations leading up to the final signing of the mid-September 2008 Global Political Agreement's agenda for Zimbabwe's Inclusive Government, which was finally implemented in mid-February 2009 (Johwa and Muleya 2008; Mbeki 2008). Mbeki wrote in the language of the NDR (to be explicated below), for example that 'you and I know that objectively [thus invoking the "science" that is part of the NDR package], Zimbabwe desperately needs the establishment of this Inclusive Government, and that this is the most urgent demand of the masses [the NDR always seeks to speak on behalf of the "masses", but there is no indication that the "masses" voted for a coalition government, let alone "demanded" it] …'. Again in the language of the NDR, Mbeki advised Tsvangirai to find 'the sense of patriotism among yourselves as leaders of the people of Zimbabwe and as African patriots, which will inspire you, despite and beyond personal and partisan interests, to implement the agreements you have concluded'. The final two blows consisted of more patriotism versus its opposite, something approaching treason (or more loosely,

cosmopolitanism), and an upper-cut from the realms of ubuntu: 'It may be that, for whatever reason, you consider our region and continent as being of little consequence to the future of Zimbabwe, believing that others further away, in Western Europe and North America, are of greater importance' – thus the by then familiar accusations of the MDC being 'puppets' of the west; and 'all of us will find it strange and insulting that because we do not agree with you on a small matter, you choose to describe us in a manner that is most offensive in terms of African culture, and therefore offend our sense of dignity as Africans, across our borders', again, an assumption that Thabo Mbeki speaks for 'all of us' amidst an invocation of a mythical African culture in which criticism is muted in the interests of mutuality (cf. Metz 2007).

8. The discussion paper is discussed at more length previously by this author (Moore 2010) in the context of South Africa's foreign policy: the next few paragraphs are derived from that article and a re-reading of the original document.
9. He adds, however, that the issues of 'white property rights and the relative autonomy of the state autonomy' had not been resolved in the first phase, and would thus have 'great significance' for the second phase.
10. One assumes that this would be the case if the international community co-operated with Mbeki's plans to revive a 1998 donor's convention recommending compensation for white commercial farmers for land that would be used ostensibly for resettlement. The recommendations were never implemented, although Mbeki's 2000 State of the Nation speech said he had revived them in April, and in return gained a promise from Mugabe that the next round of elections would be free and fair. (Thabo Mbeki, 'State of the Nation Address', 4 May 2000, http://www.thepresidency.gov.za/president/sp/2000/tm0504.html, accessed August 20, 2009).
11. The treatise may be compared with a published document that emerged from earlier struggles within ZAPU's army bearing many similarities with the ones outlined in Mhanda's writings (Tshabangu 1979). Similar differences of opinion leading to conflict emerged in the South West People's Organisation (Leys and Saul 1995) and the African National Congress (Trewhela 2011).
12. But see, in *Dzino*'s appendix, a 22 September 1976 Mozambican Information interview with Machingura – 'The Zimbabwe People's Army: An Interview with Dzinashe Machingura' – which gave a very radical edge to ZIPA's perspective. It was widely circulated in international solidarity movements, undoubtedly also among American policy-makers who would have been alarmed, especially given the context of the Cold War and the prospect of unity among the liberation armies leading to greater USSR involvement. See also Ranger (1980), Saul (1979a, b), and Moore (2011, forthcoming in Basset and Clarke).
13. See Peter McKay (2009) for a fascinating account of one British subject's involvement with the nationalists at this stage.
14. One of the main reasons ZIPA was formed was to unify the armies of the parties separated in 1963. Indeed, Mhanda and his comrades' attempts to keep this unity alive were some of the reasons for their incarceration.
15. Blessing-Miles Tendi (2010, 163–8) tells the ZIPA tale, but gets the date of ZIPA's formation wrong: it was 25 November 1975, not 1976 (Tendi 2010, 164).
16. For Kissinger, militant Africans' demands would lead to more Russian meddling and 'chaos ... and the whole enterprise after all only makes sense as a firebreak to Africans radicalism and Soviet intervention' (Kissinger, letters to Crosland, 1976, London school of Economics Archives, cited in Moore forthcoming).
17. See Scarnecchia (forthcoming) for an archivalanalysis of how Mugabe convinced western diplomats of his leadership capabilities at the Geneva conference.
18. Mhanda's memoir reveals many more details of these events (2011).
19. This was also the main theoretical base for disputes among Marxists in Russia before the revolution: see for example Service (2010, 163) on Lenin's and Trotsky's resolution of the problem of substituting for the bourgeoisie's development role.
20. This might be its Achilles Heel, although this is not considered by Mhanda directly.
21. Mhanda's treatise does not state outright why the narrow nationalists do not undertake good social analysis. This could be due to the fact that such work would reveal its

weaknesses, but it also that the very weakness of the petty bourgeois nationalist leadership leads inevitably to poor analysis!
22. Unless one assumes, with Moyo and Yeros (2005), Scoones et al. (2010), and Sadomba (2010) that the land invasion project has been more or less successful and is thus the core of the NDR. Moyo and Yeros use the phraseology of the NDR in their work and thus should warrant inclusion in this article. Space disallows this discussion here, as does the fact that Davies (2005) and Moore (2004) have engaged with their interpretations already, to an extent.
23. In more detail, yet still abstract, the treatise goes on:

> The active participation of the fighters in the struggle and their intercourse with the revolutionary experiences of other people's struggles gave rise to the emergence of the embryonic revolutionary forces within the liberation struggle.... The polarised political forces within the nationalist movement coexist peacefully for some time, but in the course of the struggle, a point is subsequently reached when they can no longer exist in harmony and promote the further development of the struggle. The relations between the two poles come to a head when on the one hand, the old guard nationalist political forces can no longer cope with the struggle and fail to direct its further development in the required direction and on the other, when the emergent political forces gather in strength and for all practical purposes no longer exclusively rely on the old guard leadership in the prosecution of the war. At this stage, the uneven political development precipitates a crisis. The old guard nationalist leadership begins to fetter the development of the struggle whilst at the same time the emergent revolutionary forces are filled with revolutionary enthusiasm and become intolerant of the stagnation of the struggle and fervently desire to carry it to its logical conclusions (Mhanda 1978, 53–4).

As Mhanda indicates, the crisis could be resolved peacefully with the 'emergent revolutionary forces gaining the upper hand' or less peacefully with 'open antagonism which can only be resolved by precipitate revolutionary action'. He does not consider what happened to his comrades and him, but says in spite of setbacks and 'temporary defeat' the emergent revolutionary forces will triumph 'sooner or later'.
24. This is my interpretation rather than something spelled out clearly in the 'treatise', although it is clearly between the lines in it, and very clear in Mhanda's subsequent political career.
25. Regardless, one supposes, of their democratic credentials.
26. A vision statement published by the ZLP in 2006 put these democratic ideals forward:

> True democracy is founded on and characterised by full consultation, participation, and involvement of all stakeholders in decision-making processes on matters that affect people's livelihoods and the well-being and fate of the nation. It is permeated by total accountability to the people, the repository of political power, from beginning to end and has as its heart and soul, the full respect for civil liberties and democratic values and the dignity of the human being.

Taken to its logical extreme this formulation is much more than 'liberal' (some observers state that Mhanda is simply a liberal now). If all 'stakeholders' participate in matters affecting their livelihoods, that includes the workplace and is thus democratic socialism.
27. Raftopolous (2006) notes the gap between the human rights and the political economy perspectives that have emerged in Zimbabwe, as does Moore (2004) in his characterisation of the opposing camps as 'agrarian patriots' versus 'critical cosmopolitans' – to which could be added 'uncritical cosmopolitans'!

Note on contributor

David Moore is Professor of Development Studies and head of that department at the University of Johannesburg. He has researched and written on Zimbabwean politics since 1984. His next output will be 'The ZIPA Moment in Zimbabwean History, 1975–1977: Mugabe's Rise and Democracy's Demise' forthcoming in Carolyn Basset and Marlea Clarke, eds., Legacies of Liberation: Post-colonial Struggles for a Democratic Southern Africa, Toronto and Cape Town: Fernwood and HSRC, forthcoming. His most recent one was 'Bloody African Development: War and Accumulation on the Dark Continent', New Political Economy, 16, 1 (February 2011).

References

Basset, C., and M. Clarke, ed., Forthcoming. *Legacies of liberation: Post-colonial struggles for a democratic Southern Africa.* Toronto and Cape Town: Fernwood and Human Sciences Research Council.
Chan, S. 2011. *Old treacheries, new deceits: Insights into Southern African politics.* Johannesburg: Jonathan Ball.
Chirkin, V.Y., and Y.A. Yudin. 1978. A socialist-oriented state: Instrument of revolutionary change. Moscow: Progress Press.
Compagnon, D. 2010. *A predictable tragedy: Robert Mugabe and the collapse of Zimbabwe.* Philadelphia: University of Pennsylvania Press.
Daily News. 2011. 'Concerned Africans CriticiseNato', (Durban) 24 August 2011.
Daniel, J., P. Naidoo, D. Pillay, and R. Southall, ed., 2011. *New SA review 2: New paths, old promises.* Johannesburg: Wits University Press.
Davidson, B., J. Slovo, and A. Wilkinson. 1976. *Southern Africa: The new politics of revolution.* Harmondsworth: Penguin.
Davies, R. 2005. Memories of underdevelopment: A personal interpretation of Zimbabwe's economic decline. In *Zimbabwe: Injustice and Political Reconcilliation*, ed. B. Raftopoulo and T. Savage, 19–42. Cape Town: Institute for Justice and Reconciliation.
Freeman, L. 2005. South Africa's Zimbabwe policy: Unraveling the contradictions. *Journal of Contemporary African Studies* 23, no. 2: 147–72.
Gevisser, M. 2007. *Thabo Mbeki: The dream deferred.* Johannesburg: Jonathan Ball.
Habib, A. 2009. South Africa's foreign policy: Hegemonic aspirations, neoliberal orientations, and global transformation. *South African Journal of International Affairs* 16, no. 2: 143–59.
Hamill, J., and J. Hoffman. 2009. 'Quiet Diplomacy' or appeasement? South African policy towards Zimbabwe. *Round Table* 98, no. 402: 1–12.
Hamill, J., and J. Hoffman. 2011. The African National Congress and the Zanufication debate. In *New SA review 2: New paths, old promises*, ed. J. Daniel, P. Naidoo, D. Pillay, and R. Southall, 50–67. Johannesburg: Wits University Press.
Kirchick, J. 2011. South Africa Stands with Gaddafi, The Atlantic Wire, 6 September, http://www.theatlantic.com/international/archive/2011/09/south-africa-stands-with-qaddafi/244584/ (accessed September 6, 2011).
Johwa, W., and D. Muleya. 2008. Zimbabwe: Mbeki letter angers Tsvangriai, *Business Day*, 26 November.
Judt, T. 2008. *Reappraisals: Reflections on the forgotten twentieth century.* London: Penguin.
Leys, C., and J.S. Saul. 1995. *Namibia's liberation struggle: The two-edged sword.* London: James Currey.
Lipton, M. 2009. Understanding South Africa's foreign policy: The perplexing case of Zimbabwe. *South African Journal of International Affairs* 16, no. 3: 331–46.
Mbeki, G. 1964. *The peasants' revolt.* Harmondsworth: Penguin.
Mbeki, T. 2001. How will Zimbabwe defeat its enemies? A discussion document. African National Congress mimeograph July 10; reprinted with some alterations as The Mbeki-Mugabe Papers: A Discussion Document, New Agenda, 2nd Quarter, 2008: 56–75.
Mbeki, T. 2008. Full text: Mbeki's letter to Morgan Tsvangirai, 22 November, http//:www.newzimbabwe.com/pages/mbeki247.19082 (accessed August 24, 2009).

McKinley, D. 2004. South African Foreign Policy towards Zimbabwe under Mbeki. *Review of African Political Economy* 31, no. 100: 357–64.

Metz, T. 2007. Toward an African moral theory. *Journal of Political Philosophy* 15, no. 3: 321–41.

Mhanda, W. 1978. A treatise on Zimbabwe's national liberation struggle: Some theoretical problems. Mimeograph.

Mhanda, W. 2011. *Dzino: Memories of a freedom fighter*. Harare: Weaver Press.

Moore, D. 1995a. Democracy, violence and identity in the Zimbabwean war of national liberation: Reflections from the realms of dissent. *Canadian Journal of African Studies* 29, no. 3: 375–402.

Moore, D. 1995b. The Zimbabwe people's army: Strategic innovation or more of the same? In *Soldiers and the Zimbabwean Liberation War*, ed. N. Bhebe and T. Ranger, 73–86. Harare and London: University of Zimbabwe Press and James Currey.

Moore, D. 2001. Democracy is coming to Zimbabwe. *Australian Journal of Political Science* 36, no. 1: 163–9.

Moore, D. 2004. Marxism and Marxist intellectuals in schizophrenic Zimbabwe: How many rights for zimbabwe's left? A comment. *Historical Materialism* 12, no. 4: 405–25.

Moore, D. 2010. A decade of disquieting diplomacy: South Africa, Zimbabwe and the ideology of the national democratic revolution, 1999-2009. *History Compass* 8, no. 8: 752–67.

Moore, D. 2011. Introduction. In *Dzino: Memories of a freedom fighter*, ed. W. Mhanda. Harare: Weaver Press.

Moore, D. Forthcoming. The Zipa moment in Zimbabwean history. In *Legacies of Liberation: Post-colonial Struggles for a Democratic Southern Africa*, ed. C. Basset, and M. Clark. Toronto and Cape Town: Fernwood and Human Sciences Research Council.

Moyo, S., and P. Yeros, ed., 2005. *Reclaiming the land: The resurgence of rural movements in Africa, Asia and Latin America*. London: Zed Press.

Moyo, S., and P. Yeros. 2005. Land occupations and land reform in Zimbabwe: Towards the national democratic revolution in Zimbabwe, In Moyo and Yeros, 2005: 44–77.

Phimister, I., and B. Raftopoulos, ed., 1997. *Keep on knocking: a History of the labour movement in Zimbabwe, 1900-1997*. Harare: Baobab.

Phimister, I., and B. Raftopoulos. 2004. Mugabe, Mbeki and the politics of anti-imperialism. *Review of African Political Economy* 31, no. 101: 385–400.

Pillay, D. 2011. The tripartite alliance and its discontents: Contesting the 'National Democratic Revolution' in the Zuma Era, In Daniel, Naidoo, Pillay, and Southall, 2011: 31–49.

Raftopoulos, B. 2009. The crisis in Zimbabwe 1998–2008. In Raftopoulos and Mlambo 2009: 201–32.

Raftopoulos, B. 2010. The global political agreement as a 'passive revolution': Notes on contemporary politics in Zimbabwe. *The Round Table* 99, no. 411: 705–18.

Ranger, T. 1980. The changing of the old guard: Robert Mugabe and the revival of ZANU. *Journal of Southern African Studies* 7, no. 1: 71–90.

Sachikonye, L. 2010. *When a state turns on its citizens: 60 years of institutionalised violence in Zimbabwe*. Harare: Weaver; Johannesburg: Jacana.

Sadomba, W. 2010. *War veterans in Zimbabwe's revolution: Challenging neo-colonialism and settler and international capital*. London: James Currey; Harare: Weaver; Johannesburg: Jacana.

Saul, J.S. 1979a. *The State and Revolution in Eastern Africa*. New York: Monthly Review Press.

Saul, J. 1979b. Transforming the struggle in Zimbabwe. In *State and revolution in East Africa*, ed. J. Saul, 232–48. London: Heinemann.

Scarnecchia, T. 2008. *The urban roots of democracy and political violence in Zimbabwe: Harare and Highfield, 1940-1964*. Rochester: University of Rochester Press.

Scarnecchia, T. Forthcoming. Imperialists and allies: Robert Mugabe's diplomacy with Americans and Africans at the Rhodesia Geneva Talks 1976.

Service, R. 2010. *Trotsky: A biography*. London: Pan Books.

Scoones, I., N. Marongwe, B. Mavedzenge, J. Mahenehene, F. Murimbarimba, and C. Sukume. 2010. *Zimbabwe's land reform: Myths and realities*. London: James Currey; Johannesburg, Jacana.

Slovo, J. 1976. South Africa—No middle road. In *Southern Africa: The new politics of revolution*, ed. D. Davidson, J. Slovo, and A. Wilkinson, 106–210. Harmondsworth: Penguin.

Solodovnikov, V., and V. Bogolslovsky. 1975. *Non-capitalist development: An historical outline*. Moscow: Progress Press.

Southall, R. 2004. The ANC and black capitalism in South Africa. *Review of African Political Economy* 31, no. 100: 313–28.

Southall, R. 2008. The ANC for sale? Money, morality and business in South Africa. *Review of African Political Economy* 35, no. 2: 281–99.

Southern African Liaison Office. 2009. Country Focus Paper: South Africa's Relations with Zimbabwe, Johannesburg: SALO, http://cage.dcis.gov.za/documents/pdf/SALO_Country_Focus_Paper-Zimbabwe_FULL.pdf (accessed February 11, 2010).

Suttner, R. 2010. Debating NDR: 'National', 'democratic', 'revolution' are concepts, but do not have fixed meanings, Saturday Dispatch (East London), 4 December: 16.

Trewhela, P. 2011. *Inside Quatro: Uncovering the exile history of the ANC and SWAPO*. Johannesburg: Jacana.

Tendi, B-M. 2010. *Making history in Mugabe's Zimbabwe: Politics, intellectuals and the media*. Bern: Peter Lang.

Tshabangu, O. 1979. *The March 11 movement in ZAPU. Revolution within the revolution for Zimbabwe*. Heslington: Tiger Papers.

Reflections on the concept of progress – and Zimbabwe

John Hoffman

Emeritus Professor of Political Theory, University of Leicester, Leicester, UK and Research Associate, University of Johannesburg, South Africa

> The notion of progress is best understood as a concept which is contradictory and on-going. Writers such as John Gray are wrong to conclude that every notion of progress has to be mechanical and unilinear. Progress is what I call a 'momentum concept' – an on-going, unstoppable process. In the case of Zimbabwe, the attainment of political independence was a vital step but the struggle for democracy and self-government will continue in a post-Mugabe era.

Introduction

This short article will seek to do two things. The first is to examine the concept of progress, and the second is to link the concept specifically to Zimbabwe.

Too many commentators view progress in negative terms. While they are right to dismiss the naïve and linear concept of progress linked to the European Enlightenment, they display an unwillingness to reconstruct the concept along what I will call post-liberal lines. When we do this (with more than a little help from Marx and Engels), we see that progress is a contradictory concept but a meaningful one all the same. There is no 'end of history'. The existence of problems is part of the 'human condition': the solution of one problem inevitably leads to the existence of others. I will link the concept of progress with the idea of a momentum concept in order to show that while we move forward, there is no final resting point – no millennium in which progress comes to an end.

The struggle for democracy in Zimbabwe demonstrates, in my view, just how contradictory progress is, since the national liberation war to end colonialism was a momentous step forward even though it has brought about an autocracy which the Movement for Democratic Change (MDC) is currently challenging.

An analysis of progress

We should certainly be critical of the European Enlightenment. This Enlightenment enshrined the basic principles of classical liberalism, and although it challenged the despotic and hierarchical character of the medieval period, it substituted a despotism and repressive hierarchy of its own.

The problem with Enlightenment thought is that it was abstract – by which I mean that it abstracted from the social realities of power. Beneath the benevolent dictums of freedom, equality and the individual lay the grisly realities of class division, patriarchy, and colonialism. Above all, it had a naïve and linear concept of progress – a belief that liberal societies would usher in a higher order in which human nature would be perfected and people would only obey laws which they had prescribed to themselves.

Along with an abstract view of reason went an abstract view of progress. Gray, for example, characterises progress as a modernist myth (1993, 138), the imposition of a plan of life in which the prejudices and anxieties of the late-nineteenth-century European intelligentsia are made mandatory for all (1996, 260). While progress is a fact in science, he argues, when it comes to ethics and politics, it is a superstition (2003, 3). As an idea, it is usually accompanied by a vulgar and unreflective meliorism that assumes that progress entails endless economic growth (1995, 108).

This is certainly true of the classical liberal and Enlightenment view of progress. While Rousseau dissented from a mechanical and naïve view of progress such a position can be seen in John Stuart Mill and in most liberal theory certainly in the English-speaking world. For those who espouse a pluralist view (like Gray) history can have no meaning: it is, at best, a series of adventures in civilisation, each singular and discrete, leading nowhere (1996, 292). It is true that Christianity and the Enlightenment do have static views of the concept of progress, and this is because they postulate an ideal society embodying ahistorical notions of emancipation and freedom. But Marxism is not similar to Christianity and the Enlightenment, as Gray argues.

Marx and Engels' conception of progress

By 1843 Marx had become increasingly critical of the Enlightenment. In his work *On the Jewish Question* Marx distinguishes between political and human emancipation. Although there are (in my view) abstract echoes in the *1844 Manuscripts* of the Enlightenment, from then on Marx seeks to place the notions of reason, freedom and emancipation on a dialectical footing. Critical of the Enlightenment, he attempts to establish what I want to call a post-liberal view of the world.

Marx does not abandon the notion of progress but rather emphasises its contradictory and historical character, and the case I will make later for a momentum concept derives from the dialectical character of Marx's argument. At the end of *The Origin of the Family, Private Property and the State* Engels comments that 'every advance in production is at the same time a retrogression in the condition of the oppressed class'. What is a boon for one is necessarily a bane for the other (Marx and Engels 1968, 592). Already Rousseau had argued in his celebrated essay on the arts and sciences that progress had brought with it deceit, superficiality, greed and above all inequality (Rousseau 1968) and *The Communist Manifesto* superbly demonstrates the progressive character of capitalism despite the fact that it enshrines the exploitation of the working class.

I remember when I was doing the course on African government at the University of Cape Town arguing in an essay which a bemused Jack Simons read, that capitalism and colonialism were progressive and therefore we should not condemn them. In his attack on the British rule in India, Marx draws out the contradictory argument of the *Manifesto* – that capitalism both advances and yet tramples upon humankind. The material basis of a new world has been created, even though the effects have been devastating. Only when a social revolution has mastered the results of the bourgeois epoch, comments Marx – only then 'will human progress cease to resemble that hideous pagan idol, who would not drink the nectar but from the skulls of the slain' (2000, 366–7). It is a gross oversimplification of Marx's views to say with Gray that Marx 'defended colonial rule' (2007, 61).

It is precisely this notion of contradiction that the concept of progress as dealt with by writers like Gray lacks. The only notion of progress he can envisage is additive – one improvement after the other (2007, 188). The idea of progress, he complains, encourages us to view our lives 'as moments in a universal process of betterment'. He quotes the New Right thinker, Hayek, to the effect that progress is movement for movement's sake, a nihilistic dictum, Gray says, that has led to the destruction of modern conservatism as a result of its embrace of neo-liberalism (1995, 89). Gray quotes Santayana attacking 'mechanical progress' (1995, 89). The idea involves an 'all but irresistible tendency to improvement', and as one of the tenets of the modernist pseudo-religion of humanism, it is a sort of historical theodicy (1996, 23).

But the point about a viable concept of progress is that it is dialectical, and not mechanistic. It involves development and thus contradiction. Progress is not the linear vision of the Enlightenment – the erroneous idea that with the development of science there is a felicitous concomitant improvement in morals and social behaviour generally. Progress, in reality, involves the development of instruments of exploitation (at least under class-divided societies) and therefore the oppression of humanity, but the fact that progress is contradictory, does not make it impossible. There is no doubt that capitalism provides the *possibility* of a world in which emancipation, self-government and freedom can be won – not as the end of historical development, but as an important step forward in the infinite progress that can be made.

The point is that the notion of progress must be reconstructed.

Reconstructing the concept

Porritt's recent work on capitalism cites the words of the Sustainable Development Commission where it speaks of sustainable development as providing 'a framework for redefining progress' and redirecting our economies to enable all people to meet their basic needs. The Commission is acutely aware of the limits of the natural world but it still operates with a (post-Enlightenment) concept of progress (2006, 290). Elsewhere, Porritt quotes the words of Richard Reeves who complains that our political systems and cultures have failed to adapt to a new world in which 'economics does not equal or even equate to progress' (2006, 309). Progress can be reworked as a concept so that it incorporates a critical view of Enlightenment abstractions.

In his work on Berlin, Gray insists that the pluralist rejection of perfection is fatal to the idea of human history as at least potentially progressive (1996, 71). But why? The rejection of perfection is only fatal to the notion of progress if we assume that humankind is progressing towards a fixed goal beyond which no progress is possible. Once we challenge that abstract notion of progress, the argument falls. Gray is unable to distinguish between an abstract humanism that does indeed postulate a static notion of human emancipation, and a concrete humanism that recognises difference and contradiction and is rooted in history.

To endorse Kraus's dictum, which Gray quotes, that 'progress makes purses out of human skin' (1997, 161) is wrong. Kraus's comment involves a curious misreading of fascism and the holocaust: the Nazis may have believed that they were carrying history forward, but their policies were reactionary. They were reacting *against* progress – or the threat of it – not carrying history forward. They made their antagonism to the French Revolution and the Enlightenment crystal clear, and it is far better, in my view, to see Nazism as an extreme form of anti-liberalism in which the achievements of the bourgeois epoch are (almost all) rejected rather than built upon and transcended. Gray is fond of quoting the words of Koestler's Nazi intellectual who speaks of the grand enterprise upon which Nazism has embarked – 'there are no more impossibilities for man now' (Gray 2003, 13) – but this is linked to a genocidal project that is profoundly at odds with the rationalism and liberal ideals of the Enlightenment.

Progress is contradictory – drinking nectar from the skulls of the slain – but it is real, nevertheless. It is often tragic and bloody, always complex, but this does not negate it.

Progress as a momentum concept

In his celebrated analysis of democracy, de Tocqueville (1966) argues that democracy is a concept which has no stopping points. Democracy opposes the hierarchies of a feudal society but it also challenges the divisive nature of private property. It is true that de Tocqueville's analysis is inconsistent. He assumes that a providential force – the hand of God – lies behind this movement, and this argument points to an abstract and static reality driving democracy (1966, 8). But it is perfectly possible to formulate the notion of momentum without such a 'foundationalist' (i.e. static and ahistorical) base.

The point about the momentum concept is that it is infinitely progressive, and to put the matter philosophically, it is both relative and absolute. It is eternally restless but because it is rooted in reality, it can only manifest itself in historically specific forms. It shuns the repressive hierarchies associated with patriarchy, the state, violence and class. It looks to the future even though it works in the present.

Momentum concepts – like equality, emancipation and freedom, etc. – can never be realised. There is no point at which one can say: 'thus far and no further'. Momentum concepts are part of the historical process and hence I say that they are infinitely progressive. What bedevils the Enlightenment concept of progress is that it assumes some ultimate goal – some final resting place – a traditional notion of utopia. Hence as Gray rightly argues such a notion embodies conventional religious connotations. Marx does sometimes imply that communism is a kind of culmination of history – 'the riddle of history solved' he says in 1844 – and he could and should have made the historical character of communism clearer.

Nevertheless, the notion of progress can only be consistently handled as a momentum concept.

The national liberation struggle in Zimbabwe

I was struck even in 1990 when I was in Zimbabwe how black people often said how much better things were under the Smith regime. Reading the Zimbabwe press on the internet one often comes across comments that under Smith people had education, jobs and healthcare – under Mugabe they have nothing.

Yet it has to be said that the defeat of white minority rule by the forces of liberation was a massive historical step forward. Inevitably many of us were rather starry eyed about this. The victorious ZANU de-racialised the state (although they retained a white minister of agriculture) and made impressive (even if they were ultimately to prove unsustainable) advances in education and health. It is true that during the liberation struggle ZANU in particular employed a good deal of coercion in its battle for hearts and minds and it is important to remember that those who say that Mugabe and ZANU ruled Zimbabwe successfully for the first 10 years have forgotten the slaughter of some 20,000 civilians in Matabeleland in the *Gukurahundi* in the early 1980s. For the dying Lookout Masuku and the detained Dumiso Dabenga things looked rather different. The bestiality of the *Gukurahundi* demonstrates graphically the contradictory extremes of the notion of progress. Judith Todd in her remarkable book *Through the Darkness* cites the words of the veteran Aaron Mutiti who warned just before the 1980 elections that if Mugabe got to power, '[F]amily life, religious life, economic life as we know it, will progressively disappear' (Todd 2007, 423). Yet it has to be said that the triumph of liberation movement was progress even if it has proved to be what Hegel once called a slaughter bench of peoples.

Even if many Zimbabwean blacks argue that things are in some ways worse now than they were under white minority rule, this is still progress, for the liberation of Zimbabwe from colonial rule has created the basis for democracy. Democracy involves far more than elections. It involves greater and greater popular participation in a way that makes the state as an institution claiming a monopoly of legitimate force increasingly redundant. Engels once said that freedom has to be asserted in principle, before it can be put into practice (Marx and Engels 1975, 474). The freedom and equality, democracy and self-government which the liberation movements espoused in theory (and had begun to put into practice) make it possible for the oppressed people of Zimbabwe to demand that these values become a reality. Civil society organisations and the trade unions forged the National Constitutional Assembly (out of which developed the Movement for Democratic Change) and they were powerful enough to secure a defeat for the government in the referendum of 2000.

Mugabe himself has said that land comes before all else, defining the Zimbabwean personality and demarcating sovereignty. This is surely right and of course the land question was not resolved at Lancaster House. But a solution to this problem would have involved among other things a strategy of dividing white farmers so that those who were well meaning and sympathetic could assist in training and aiding African farmers and those who were died in the wool reactionaries could be isolated. Phillip Barclay has pointed to tax breaks which could have been given to farmers to set agricultural training programmes and encouragement and help given to black purchasers to buy land (Barclay 2010, 152). As it was, the policy of land reform adopted after 2000 had overwhelmingly negative consequences and involved a good deal of violence and appalling inroads into the rule of law. The policy has been pursued of handing land in the main over to cronies and Ministers (despite modest advances). As a result, productivity has slumped and the land issue has not been resolved.

This question of land reform was exhaustively debated at the Bulawayo conference on 'progress in Zimbabwe'. In this issue, Blair Rutherford has conceded in his review essay of *Zimbabwe's Land Reform: Myths & Realities* that although the land distribution after 2000 had positive features, it downplayed the violence involved against the white farmers and their employees. Booker Magure takes the view that the so-called land reform 'ruined' the agricultural sector, costing the country between US$20 and 30 billion. Too much land went mostly to the privileged few, and Kirk Helliker quotes Moore's witty characterisation of those who praise this process as 'patriotic agrarianists'.

Of course, it would be naïve to imagine that the ousting of Mugabe will lead to some kind of liberal or socialist promised land in which autocracy and corruption will magically disappear. I remember in September 2008 Brian Raftopolous saying to me that it is important that Tsvangarai does not concentrate power in an elitist manner and all we can say for certain is that a post-Mugabe Zimbabwe will be difficult and dangerous. A crucial step forward: but one inevitably littered with mistakes, wrong turnings and blind alleys. Already there are ambiguities and contradictions within the unity government and the MDC itself. A post Mugabe government will continue the historical process, with tremendous problems to overcome. The legacies of the Mugabe period are formidable: economic and environmental catastrophe; non-functional education and health systems; poverty and patriarchy – the latter in its colonial and post-colonial manifestations; starvation and unemployment; corruption and violence; brow-beaten and terrorised women; the question of what to do with supporters of ZANU, etc. A hard-headed notion of progress, rooted in painful and complex realities, is needed as never before.

Despair and nihilism are not helpful, but nor is naïve optimism and wishful thinking. Ian Phimister is so right in his paper to the conference (see also in this issue) to attack the so called 'patriotic' historians and their nationalist progenitors who naively assume that with the victory of the anti-colonial struggle, history somehow comes to an end. Liberation, like progress itself, is a momentum concept. We must strive to advance it without ever thinking that it can become a static reality. Attaining liberal institutions in Zimbabwe would constitute a massive advance – but they will hardly be the end of the road.

Note on contributor

John Hoffman is Emeritus Professor of Political Theory at the University of Leicester, UK. He has recently published a book on John Gray and is currently working on a book on Thabo Mbeki's Quiet Diplomacy with a colleague, James Hamill, who teaches in the Department of Politics and International Relations at the University of Leicester. Professor Hoffman is also a Research Associate of the Department of Anthropology and Development Studies, University of Johannesburg.

References

Barclay, P. 2010. *Zimbabwe: Years of hope and despair.* London: Bloomsbury.
Gray, J. 1993. *Beyond the new right.* London: Routledge.
Gray, J. 1995. *Enlightenment's wake.* London: Routledge.
Gray, J. 1996. *Post-liberalism.* London: Routledge.
Gray, J. 1997. *Endgames.* Cambridge: Polity.
Gray, J. 2003. *Al Quaeda and what it means to be modern.* London: Faber and Faber.

Gray, J. 2007. *Black mass*. London: Allen Lane.
Marx, K. 2000. *Selected writings*. Ed. D. McLellan. 2nd ed. Oxford: Oxford University Press.
Marx, K., and F. Engels. 1968. *Selected works*. 1 vol. London: Lawrence and Wishart.
Marx, K., and F. Engels. 1975. *Collected works*. 4 vol. London: Lawrence and Wishart.
Porrit, J. 2006. *Capitalism as if the earth matters*. London: Earthscan.
Rousseau, J.J. 1968. *The social contract and discourses*. London: Dent.
Tocqueville de, A. 1966. *Democracy in America*. 1 vol. London: Fontana.
Todd, J. 2007. *Through the darkness*. Cape Town: Zebra Press.

Shifting the debate on land reform, poverty and inequality in Zimbabwe, an engagement with *Zimbabwe's Land Reform: Myths and Realities*[1]

Blair Rutherford

Sociology and Anthropology, Carleton University, Canada

> *Zimbabwe's land reform: myths and realities*[2] purports to overturn the western media and academy's 'myths' of agrarian failure and cronyism in Zimbabwe's fast-track land reform with a study rooted in the 'reality' of its outcomes in the Masvingo area. Yet the positivist picture painted by Scoones, Marongwe, Mavedzenge, Mahenehene, Murimbarimba, and Sukume is another *position* in portrayals of a complex process entangling many local material struggles–including those seen as successful examples of the yeomanry admired by the authors–with the equally important processes of authoritarian nationalism they side-line. 'Myth making' is not counter to 'reality', but positions particular claims within it. By concentrating on the 'local' and celebrating what they see as non-technocratic successes, the authors ignore the context and politics of the state–which they later invoke to develop adequate supportive policy and stability for the new farmers. Their reality ignores as much as the myths they try to challenge, and thus fails to assist to develop the policies they would like.

Since 2010, there has been a significant shift in the academic terrain concerning the characterisation of the wide-scale transfer of land that has occurred in Zimbabwe since 2000. Aside from the work of Sam Moyo and his co-authors which has been generally supportive of what they call the 'fast track land reform' of the last 11 years (e.g., Moyo 2001, Moyo 2011; Moyo and Yeros 2005a, b), until the last year or so most academic analysts have been very critical of the process of this massive land redistribution. The shift is that some of those who had condemned the identified and widely reported violence, the chaos, the corruption and the economic disruptions caused by the forcible transfer of land from many large-scale commercial farmers, who were almost exclusively white, to black farmers have become less critical. They have begun focusing instead on the more positive outcomes for the new farmers on the transferred land (compare, e.g., Cousins 2006 and Cousins 2010). The work that has been pivotal in this shift is the recently published book *Zimbabwe's Land Reform: Myths and Realities* written by Scoones et al. (2010).

Whereas Moyo's work has often been challenged by many academics on the grounds that it has been appraised, rightly or wrongly, as too sympathetic to the ZANU (PF) regime, Scoones et al. (2010) has been much more positively received. For instance, the following academics praise this book in its inside and outside covers, reading like a list of a 'who's who' of the leading scholars of the politics of land in Zimbabwe (and in Africa) over the last four decades: Bill Kinsey, Robin Palmer, Sam Moyo, Henry Bernstein, Mandivamba Rukuni, Pauline Peters, Jocelyn Alexander, JoAnn McGregor, Ben Cousins, Admos Chimhowu, Amanda Hammar, and Joost Fontein, amongst others. Other than Moyo, none of these scholars have been challenged in academic debate to the best of my knowledge as supporters of the ZANU (PF) government and indeed a number of them have strongly challenged some of the work by Moyo and his co-authors. Of course, these blurbs of praise for the book do not indicate complete acceptance of its arguments and analysis. They do, however, show that *Zimbabwe's Land Reform* needs to be taken as a book that if not building bridges between different scholars of rural Zimbabwe in the last 11 years is at the very least a defining part of a moment in which a rethinking of analyses and interventions is occurring.

While some have used this book to laud the ZANU (PF) government actions and to attack its critics (e.g., Freeman 2010), I am more interested in other positionings of this book as a way to better critically assess its arguments and evidence. In so doing, I seek to contribute to the ongoing re-assessment of the land redistribution and conflicts in Zimbabwe.

Positionings is my touchstone in this paper. I use it loosely to explore some of the discursive, material, and political practices through which this book engages with its topic–how it positions its argument, its evidence, and its own intellectual, if not political, project. This term allows me to try to tease out some of its insights, its receptions, and its blind-spots.

Let me begin by briefly noting my own positioning in this scholarship. My own research on Zimbabwean farm workers began in 1992 and included periods of field research in 2000, 2002, and 2003, before I was forced by the politics in the countryside to cross the Limpopo River and refocus my research on the growing number of Zimbabweans working on the farms in northern South Africa. In my writings concerning the changing situation of farm workers in the violent land redistribution exercises in Zimbabwe, I have aimed, perhaps not always successfully, to show the complicated politics shaping how they have been positioned and have been positioning themselves in the changing agrarian landscape. I have sought to attend to some of the 'entanglements' (Moore 2005) of wider national-scale actions with more localised manoeuvres and conditions in particular farming areas through a historically situated ethnographic analysis (Rutherford 2001, 2004, 2008, Rutherford 2011).

I find *Zimbabwe's Land Reform* to be extremely rich in detail, insight and analysis into some of the complicated social landscapes of the agrarian relations emerging in Masvingo, south-eastern Zimbabwe. I am not surprised that it is making a significant contribution to the academic analyses of rural Zimbabwe and likely will have resonance in various policy-making and implementation practices of governmental, donor and non-governmental actors. However, I will not dwell on, or profile, the many strengths of this strong book. Instead, I want to concentrate on other elements of the book which I find to be problematic and needing greater scrutiny and discussion.

As the subtitle of *Zimbabwe's Land Reform: Myths and Realities* suggests, Scoones et al. (2010) seek to marshal scholarly evidence to challenge what they call the dominant 'myths' concerning Zimbabwe's land reform since 2000 found in the media and made by other commentators. Drawing on field data from Masvingo province, they aim to undermine the following five claims, which they deem to be 'myths':

Myth 1: Zimbabwean land reform has been a total failure
Myth 2: The beneficiaries of Zimbabwean land reform have been largely political 'cronies'
Myth 3: There is no investment in the new resettlements
Myth 4: Agriculture is in complete ruins, creating chronic food insecurity
Myth 5: The rural economy has collapsed (2010, 8).

Noting that knowledge is always 'socially and politically constructed' and that 'personal, institutional and political location' of this construction 'matters', they analyse 'the creation of myths and their portrayal through policy narratives' as 'an important first step in unpacking the complexity of Zimbabwe's land reform story' (2010, 7). Against such 'biased lenses' (2010, 8), the ontological anchor for their work is what they call 'empirical realities', which entails their focus being more on the consequences of the 'land reform' than the disputed social and political practices that have been involved in it. As Scoones succinctly told a BBC reporter challenging their book in a television interview in 2011, 'We are looking at outcomes not processes' (Royal African Society n.d.).

A discourse analysis, sensitive to what is often called post structural critique, could of course show the sleight of hand at work, the professed attention to the constructed-ness and the policy narratives of such 'myths' while somehow the knowledge produced by Scoones et al. (2010) escape such located-ness. By positioning their argument as an eschewal of allegiance to a singular theoretical perspective (without reflecting or perhaps purposively downplaying their own positionings), and adopting instead an 'empirical stance' (2010, 14), they seek to locate their analysis outside a social and political construction of knowledge. In their writing, their 'empirical stance' permits allegiance to 'facts' and the dismissal of many other critical engagements with the agrarian politics as 'myth'.

However, for me, rather than trying to simply deconstruct this constitutive other, this disavowal of their own 'policy narrative'—one that can be described as that of a positivistic policy science given their proclaimed allegiance to empirical realities against what they call bias—I seek to understand what this discursive positioning enables, what it occludes, and what it limits in this otherwise very strong book.

Enabling

What their discursive and analytical strategy enables is the very refined focus on many of the material practices found in what now are the new resettlement areas. In their words, they 'focus on ground-level, field realities. Our aim is to chart a way forward, and not dwell excessively on the interpretations of past events'. By eschewing the 'intense debates that have surrounded Zimbabwe's land reform' which they dismissively reduce as 'myths', they argue their 'book is intended as a modest contributions to the rebuilding of Zimbabwe. Through solid evidence from the field, we hope to illuminate some fairly basic questions: who got the land, what did people do with it, and what are the implications for broader development options?' (2010, 31). I suggest this modest aim, this explicit disavowal of the debates and the processes of land reform, and the focus instead on 'hard realities' is both the strength and ultimately their weakness when they start laying out the implications for 'development options'.

This book provides an incredible wealth of detail of the diverse economic practices emerging from and intersecting with the social relations and environmental conditions shaping the agrarian dynamics in Masvingo while attending to the uncertain and disputed authority relations seeking to govern diverse farming areas. For me, the exemplary strength of this book is that it shows in a refined analysis the particular socio-political and class positionings of individuals and households and some of the shifts over the last 10 years in their 13 case study sites across different ecological and socio-geographical zones in Masvingo Province. They clearly show that since 2000 rural Masvingo has experienced a range of economic activities where new commodity chains have been forged and livelihood strategies expanded, yet with class inequalities continuing.

Moreover, they argue that 'accumulation from below' is occurring in the new resettlement areas, as a more extensive range of agricultural activities, including significant investments, have been happening on what had largely been large-scale white-owned cattle farms in Masvingo. They note this type of 'green revolution' is 'one based on skill, effort and hard labour, and the benefits of new land' rather than driven by technocratic planning and significant donor or private sector investment in agricultural intensification (2010, 124).

They thus position the reader in a wealth of information, of quantitative evidence generated through surveys and summarised cases emerging through interviews. In the pages of this book, one finds: investments in cattle, ox ploughs and other means of production, trees planted, access to water, trends to draught power strategies, fertiliser purchase, crop production figures, percentage sold, herd composition of cattle, labour hiring, labour dynamics, schematics of commodity chains for key crops and livestock, non-farm income, remittances, household migration patterns, to name but a few. Through innumerable tables and their thoughtful analysis of the information, Scoones et al. (2010) positions the reader into the fluid, material terrain of the resettlement schemes. They show economic differentiation, impoverishment, and productivity gains. They also attend to differentiated gains by women in the new resettlement areas, potentially enabled by the contested authority relations in these spaces that allow more women to acquire access to land compared to those in the Communal Lands. By prioritising all this evidence, the book opens new vistas into the differentiated lives of these new resettlement households.

By locating their analysis in the materiality of farming and showing the gains in terms of access to the means of production and increased productivity for many of the new resettlement farmers surveyed, the book achieves its goal of disputing dominant 'doomsday' portrayals of rural Zimbabwe in the last 11 years–their 'five myths'–while providing many scholars and practitioners with new information and much new insight into rural Zimbabwe. For example, against MYTH 1 (re: 'land reform has been a total failure), they show that there has been an incredible redistribution of land on the national scale (145,000 A1 farms and 16,000 commercial A2 farms established in Zimbabwe),[3] with about half of the 177 sampled households in their research being on an 'upward trajectory.' There is economic differentiation based in part on pre-existing access to assets, labour and capital (2010, 125), with 35% of their sample households accumulating through agriculture (with only 1.4% doing so through patronage connections) and a further 21.4% accumulating through combining farming with non-farm livelihood strategies (2010, 227). In contrast, 34% of the households are barely able to make ends meet and 10% left the farms for various reasons.

Rather than viewing rural Zimbabwe as a site of chaos and economic stagnation, their book provides a sense of dynamism. As they argue, 'There are problems, for sure, but there has been an unleashing of innovation, diversity and entrepreneurship, with new market connections and governance arrangements being forged' (2010, 164). In contrast to the conventional tale of complete ruination of rural Zimbabwe common in many media stories found in the global North,[4] such an argument and a marshalling of evidence are exciting and can be persuasive. However, they can also distract the reader from some of the displacement occurring in the book's own analytical arguments.

Occluding

Their focus on the 'outcomes' of the land reform occludes their additional insightful engagement with multiple and diverse historical processes informing the 'solid evidence from the field' as well as their own political sympathies. Despite the downplaying of process, they show the very different dynamics in the different resettlement areas studied, noting this history informs the particular consequences in each site: 'There is no single story of the process of land reform across our sites. Each was different. But understanding what happened when land was taken is critically important for understanding what happened next' (2010, 43). For me, this attention to the history, to the process, is another strength of the monograph as they are able to analyse the differential consequences of land redistribution on class, gender, and productivity axes. It is an analytical tactic that provides insight into these rather fluid and contested social territories of the new resettlement areas. But this attention to the plurality of contingent histories of each resettlement site becomes a reason to disavow wider-scale analysis, as they tellingly argue:

> What prevailed in a particular place was highly contingent on circumstance and context, and there was much blurring of boundaries and local contestation of authority and legitimacy. The politics of land in this period was therefore not straightforward. Any simple generalisation is almost certainly untrue for a range of particular settings. For this reason, we start with the empirical particularities and avoid making any wider, sweeping generalisations about political motivations and dynamics. It was the particular circumstances prevailing on a particular farm that is important, for it is these that have affected people's livelihood pathways over the following decade. (2010, 45)

The authors thus seem to assume that their focus on the empirical particularities–the dismissal of 'sweeping generalisations'–permits them to show the reality of land reform in Zimbabwe. But their empirical focus carries with it a particular political story of its own, namely that of yeomen effort on the part of (many of) the resettlement farmers, a story-line they regularly repeat. Their sympathy to the land invaders, allocators and farmers comes through in their vignettes of how each resettlement farm was acquired. For instance, the invaders were said to 'encourage' others to join them, be 'charismatic', while in contrast white commercial farmers would 'bribe' or used 'hired thugs' against the invaders (2010, 48, 49) and thus clearly are morally, if not politically suspect. Farm workers who resisted the invasion were said to be 'very loyal to their employers' (2010, 49) and not, say, trying to grapple with uncertain and ambiguous power relations and threats from all sides (e.g., Rutherford 2008). In short, the book positions itself in support of the resettled farmers, those who can 'accumulate from below' despite the lack of government or donor support, showing how some 'have seriously invested in their new farms, and despite all odds, have made a go of it, with great plans for the future' (2010, 52). In contrast to, perhaps, an analytical strategy seeking to engage with the contradictions and inequalities emerging from the agrarian reform, while acknowledging the empirical variation in the agricultural means of production of resettled households, the book emphasises the durability and economic achievements of 'the' resettled farmer. Of course, there is nothing inherently wrong with such a political positioning, of lauding the massive land transfer since 2000 as some form of 'land reform' enabling an 'accumulation from below'. However, it is a positioning, a stand, one not explicitly stated, and which is occluded by their dichotomy of empirical realities and biased myths.

The ability of this dichotomy of empirical realities and biased myths to gloss over the 'personal, institutional and political location' of the construction of knowledge also comes through in the Preface. They note in passing that three of the co-authors, the men who led the research field team in Masvingo, have all gained land through the resettlement process: Mavedezenge is an A1 resettlement farmer, Murimbarimba is a fulltime A2 sugar cane farmer, and Mahenehene has a plot in an 'informal site' (2010, xi). Some might suggest that greater discussion of this material stake and personal benefit from these wider processes would follow their own argument about the importance of the located-ness of knowledge production, but it is not discussed further in the book.[5] Instead in the following paragraph the authors do note the divergent backgrounds and politics of members of the research team but suggest that these were ultimately subsumed by their allegiance to empirical reality:

> We were always there to challenge each other's assumptions and biases, but what held the ground together was the commitment to explore the empirical realities on the ground, and root our analysis and policy recommendations in such solid evidence. (2010, xii)

Thus empirical realities trump (personal) bias once again, disavowing the authors pronounced grounding in the social construction of knowledge positioning.

I thus suggest that the authors' positioning of the book as a detached promotion of the empirical realities contradicts their textured analyses of contested histories and masks their own politics. This leads me to show how their immersion in the material details also limits their book.

Limiting

Such political sympathies are not what concerns me in themselves, although they undermine their assumed positivist stance. What is problematic to me is that the constitutive contrast between myths and reality leads them to associate analyses of state-abetted violence with the former, juxtaposing this in contrast to their own 'realist' analysis of 'outcomes'. I suggest this analytical positioning prevents them from addressing the wider-scale politics and power relations which have been so crucial for these micro-dynamics into which they provide much insight. This, I would suggest, leads them to make some questionable analyses and prognoses.

In their case studies, they do note in passing the political violence and lack of enforcement of laws. But they characterise the Zimbabwean state from 2000 to 2008 as creating 'policy distortions' (2010, 94) rather than, say, being intensely politicised by the ZANU (PF) regime. The following passage, discussing the dynamic between national-scale state actions and the particularities of land redistribution sites is apt:

> For the most part, the post-2000 resettlement did not suffer from top-down technocratic intervention; indeed the absence of almost any external support was a feature of it. The outcome resulted from a complex trade-off between local conditions, particular histories and contingent circumstances and the structuring forces of nationalist politics, technocratic planning models and local institutional arrangements, mediated by diverse forms of 'traditional' and 'modern' political authority, gender dynamics and social relations. With the state and other actors now re-engaging, we must ask what else should be done. (2010, 237)

'Nationalist politics' is what others have called a regime deploying violence to try to eliminate the opposition MDC. How that played out was definitely contingent but 'trade-off' gives a sense of collective deliberation rather than hierarchical deployment of threats, violence, and counter-violence, at times with direct support of sections of the security apparatuses of the state (see, e.g., Moore 2004; Hellum and Derman 2004; Bond and Saunders 2005; Kriger 2006; Raftopoulos 2006; Scarnecchia 2006; Hammar 2008; Sachikonye 2011). Yet *Zimbabwe's Land Reform* consistently steers away from squarely examining such national-scale politics on setting the contours and ongoing status of the massive land redistribution, even when mentioning its influence. Take the following passage, for example:

> The heightened political tensions around the 2008 elections, and the prospect of an inclusive government that might end land-based patronage, resulted in a range of speculative land claims by politically-connected elites. While there remains debate about the origins and motivations of the land occupations in 2000, there was little doubt about the politically-motivated origins of this new 'land grab'. (2010, 199)

Here they seem to suggest that the violence unleashed by the ZANU (PF) government and its allies after March 2008–coded as 'heightened political tensions' which euphemises significant terror, violence, and murder (Human Rights Watch 2011)–led to politically connected expropriation of land. Yet in so doing, they note it was inspired by fear of the cessation of already existing 'land-based patronage' connected to the fast-track land resettlement starting in 2000.

Another example of downplaying the importance of national-scale politics comes when they use the wide-scale urban evictions that displaced 100,000s of people in 2005 (called *Operation Murambatsvina*) as a way to comment on the 'ambiguous character' of the state: 'at one time backing the land invasions and the new resettlements and at the next moment invoking draconian planning laws to undermine development efforts on the ground' (2010, 211). Given that they refuse to engage in discussions of the politics of the process of land redistribution, they simply view the forced urban removals as an example of some excessive technocratic impulse of an otherwise supportive state and not, say, as a regime seeking to bolster its survival through violence and power (Vambe 2008).

I suggest this analytical limit results from their stated intention to provide policy prescriptions based on evidence–the 'realities' of their subtitle–for 'a fundamental rethinking of the future for rural Zimbabwe' (2010, 232). Their positioning within the minutia of material practices is equated with empirical realities for better interventions: 'the aim of challenging myths with data on complex realities is not to create new myths. Our aim, instead, is a more dispassionate, evidence-based assessment rooted in careful sampling and analysis' (2010, 238). Even though they observe in passing that land has become a key source of political patronage and violence, intimidation and 'abuse of the rule of law' which 'has undermined the land reform programme's credibility and legitimacy both nationally and internationally', they plead this should not prevent one from looking at the 'wider story which this book has tried to tell' (2010, 252).

They even call for a more 'solid, coherent political consensus.... [A] more effective, longer-term political settlement is clearly required, rooted in more widely accepted forms of public authority' (2010, 236). But as they have not analysed the politicisation of state practices and structures–even if in passing they note that politics 'has been so fraught' and any association with the 'opposition MDC, has become an invitation to retribution and trouble' (2010, 251)–they instead seem to suggest that a proper developmental state will emerge after serious consideration of the importance of supporting the welfare and accumulation strategies of its rural citizens. As they opine,

> Reconstruction must take account of what has gone before: the disruptions, forms of violence, as well the innovations in institutions and processes. Future development must therefore sensitively, carefully and strategically intervene in ways that allow a functional, responsive and accountable state to emerge. (2010, 189)

How so, one may ask?

And it is here where one sees the wider politics of this book. By eschewing a critical analysis of partisan state practices–relegating those largely to the realm of myth-making and distracting debates over process–Scoones et al. (2010) present their thoughtful policy suggestions as if there is a policy community in and outside of Zimbabwe keen to listen and having apolitical policy apparatuses, the civil service, and administrative capacities at the ready to implement them. As they conclude:

> The first decade has been difficult, and many important lessons have been learned. The next decade, given the right support and policy environment, combined with political and economic stability, must be the moment when the real benefits of redistributive land reform and a reconfigured agricultural economy can be shown.... If the myths continue to trump the realities, however, misguided policy and inappropriate support will be the result. If the reverse is true, there are real prospects for a bright future for rural livelihoods in the new resettlements in Zimbabwe. (2010, 253, 256)

Concluding thoughts

In conclusion, I think that *Zimbabwe's Land Reform* has played an important role in convincing more scholars to rethink some of the results of the last 11 years in rural Zimbabwe, while perhaps also influencing others in the donor community who have been keen to try to re-engage with Zimbabwe since the government of national unity began in February 2009. I think the authors should be praised for prompting readers, including critical academics, into more publicly recognising what should be an obvious point: 'for those who have remained [on the distributed land] there is near universal recognition that gaining access to land has improved people's lot' (2010, 76).

One could also suggest that their disavowal of analysing the politics of land redistribution and its relationship to wider state practices may well be an explicitly strategic way to try to gain a sympathetic hearing of those officials in Zimbabwean authority structures and the donor community. However, one could also think of it as a constructed policy narrative that will have difficulty leading to their recommended interventions, as the national-scale politics are deeply entangled with the contingent realities they intimately discuss (and which at times they, perhaps inadvertently, show).

An alternative for *Zimbabwe's Land Reform: Myths and Realities* might have been to argue that transformations of rural Zimbabwe resulting in more households able to accumulate in part or whole through farming took place because of an authoritarian regime that does not hesitate in using violence to try to destroy its political opposition. However, such a policy narrative would require a more explicitly critical analysis of the national-scale actions and their entanglement in the politics of diverse localised sites (e.g., Fontein 2009; Zamchiya forthcoming) if one wants to advocate for the building of some sort of accountable, developmental state. I would garner, however, that this type of narrative would not necessarily build bridges amongst the existing diversity of scholars and likely be less useful for generating resources and support for resettlement farmers amongst donors and the government of Zimbabwe. To me, this suggests that 'myth making' is not counter to 'reality'. Rather it positions particular claims within it.

Acknowledgements

This paper was first given at the Canadian Association of African Studies annual meeting at York University, Toronto, Canada, 7 May 2011. I thank those attending and the other presenters on the panel for the constructive feedback. I also thank Amanda Hammar, Jocelyn Alexander, and Norma Kriger for their helpful, critical comments. Responsibility for the final paper, of course, is mine alone.

Notes

1. Paper first presented at the Canadian Association of African Studies annual meeting at York University, Toronto, Canada, 7 May 2011.
2. *Zimbabwe's Land Reform: Myths and Realities* by Ian Scoones, Nelson Marongwe, Blasio Mavedzenge, Jacob Mahenehene, Felix Murimbarimba and Crispen Sukume, Woodbridge, Suffolk, James Currey, 2010, 304 pp., ISBN 9781847010247.
3. A1 and A2 are the designations for different type of land resettlement schemes, which they define as 'A1, small-scale farming, either in villagised arrangements or as self-contained

plots and A2, small- and medium-scale commercial farms' (2010, 3–5). It should be noted that other scholars, including those who raise more critical questions about the land reform since 2000, also have noted this incredible transfer of land (e.g., Alexander 2006; Waeterloos and Rutherford 2004).
4. As I write, for example, *The Economist* just published an article excoriating the implementation of an indigenisation law in Zimbabwe, starting it off with these frightening words, 'A DECADE ago Robert Mugabe's regime seized most of Zimbabwe's white-owned commercial farms. The president promised to give the land to the landless, but instead gave much of it to his wealthy cronies. The country's largest industry was wrecked, creating deadly food shortages (see picture)'. The 'picture' is a photo of two relatively nice-looking wrought-iron gates ajar, surrounded by one- to two-metre high grass marked with the alarmist caption 'This is what happened to the farms. The mines may be next'. (The Economist 2011). For a sharp analysis of the polarised media reporting on Zimbabwe concerning land redistribution after 2000, see Willems 2004).
5. Indeed two reviewers of my article kindly pointed out to me this located positioning of some of the co-authors of the book, suggesting it requires at least mentioning, if not analysis.

Note on contributor

Blair Rutherford is professor of Anthropology and director of the Institute of African Studies at Carleton University in Ottawa, Canada. He has published widely on the cultural politics of land, labour, and citizenship in Zimbabwe and South Africa.

References

Alexander, J. 2006. *The unsettled land: State-making & the politics of land in Zimbabwe, 1893-2003*. Oxford: James Currey.
Bond, P., and R. Saunders. 2005. Labor, the state, and the struggle for a democratic Zimbabwe. *Monthly Review* 57, no. 7: 42–55.
Cousins, B. 2006. Debating the politics of land occupations. *Journal of Agrarian Change* 6, no. 4: 584–97.
Cousins, B. 2010. Time to ditch the 'disaster' scenarios. *Mail & Guardian*, May 21. http://mg.co.za/article/2010-05-20-time-to-ditch-the-disaster-scenarios (accessed September 2, 2011).
The Economist. 2011. A new plan to wreck one of Africa's unluckiest countries. *The Economist*, September 3. http://www.economist.com/node/21528303 (accessed September 4, 2011).
Fontein, J. 2009. 'We want to belong to our roots and we want to be modern people': New farmers, old claims around Lake Mutirikwi, Southern Zimbabwe. *African Studies Quarterly* 10, no. 4: 1–35.
Freeman, N. 2010. Zimbabwe's road to vindication. *Race and History*, December 15. http://www.raceandhistory.com/Zimbabwe/2010/1512.html. (accessed September 2, 2011).
Hammar, A. 2008. In the name of sovereignty: Displacement and state making in post-independence Zimbabwe. *Journal of Contemporary African Studies* 26, no. 4: 417–34.
Hellum, A., and B. Derman. 2004. Land reform and human rights in contemporary Zimbabwe: Balancing individual and social justice through an integrated human rights framework. *World Development* 32, no. 10: 1785–805.
Human Rights Watch. 2011. *Perpetual fear: Impunity and cycles of violence in Zimbabwe*. New York: Human Rights Watch.
Kriger, N. 2006. From patriotic memories to "patriotic history" in Zimbabwe, 1990-2005. *Third World Quarterly* 27, no. 6: 1151–69.
Moore, D. 2004. Marxism and Marxist intellectuals in schizophrenic Zimbabwe: How many rights for Zimbabwe's left? A comment. *Historical Materialism* 21, no. 4: 405–25.
Moore, D.S. 2005. *Suffering for territory: Race, place, and power in Zimbabwe*. Durham, NC: Duke University Press.

Moyo, S. 2001. The land occupation movement and democratisation in Zimbabwe: Contradictions of neoliberalism. *Millennium* 30, no. 2: 311–30.

Moyo, S. 2011. Land concentration and accumulation after redistributive reform in post settler Zimbabwe. *Review of African Political Economy* 38, no. 128: 257–76.

Moyo, S., and P. Yeros. 2005a. Land occupations and land reform in Zimbabwe: Towards the national democratic revolution. In: *Reclaiming the land: The resurgence of rural movements in Africa, Asia and Latin America.* ed. S. Moyo and P. Yeros, 165–205. London: Zed Books.

Moyo, S., and P. Yeros, ed., 2005b. *Reclaiming the land: The resurgence of rural movements in Africa, Asia and Latin America.* London: Zed Books.

Raftopoulos, B. 2006. The Zimbabwean crisis and the challenges for the left. *Journal of Southern African Studies* 32, no. 2: 203–17.

Royal African Society. n.d. Zimbabwe's land reform: Challenging the myths. http://www.royalafricansociety.org/component/content/article/728.html (accessed September 2, 2011).

Rutherford, B. 2001. *Working on the margins: Black workers, white farmers in postcolonial Zimbabwe.* London: Zed Books and Harare: Weaver Books.

Rutherford, B. 2004. Desired publics, domestic government, and entangled fears: On the anthropology of civil society, farm workers, and white farmers in Zimbabwe. *Cultural Anthropology* 19, no. 1: 122–53.

Rutherford, B. 2008. Conditional belonging: Farm workers and the cultural politics of recognition in Zimbabwe. *Development and Change* 39, no. 1: 73–99.

Rutherford, B. 2011. On the promise and perils of citizenship: Heuristic concepts, Zimbabwean example. *Citizenship Studies* 15, nos. 3–4: 499–512.

Sachikonye, L. 2011. *When a state turns on its citizens: 60 years of institutionalized violence in Zimbabwe.* Johannesburg: Jacana.

Scarnecchia, T. 2006. The 'Fascist Cycle' in Zimbabwe, 2000-2005. *Journal of Southern African Studies* 32, no. 2: 221–37.

Scoones, I., N. Marongwe, B. Mavedzenge, J. Mahenehene, F. Murimbarimba, and C. Sukume. 2010. *Zimbabwe's land reform: Myths & realities.* Oxford: James Currey.

Vambe, M., ed. 2008. *The hidden dimensions of Operation Murambatsvina in Zimbabwe.* Harare: Weaver Press.

Waeterloos, E., and B. Rutherford. 2004. Land reform in Zimbabwe: Challenges and opportunities for poverty reduction among commercial farm workers. *World Development* 32, no. 3: 537–53.

Willems, W. 2004. Peasant demonstrators, violence invaders: Representations of land in the Zimbabwean press. *World Development* 32, no. 10: 1767–83.

Zamchiya, P. Forthcoming. A synopsis of land and agrarian change in Chipinge district, Zimbabwe. *Journal of Peasant Studies.*

Index

References in **Bold** represent illustrations.

accumulation 2, 4; disposession 31
Affirmative Action Group (AAG) 54, 70, 72, 77, 78
Africa: agriculture 101–2; business-class development 68–71
Africa Consolidated Resources (ACR) 57
African National Congress (ANC) 122
African Voice, The (Ranger) 28
African Youth League (AYL) 125
agrarian policies: Rhodesian 104
agrarianists: patriotic 144
Agribank 77
agriculture: African 101–2; decline 71; science 102; subsidies 52
Agritex 104
Air Zimbabwe 77, 93
Alexander, J. 104, 113
alternative histories 30–1
amafusi (abandoned land) 109, 110
anarchism 37
Anatomy of Terror report (2011) 17
Anglo-American Corporation 55
asset freezing 86
authority: traditional 106–7

bank transfers ('burning money') 92
Bankers Association of Zimbabwe (BAZ) 74
banking sector: dollarisation 93; economic crisis 91–4; empowerment policy 74–5; workers' agency during economic crisis 93–4; workers during economic crisis 92–3
Barclay, P. 143
Beach, D. 29
Becoming Zimbabwe (Raftopoulos and Mlambo) 31
Berry, S. 102
best practice agenda 50
Bilateral Investment Treaties (BITs) 73
Biti, T. 16, 75, 77
Black Friday 55, 85
black market 89
Black Mass: Apocalyptic Religion and the Death of Utopia (Gray) 1

Boka, R.: scandal 54–5
briefcase businessmen 52, 53
British South Africa Company (BSAC) 51
burning money 92
business-class development: African 68–71
business-state relations: neo-patrimonialism 68

Catholic Relief Services (CRS) 18
Central Intelligence Organisation (CIO) 17
Chamber of Mines of Zimbabwe (COMZ) 71, 79
Chan, S. 122
Chatterjee, P. 38
Cheater, A. 107, 112
Cheeseman, N. 12
Chiadzwa mines 21
Chigwell Farm (Chegutu) 73
Chipangano 2, 5; Mbare 20
Chitungwiza 84
Chiyangwa, P. 54
cholera epidemic (2008–9) 2, 73
Christian Care 18
Christianity 140
citizens: subjects 36
civil service: mining revenue paying 16–17; preventing removal 15–16
civil society 38–44; radical (state-centric and society centric) 37–8
Cliffe, L. 30
Cobbing, J. 28
Cold Storage Commission (CSC) 55
Cold War (1945–91) 120
colonialism: settler 68
Commercial Farmers' Union of Zimbabwe (CFU) 73
communal area reforms 103–5
communal land 99, 104, 107
Communal Land Acts: (1981) 103, 109, 110; (1982) 113
Communal Lands Development Plan (1984–5) 104
communal tenure 100

INDEX

Communist Manifesto 140
communitarian relations 36
Confederation of Zimbabwe Industries (CZI) 76
Congo *see* Democratic Republic of Congo
Congo-Duka 58
Congress of South African Trade Unions (COSATU) 121
corruption 53
Crack Unit on Price Controls 56
Crosland, A. 127
cross-border trading 90
Cupertino 123
currency: foreign 90, 92

David Whitehead Textiles 76
Davies, R. 53
democracy 131; de Tocqueville analysis 142
Democratic Republic of Congo (DRC) 3; war (1998–2003) 58, 85
Denga, P. 20
development: African business-class 68–71
developmental patrimonial regimes 50
diamonds 16, 57; mining 21–3
dispossession: accumulation 31
District Councils Act (1980) 113
dollar: Zimbabwean 55, 56
dollarisation 83, 84; banking sector 93; effects 94–5; teaching sector revival 90–1
Dongo, M. 55
donors 37
DR Congo 3; war (1998–2003) 58, 85
drought 105; relief 104

earnings 54
Econet 54, 78
economic collapse: land reform programme 71–4
economic crisis (1997–2008) 83–95; banking sector 91–3; synopsis 85–7; teachers and bank workers' agency 93–4; teaching sector 87–8; urban studies 84–5
economic structural adjustment programme (ESAP) 53, 54, 55, 62, 86
economy: foreign-owned 52–3; indicators (1980–2006) *54*; macroeconomic indicators (1980–2006) *86*
elite accommodation 55
employment 54
Empowerment Corporation 54
empowerment law 75
empowerment policy 67–8; banking sector 74–5; business-class development 68–71; conclusion 80; land reform 71–4; manufacturing sector 76–9; mining sector 79–80

Engels, F.: *The Origin of the Family, Private Property and the State* 140
Epworth: politics 19
European Enlightenment 139–42
evictions 21, 72

farms: compulsory acquisition 85; evictions 72
fast track indigenisation programme 80
fast-track land reform process 2, 38–9, 71, 88, 147, 153
food aid 17–18
Food for Work programmes 113
foreign currency dealing 90, 92
foreign direct investment (FDI) 78, 79, 80
forex rents 54
French Revolution (1789–99) 142
Fukuyama, F. 27

Gates Foundation (B&MGF) 21
GDP (gross domestic product) 77
general election (2000) 58
Giddens, A.: structuration theory 84, 93, 94
Global Political Agreement (GPA) 11, 12; and Inclusive Government (IG) 14–15
Godwin, P. 1
Gono, G. 71, 74, 75, 92
governance: good enough 50
Government of National Unity 83, 90
Gray, J. 140, 141, 142; *Black Mass: Apocalyptic Religion and the Death of Utopia* 1
Green Bomber militias 2
green revolution 104
Growth with Equity principle 87
Gukurahundi 6
Gumede, M. 106
Gwayi reserve 101
Gwayi Valley: map **105**; worker peasantry 105–6

Hamadziripi, H. 5
Handley, A. 68
Hanke, S. 86, 91
Harare Province 20
Harvey, D. 31
headmen: land administration 110–11
Helliker, K. 144
hidden transcripts 6, 99, 100, 114
history: alternative 30–1; becoming 31; nationalist 28–30; patriotic 27–8, 144; radical 30–1
HIV-AIDS 124
Hlahla, B. 23
Hoffman, J. 2, 6, 30, 31
households 106–7; behaviour and land claims 109–10

INDEX

housing 21
humanism 141
hyper-inflation 56, 77, 84, 86, 89, 92

IMF (International Monetary Fund) 87
imperialism: struggle against 39, 43
import substitution 53
Inclusive Government (IG) 11, 14–19; and Global Political Agreement (GPA) 14–15
indigenisation 69–70, 78, 79; *fast track* programme 80; law 72
Indigenous Business Development Centre (IBDC) 54, 70
Industrial Conciliation Acts 51
inflation: hyper- 56, 77, 84, 86, 89, 92
informal political networks: concept 12
informal sector: teaching 89–90
International Centre for Settlement of Investment Disputes (ICSID) 73
investment: foreign direct (FDI) 78, 79, 80

Jones, J. 84
Joshi, J. 57
Justice for Agriculture (JAG) 73

Kabila, L. 58, 85
Kanyenze, G. 93
Kasukuwere, S. (Minister) 75
Kenya 102
Khan, M.H. 50, 59
Khumalo, M. 106
kinship 106–7
Kissinger, H. 127
Kombayi, P. 5
Kondozi estate 73, 75
Koning, P. 91
kraal building 106, *107*
kraal court 110
kraal dynasties *107*
Kriger, N. 30
kukiya-kiya 84, 85, 94
Kurotwi, Major L. 22

Lancaster House 51; Constitution 62, 102; settlement 59
land: administration and headmen 110–11; claims and households' behaviour 109–10; communal 99, 104, 107; differing claims 108; expropriation 106; governance and legislation *111*; informal ownership 110; intra-household allocations 109; leases 108; management and ambiguity 111–12; occupations 39; redistribution and political progression 43; rental market 107–8; ZANU-PF 38
Land Acquisition Act (1992) 72
Land Apportionment Act (1930) 51, 101

land reform 143, 144; economic collapse 71–4; *fast-track* process 2, 38–9, 71, 88, 147, 153; myths 148
Land Tenure Act (1969) 51
landholding: secure 99
leases: land 108
legislation: land governance *111*
liberation: loyalty to 27; war 112

M&S Syndicate 57
Machingura, Dzinishe 'Dzino' 124–8
madiro: promotion 112
Magure, B. 144
Makumbe, J. 3
Mamdani, M. 36, 40
Mandaza, I. 39, 40, 42, 43, 69, 71; *Zimbabwe. The Political Economy of Transition* 30
Mandela, N. 119
Mandiwananzira, S. 79
manufacturing sector: empowerment policy 76–9
Maramba Pfungwe (constituency) 18
Marange 22, 23
market stall allocation 21
Marx, K. 27; *On the Jewish Question* 140
Marxism 120, 128, 130, 140
Masiyiwa, S. 54
Masvingo Province 150
Matabeleland 29
Matabeleland Today (Ranger) 28
Matabeleland-Order-In Council (1894) 101
Matyszak, D. 12, 14
Mawere, M. 69
Mbada Mining 57
Mbare 21
Mbeki, G. 119, 120, 121
Mbeki, T. 2, 121, 122–4
mechanical progress 141
Melber, H. 27
Mhanda, W. 124–8, 130, 131; *A Treatise on Zimbabwe's National Liberation Struggle: Some Theoretical Problems* 124
Mhlanga, R. 57
Midzi, A. 19, 20, 21
migration: teaching sector 88–9
Mill, J.S. 140
Millennium Economic Recovery Programme (MERP 2001) 123
mining sector: empowerment policy 79–80
Ministry of Lands, Resettlement and Rural Development: *Communal Lands Development Plan* (1984–5) 104
Mlambo, A.: *Becoming Zimbabwe* 31
Mnangagwa, E. 19, 58
Moore, D. 30
Movement for Democratic Change (MDC) 139; election withdrawal (2008) 11; forming

INDEX

132; intimidation of MPs 21; torture 5; ZCTU 55
Moyo, J. 38, 39, 42, 43, 70
Moyo, P. 84, 85
Moyo, S. 147
Mozambique 4, 127
Mpofu, O. 16, 22
Mugabe, R. 3, 51, 85
Mugabeism 4
Mujuru, General S. (also R. Nhongo) 5, 19, 22
Munslow, B. 68
Musvaire, W. 18
Mutambara, A. 11
Muzenda, S. 5
Muzorewa, Bishop A. 128
Mwonzora, D. 20

National Constitutional Assembly (NCA) 132, 143
National Democratic Revolution (NDR) 39, 119–22; Dzino's view 124–8; Mbeki's view 122–4; National Liberation struggle 128–32; perspectives and praxis 132; South Africa 119
National Liberation struggle 128–32, 142–4
nationalism 39; reformist 129
nationalist history 28–30
nationalist politics 153
Native Land Husbandry Act (1951) 101, 111
Native Purchase Area: farmers 69
Nazism 142
Ncube, S. 112
Ncube, W. 76
Ndebele communities 106
Ndebele Rising (1896–7) 28–9
Ndlovu-Gatesheni, S. 27
neo-patrimonialism 49; business-state relations 68
networks: informal political 12
Nhongo, R. *see* Mujuru, S.
Nkomo, J. 6, 51
Noczim 77
Non-Governmental Organisations (NGOs) 37
Nyanhongo, H. 19, 20, 21
Nyoni, P. 56

On the Jewish Question (Marx) 140
OomGov 119, 120
Operation Maguta 18
Operation *Mari Wakaiwanepi?* 57
Operation Reduce Prices 56
Operation Restore Order 56
Operation Sovereign Legitimacy 58
Origin of the Family, Private Property and the State, The (Engels) 140
ownership: individualised 107–9

Partnership Africa Canada (PAC) 57
patrimonial regimes: developmental 50
patriotic agrarianists 144
patriotic history 27–8, 144
patronage: political 53
Peasant Consciousness and Guerrilla War (Ranger) 28
Peasant Revolt in South Africa (Mbeki) 119
peasantry: worker 101, 105–6
People's Markets 54
Pfidze, Captain 18
Phimister, I. 39, 144
Police Internal Security Intelligence (PISI) 18
political networks: informal 12
Political Parties Finance Act (1992) 58
political patronage 53
politics: nationalist 153
Poverty Datum Line (PDL) 86
price fixing 52
progress: analysis 139–40; Marx and Engels 140–1; momentum concept 142; reconstructing concept 141–2
Progressive Teachers Union of Zimbabwe (PTUZ) 87, 90
property rights 43
protobourgeoisie: post-colonial 70
Public Service Commission 19
public transcripts 100, 114

radical history 30–1
Raftopoulos, B. 12, 31, 39, 144; *Becoming Zimbabwe* 31
Ranger, T. 4, 111; *The African Voice* 28; *Matabeleland Today* 28; *Peasant Consciousness and Guerrilla War* 28; *Revolt in Southern Rhodesia* 28, 29; *Voices from the Rocks* 28
Real Time Gross Settlement (RTGS) 92
Reeves, R. 141
reformist nationalism 129
reforms: communal area 103–5; post-independence 113–14
rent flows: changing alliances (new millennium) **60**; Zimbabwe (1980s) **52**
rental market: land 107–8
rents: Zimbabwe history 51–7
Reserve Bank of Zimbabwe (RBZ) 71–4, 87, 92
Revolt in Southern Rhodesia (Ranger) 28, 29
Rhodes, C. 51
Rhodesian agrarian policies 104
Riddell Commission (1981) 86
rights: property 43
robber barons 53
Robins, S. 30
Robinson, P. 86
Rousseau, J-J. 140

INDEX

rural areas: violent control 17–19
rural development interventions 100–1
Rural District Council Act (1988) 113
rural social engineering: background 101–2
Rutherford, B. 144
Rwanda 50, 61

Sable chemicals 77
Sachikonye, L. 30; *When a State Turns on its Citizens* 4
sanctions 86
Saul, J. 31
Saunders, R. 79, 80
Savanhu, T. 20
Scoones, I.: *Zimbabwe's Land Reform: Myths and Realities* 147–55
Scott, J. 101, 114
settler colonialism 68
settler economy 101
Shanghai reserves 101, 106
share-cropping 109
Shona rising 29
Simons, J. 140
Sithole, M. 3, 92
Sithole, N. 128
Smith, Ian 126, 127
social engineering 100; rural 101–2
social imperialism 120
socialism 120, 129
soil quality 105
Solidarity Peace Trust (SPT) 20
South Africa: National Democratic Revolution (NDR) 119
South African Communist Party (SACP) 121
South African Development Community (SADC) 11, 67, 85, 122, 132
Southall, R. 1
sovereignty 27
Stanbic 75, 91–3
state: post-colonial policies 102–3; violence 43
Stoneman, C. 30
structural adjustment programme (SAP) 53, 54, 55, 62, 86
structuration theory (Giddens) 84, 93, 94
subjects: citizens 36
subsidies: agriculture 52
Sunrise I-III 87
Sustainable Development Commission (CSD) 141

Tanzania 50, 61
Tawengwa, S. 54
teaching sector: agency 93–4; economic crisis 87–8, 93–4; informal sector 89–90; migration 88–9; revival after dollarisation 90–1
Tendi, B-M. 12, 28

tenure: communal 100; relations 100, 107
Third *Chimurenga* 86, 99, 124
Through the Darkness (Todd) 143
Tocqueville, A. de 142
Todd, J.: *Through the Darkness* 143
Tongogara, J. 5
Total Control of our Resources through Indigenisation and Empowerment conference (Mutare 2010) 79
trade unions 38, 39, 125
trading: cross-border 90
traditional authority 106–7
Traditional Leaders Act (1998) 105, 114
Treatise on Zimbabwe's National Liberation Struggle: Some Theoretical Problems, A (Mhanda) 124–8
Tribal Trust Land Act (1967) 102, 111
Tsvangirai, M. 6, 11

Uganda 3
unemployment 70
Unilateral Declaration of Independence (UDI) 126
United Merchant Bank 54
Upfumi Kuvadiki 20, 79
urban politics: violence 19–21
urban studies: economic crisis 84–5

Venezuela 37
villagisation 104
violence: rural areas 17–19; state 43; urban areas 19–21
Voices from the Rocks (Ranger) 28
Vorster, J. 127

Wainwright, H. 38
war of liberation 112
War Victims Compensation Fund scandal (1997) 55
When a State Turns on its Citizens (Sachikonye) 4
Worby, L.E. 100–1
Worker 9
worker peasantry: creation 101; Gwayi Valley 105–6
World Bank 101

Yeros, P. 38, 39, 42, 43

ZANU PF (Zimbabwe African National Union Patriotic Front) 2; commercial empire 57–9; land 38; Leadership Code 53; parallel government 15; power-sharing politics 11–23, 59; pseudo-socialist transformation agenda 100
ZIDCO 57
Zimbabwe: comparative perspective 59–61

INDEX

Zimbabwe African National Liberation Army (ZANLA) 5, 127
Zimbabwe African People's Union (ZAPU)) 51, 126
Zimbabwe Banking and Allied Workers' Union (ZIBAWU) 93
Zimbabwe Congress of Trade Unions (ZCTU) 55, 84
Zimbabwe Defence Force (ZDF) 58
Zimbabwe Defence Industries (ZDI) 58
Zimbabwe Indigenous Economic Empowerment Organisation (ZIEEO) 79
Zimbabwe Mining Development Corporation (ZMDC) 16, 58
Zimbabwe Mirror 42
Zimbabwe National Liberation War Veterans Association (ZNLWVA) 55
Zimbabwe People's Army (ZIPA) 4, 124, 127, 128
Zimbabwe Stock Exchange (ZSE) 91
Zimbabwe Teachers Association (ZIMTA) 87
Zimbabwe. The Political Economy of Transition (Mandaza) 30
Zimbabwe United Passenger Company (ZUPCO) 77
Zimbabwe Unity Movement (ZUM) 5
Zimbabwean Electricity Supply Authority (ZESA) 77
Zimbabwe's Land Reform: Myths and Realities (Scoones et al) 147–55
Zimbank 93
Zimplats 80

www.routledge.com/9780415627917

Related titles from Routledge

Outcomes of post-2000 Fast Track Land Reform in Zimbabwe
Edited by L. Cliffe, J. Alexander, B. Cousins and R. Gaidzanwa

The struggle over land has been the central issue in Zimbabwe ever since white settlers began to carve out large farms over a century ago. Their monopolisation of the better-watered half of the land was the focus of the African war of liberation war, and was partially modified following Independence in 1980. This collection addresses questions emerging from the aftermath of land redistribution under Zimbabwe's Fast Track Reform and from the consequences for the agrarian economy, rural society and the nature of politics.

This book will be an essential starting place for analysts, policy-makers, historians and activists seeking to spotlight the key issues for the next decade.

This book was published as a special issue of the *Journal of Peasant Studies*.

November 2012: 246x174: 288pp
Hb: 978-0-415-62791-7
£90 / $145

For more information and to order a copy visit www.routledge.com/ISBN 9780415627917

Available from all good bookshops

www.routledge.com/9780415524848

Related titles from Routledge

Zimbabwe Since the Unity Government
Edited by Stephen Chan and Ranka Primorac

Zimbabwe has moved from a condition of restricted expression to one of many contradictory expressions. Politics has lost none of its compromises and conflicts, but it has been amplified by an explosion of voices. For the first time, a genuine debate is possible among many actors, insiders and outsiders, and the question marks over Zimbabwe and its future are no longer in terms of a narrow choice between one party and another, one outlook or another. Compromise government has meant complexity of debate. This does not preclude disillusionment within debate, but it does include vigour and imagination in debate.

This book includes essays from renowned scholars, governmental and diplomatic figures, and prioritises contributions by Zimbabweans themselves. The contributions provide a blend of academic and practitioner observation and judgement which no other volume has done.

This book was published as a special issue of *The Round Table*.

September 2012: 246 x 174: 144pp
Hb: 978-0-415-62484-8
£85/$145

For more information and to order a copy visit
www.routledge.com/9780415624848

Available from all good bookshops